Foundational Issues in Christian Education

Foundational Issues
in Christian Education
An Introduction in Evangelical Perspective

Robert W. Pazmiño

1988

BAKER BOOK HOUSE
Grand Rapids, Michigan 49506

Library of Congress Cataloging-in-Publication Data

Pazmiño, Robert W.
    Foundational issues in Christian education: an introduction in
  evangelical perspective / Robert W. Pazmiño.
        p.   cm.
    Bibliography: p.
    Includes index.
    ISBN 0-8010-7103-8
    1. Christian education. I. Title.
  BV1471.2.P39 1988   88-16753
  268—dc19   CIP

TO

ALBERT A. PAZMIÑO

1909–1986

My Father and a Modern Day Andrew

Contents

Introduction   9

1. Biblical Foundations   17
   The Old Testament   18
   The New Testament   29
   An Integrated Model   40

2. Theological Foundations   49
   Four Theological Distinctives   49
   An Orthodox Foundation   60
   A Reforming View of Education   63
   Insights from Paulo Freire   68

3. Philosophical Foundations   75
   General Definitions   75
   Philosophical Questions   82
   Modern Philosophies of Education   106
   The Choice of Philosophies   111

4. Historical Foundations   115
   History and Historical Method   116
   History and Education   117
   History and Christian Education   119
   The Old Testament   122
   The Greek Heritage   124

The New Testament   126
Early Christianity   128
The Middle Ages   130
The Renaissance   133
The Reformation   135
The United States   139
Recent Evangelical Educators   143
Continuity and Reaffirmation   149

5. Sociological Foundations   151
The Social Construction of Reality   152
Contextualization and Decontextualization   157
The Sociology of Knowledge   159
The Sociology of Education   165
A Model for Sociological Inquiry   176

6. Psychological Foundations   177
Four Approaches to Integration   178
Questions of Developmental Psychology   179
Cognitive Development: Jean Piaget   183
Psychosocial Development: Erik Erikson   185
Moral Development: Lawrence Kohlberg   187
Faith Development: James Fowler   192
Developmental Presumptions   196
An Interactive Biblical Model   198

7. Curricular Foundations   205
Basic Questions   207
Proposed Metaphors for Curriculum   210
The Place of Values in Curricular Planning   214
The Hidden Curriculum   216
A Larger Vision   218

Select Bibliography   223

Index   229

Introduction

In a front-page article in the *New York Times* entitled "Mainstream U.S. Evangelicals Surge in Protestant Influence," Kenneth A. Briggs elaborated how mainstream evangelical Protestants had emerged as the most powerful new force in American Protestantism. Briggs cited a number of developments indicating a new vitality on the part of those standing between liberals and fundamentalists as a mediating force in Protestant church life in the United States.[1] Briggs's article represents a growing national interest in evangelicals that began with Jimmy Carter's presidency and continues to this day.

Carter identified himself as an evangelical Christian in the Southern Baptist tradition. One week after he was elected in 1976, a *Newsweek* front-cover story was entitled "Born Again! The Evangelicals."[2] In December 1977 a cover story of *Time* drew national attention with its description of evangelicalism as the "New Empire of Faith."[3] With this increased national interest and the possible contribution of evangelicals

1. Kenneth A. Briggs, "Mainstream U.S. Evangelicals Surge in Protestant Influence," *New York Times*, 14 March 1982, 1, 50.
2. *Newsweek*, 25 October 1976.
3. *Time*, December 1977, 52–58. The *Newsweek* and *Time* articles are both cited in Marvin J. Wilson, "An Evangelical View of the Current State of Evangelical-Jewish Relations," *Journal of the Evangelical Theological Society* 25(June 1982):150.

9

to Protestant church life, evangelicals must initiate efforts to reevaluate biblical concerns in educational thought and practice. To this end evangelical Christian educators are called to reappraise their thought and practice in relation to the foundations of Christian education.

This book explores the disciplines used to form a wholistic and integrated conception of Christian education from which guiding principles and guidelines for practice can be drawn. Christian educators who are evangelical in theological orientation need to make a concerted effort to affirm those biblical insights which provide the essential authority for theory and practice. In addition, evangelicals need to incorporate insights from other disciplines. Such incorporation, however, is subject to the continuing authority of God's Word as found in Scripture. By critically exploring the various foundations that have been and are predominant in evangelical thought, educators can better deal with current needs and future challenges.

Christian educators have been conscious of the need to balance concerns for both continuity and change. Continuity is affirmed in emphasizing essential biblical truths that have guided the Christian faith and educational ministries.[4] Change is affirmed in emphasizing the need for applying biblical truths in relation to specific cultural, social, and personal variables. This effort requires careful reappraisal of biblical and theological sources as well as evaluation of the various trends confronting the wider society.

In exploring these areas it is appropriate to pose questions that have continuing significance in evangelical Christian education. A European educator once confronted an educator from the United States with the observation that "American educators are always raising questions and never answering them." In response to this observation, the educator from the United States asked, "Is that so?" To avoid this real danger, we need to propose some possible answers to the questions.

It is crucial that foundational questions be raised by Christian educators before they form a set theory and practice of Christian education. Raising these questions enables Christian educators to explore new possibilities and to consider "new wineskins" for Christian education. Through such exploration, persons concerned for education in various settings can identify principles and implications for practice.[5] The pro-

4. For an introductory discussion of evangelical perspectives in education, see George R. Knight, *Philosophy and Education: An Introduction in Christian Perspective* (Berrien Springs, Mich.: Andrews University Press, 1980), 141–227; and Harold William Burgess, *An Invitation to Religious Education* (Mishawaka, Ind.: Religious Education Press, 1975), 21–58.

5. For insights into the division of foundations, principles, and practice, see Emile Durkheim, *Education and Sociology* (New York: Free Press, 1956).

cess by which various educational questions are raised in relation to foundations, principles, and practice is suggested by Denis Lawton, who outlines these areas in terms of a systems diagram (see fig. 1).[6]

At each point in the process, thought and practice are subject to the continuing authority of God's written Word. The Bible is a critical instrument which discerns and judges the educator, the educatee, and the educational process.[7] By exploring biblical and theological foundations first, Christian educators can affirm transcultural universals which may then guide all educational conceptions and efforts. The consideration of philosophical foundations also assists the educator in specifying cultural universals. Transcultural and cultural universals are elements of continuity, less subject to change and various contingencies though not exempt from interpretation.

A second step in the educational process involves the investigation of cultural variables through the disciplines of history and sociology. This step provides the Christian educator with some sense of context, though cultural variables are more subject to the variations of time and space. Yet these cultural variables are no less the concern of the Christian educator who seeks to contextualize her or his educational efforts. Thus the Christian educator endeavors to make the universal and transcul-

FIGURE 1   **The Educational Process**

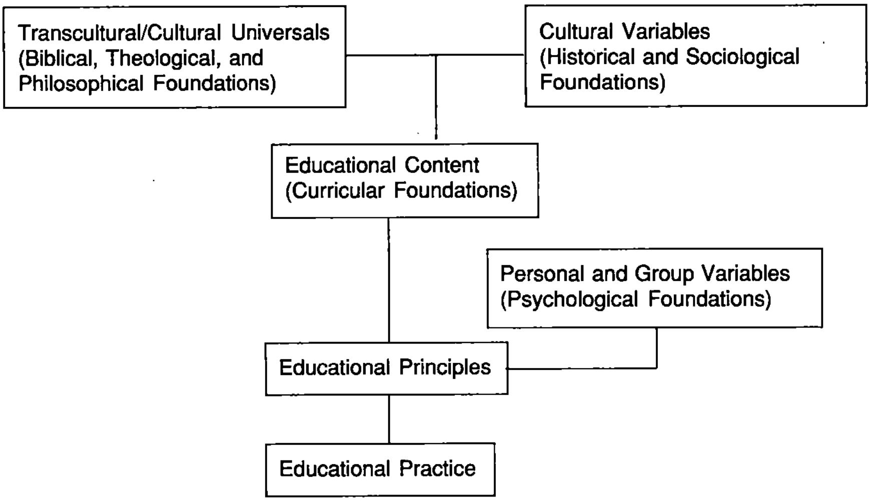

6. Denis Lawton, *Class, Culture and the Curriculum* (London: Routledge & Kegan Paul, 1975), 85–87.

7. Hebrews 4:12 and 2 Timothy 3:16 affirm this critical and evaluative function of God's written Word.

tural truths of God's revelation real to those participating in the educational event. The educator seeks to so know, understand, and love students that her or his teaching speaks directly to their needs and concerns. This, of course, does not exclude the educator's role as one who raises critical questions and provides perspectives unknown to the students. But some sense of one's location in time, space, and society is crucial for education.

The third step in the proposed model involves questions of educational content, the organized knowledge and experience shared in Christian education. This step identifies the Christian heritage. Curricular concerns at this point are organization of knowledge and identification of values and skills that are to be passed on from one generation or group to the next. In our current situation, questions of curriculum include the exposure of students to new knowledge and skills required for participation in a rapidly changing society. The inclusion of computer competency units in elementary and secondary schools is one example of curricular concern necessary given the impact of technology. Another curricular concern is the need for biblical literacy in the Christian community.

Beyond the questions of cultural universals, cultural variables, and educational content, the educator is confronted with individuals to whom she or he is responsible. The Christian educator needs to consider psychological foundations in order to discern the personal and group variables that influence education. Most particularly, the students or educatees who are present and involved voluntarily or involuntarily must be considered. In addition, educators are responsible to parents, administrators, boards, peers, pastors, and a host of other persons and groups depending upon the context of service. Psychological foundations provide insights to understand how persons develop, learn, and interact with others. Insights are also provided from sociological foundations for understanding how the teacher herself or himself relates and interacts with a variety of other persons, groups, and structures endemic to educational settings, whether in the home, the school, the church, or the community. The impact of sociological factors upon psychological foundations indicates the interactions of the various dimensions of the educational process as well as the potential limitations of a strictly systemic or analytical view of grasping the whole of education.

The Christian educator finally needs to state educational principles that have been culled from the various foundations and then apply those principles in terms of educational practice. A careful exploration of foundations is essential before specifying principles and guidelines for practice. Too often, foundational questions have been ignored or the answers to such questions have been assumed in addressing the tyranny of urgent pressures in churches, homes, schools, and other ministry settings. While these fifth and sixth steps are not the focus of this text, suggestions are made in these areas for the reader's consideration.

The entire educational process, though discussed in terms of a system, is subject to numerous contingencies which suggest that Christian education combines aspects of an art as well as a science. The Christian educator is called upon to creatively combine and integrate insights from various disciplines in the thought and practice of education. This artful integration includes disciplines beyond those identified in this book as foundations for a Christian education. Educational thought and practice have incorporated insights from such diverse studies as fine and applied arts, economics, political science, life sciences, physical sciences, systems theory, management theory, engineering, and mathematics. This reality supports the proposition that all truth is God's truth. The Christian educator can incorporate God's truth wherever it may be revealed in the created world in ways that reflect humanity's God-given creativity.

In discussing Christian education, one readily becomes conscious of its "preparadigmatic" character. Thomas Kuhn has suggested this term to describe an area of study or academic discipline which has not developed a paradigm—a dominant and widely accepted understanding, framework, or concept that serves to guide all thought and practice. In the physical and biological sciences, it is possible to identify dominant paradigms.[8] In the case of the social sciences and education, it is more difficult to identify a dominant paradigm. This is partly because the subjects for study in the social sciences and education are human beings. Human beings are infinitely more complex than physical, chemical, and biological processes. From a Christian theistic perspective, one can affirm this complexity by virtue of the fact that persons are created in the very image of God. Each person is unique and exceptions can be cited for any given paradigm or model.

This preparadigmatic stage of Christian education, which by virtue of persons' created nature may be a perennial one, implies that any educational conception or practice remains incomplete and subject to renewal and change. This is in part due to the nature of persons with their unlimited potential for good as well as evil. The realization of this potential is dependent upon the Christian educator's relationship with God and the extent to which he or she is following after God in educational thought and practice. Thus, a major challenge for Christian educators is to be faithful, obedient, and creative in their thought and practice. By drawing upon various resources, Christian educators are

8. See Thomas Kuhn, *The Structure of Scientific Revolutions*, 2d ed. (Chicago: University of Chicago Press, 1970), 10–51.

further challenged to develop an integrated understanding of Christian education that will guide practice. To ignore this challenge is to potentially be victimized by a mindless effort that fails to give glory to God.

The preparadigmatic stage of Christian education requires that each new generation of Christian educators reconsider the foundational questions. Without raising these questions, Christian educators are likely to perpetuate antiquated conceptions and practices that are not faithful to the gospel; to be subject to a cultural captivity devoid of significant impact; to be unresponsive to what the Holy Spirit is saying. Whereas this task is the particular responsibility of those professionally called to Christian education at various levels, the whole people of God must recognize their accountability for the direction and quality of Christian education in churches, homes, schools, communities, and societies. A lack of commitment to foundational issues results in limited possibilities for present and future generations.

This work is written from a bicultural Hispanic-North American perspective. The author is also an ecumenical evangelical in theological persuasion. For many this may pose an irreconcilable tension. First, Hispanics have generally been associated with Central and South America and the Caribbean rather than with North America. Second, ecumenical Christians are generally viewed as being other than those who identify themselves as evangelical. Nevertheless, it is from this vantage point that I address the current and enduring challenges of Christian education.

This work is intended to be an introductory textbook for courses at college and seminary levels. Its approach draws heavily upon secondary sources in order to provide a wide exposure for students. The author's hope is that students will be encouraged to follow up on the references provided for further study. Although the primary audience for this work are persons of evangelical persuasion, the author intends to engage the wider ecumenical community of religious educators as well.

I am grateful to those communities and individuals who have made this book possible. I am grateful to Gordon-Conwell Theological Seminary, which I have known both as a student and as a faculty member. The students in the courses I have taught have challenged me to consider various aspects of Christian education and to develop my thoughts. In particular, I thank Valerie Roberts and Kris Edscorn who provided detailed responses to the text in process. I am grateful to Andover Newton Theological School, which has supported my calling to serve a multicultural and theologically diverse church and world. I also appreciate the fellowships and congregations which have supported and guided me throughout my ministry.

I am grateful to the friends who patiently typed and edited the manuscript and who fostered the process of writing through their feedback. In particular, I thank Virginia Steadman and Deborah Perkins.

My greatest appreciation goes to my family, immediate and extended, who have loved and encouraged me in the midst of my work. My parents, Laura and Albert Pazmiño, have always believed in me and modeled the Christian life. My children, David and Rebekah, have always challenged me to be a better teacher and model in our home. Finally, I thank my wife, Wanda, for being a close companion and friend throughout the joys and struggles of my pilgrimage.

1

Biblical Foundations

In order to think responsibly about and practice education from a distinctly evangelical theological position, Christians, and in particular Christian educators, must carefully examine the biblical foundations for Christian education. Scripture is the essential source for understanding Christian distinctives in education. Therefore, it is crucial that the Christian educator's thoughts and practices be guided by God's revealed truths as he or she seeks to be obedient to Christ in the tasks of education. Christians are subject to a confusing plurality of educational theories in contemporary society. In such a situation, the exploration of biblical foundations provides an essential standard for judging education. The examination of these foundations does not result in a sterile or rigid theory and practice, devoid of creativity. Rather, Christian education patterned upon biblical foundations provides for a dynamic educational experience.

Several foundations can be identified in both the Old and New Testaments. These biblical sources provide models or paradigms even at the basic level of a commonsense reading of the text. All educators have models or paradigms that guide their thought and practice. In most cases, these models remain unexamined. The challenge for Christians is to examine their models for education, to make them explicit, and to undergird them with biblical foundations. The models suggested by various biblical foundations provide guides with which to consider past, present, and future educational efforts. What follows are a sampling of foundations which must be elaborated by educators in various settings making use of more extensive critical, canonical, and contextual studies.[1]

The Old Testament

The Book of Deuteronomy

Deuteronomy 6: An Educational Mandate   In Deuteronomy 6:1, 2, 4–9, Moses exhorts the people of Israel to remember God's activities in their history, to teach God's commands, and above all, to love, fear, and serve God:

> These are the commands, decrees and laws the LORD your God directed me to teach you to observe in the land that you are crossing the Jordan to possess, so that you, your children and their children after them may fear the LORD your God as long as you live by keeping all his decrees and commands that I give you, and so that you may enjoy long life.

> Hear, O Israel: The LORD our God, the LORD is one. Love the LORD your God with all your heart and with all your soul and with all your strength. These commandments that I give you today are to be upon your hearts. Impress them on your children. Talk about them when you sit at home and when you walk along the road, when you lie down and when you get up. Tie them as symbols on your hands and bind them on your foreheads. Write them on the doorframes of your houses and on your gates.

Moses' teaching is directed to the believing community in which persons are called to relate their faith in God to all of life. This passage from Deuteronomy provides insights about the goals, the teacher, the student, the content, and the setting of biblical education.[2] The educational mandate of Deuteronomy 6:4–9 requires passing on

1. Gabriel Fackre in *The Christian Story: A Pastoral Systematics* (Grand Rapids: Wm. B. Eerdmans, 1987), 157–210, identifies four senses of Scripture: common, critical, canonical, and contextual. This discussion is largely limited to the common sense, recognizing that evangelical constituencies make varied use of critical, canonical, and contextual insights. For further inquiry in this area, see Mary C. Boys, *Biblical Interpretation in Religious Education* (Birmingham, Ala.: Religious Education Press, 1980); and for a good example of the fruits of canonical work, see Walter Brueggemann, *The Creative Word: Canon as a Model for Biblical Education* (Philadelphia: Fortress, 1982).

2. For these insights, I am indebted to Timothy C. Tennent, "Personal Philosophy of Christian Education" (Gordon-Conwell Theological Seminary, 1984).

the commandments of God to the next generation. Its ultimate goal is to foster a love of God expressed in loyalty and unqualified obedience. To love God is to answer to a unique claim (6:4), to be obedient (11:1–22; 30:20), to keep God's commandments (10:12; 11:1, 22; 19:9), to heed them and to hear God's voice (11:13; 30:16), and to serve God (10:12; 11:1, 13). In each of these passages the word *love* refers to obedience from the heart involving all of one's being.[3] Jesus echoes this relation of love to obedience in John 14:15: "If you love me, you will obey what I command."

The love of God is expressed in obedience to God's commandments and in giving oneself wholly (heart, soul, and strength). Teaching is to be incisive in challenging hearers to a total life response to God characterized by heartfelt devotion. This teaching is the particular responsibility of parents, yet this goal has significance for all forms of education.

In the ultimate sense God is the teacher in biblical education. God is the author and discloser of all truth, and both teachers and students stand under this truth. God calls teachers and students to understand, grow in, and obey God's revealed Word. In this passage and throughout the biblical record, teachers are responsible as stewards and proclaimers of God's truth. This truth can be communicated in a variety of ways, always involving a relational dimension. A relationship of love, trust, openness, honesty, acceptance, caring, support, forgiveness, correction, and affirmation is to characterize interactions between teacher and student.[4] The teacher, like parents, is called upon to model the love of God which he or she hopes to encourage students to follow.

Through the teaching and example of the teacher, the student is called to understanding, growth, and obedience in relation to God's revealed Word. While the teacher is encouraged to diligently and incisively teach, it is assumed that the student will be open and willing to receive this instruction. Other passages of Scripture, in particular the Book of Proverbs, provide clear injunctions for children to be attentive to the instruction of their parents. Teachers in the context of Jewish life were primarily parents, and Deuteronomy 6 therefore focuses on this role. But this perspective has implications for educational relationships beyond the home, as was the case in postexilic synagogue schools.

The essential content of biblical education according to Deuteronomy 6 is the commandments, decrees, and laws of God which Moses was directed to teach. But this content is vitally related to the whole of

3. Ibid.
4. Lawrence O. Richards, *A Theology of Christian Education* (Grand Rapids: Zondervan, 1975), 314.

life. The content of God's revelation is to be taught or impressed upon students, to be talked about at various times, to be tied and bound upon one's body, and to be written in public and readily observed locations. Truth is to be integrated into all of life and is to affect the moment-to-moment and day-to-day existence of the people of God. This content is both foundational and radical. It is foundational in providing the basic truth and structure upon which all else must be built. It is radical in providing the roots from which all life is nourished or affected. Thus both stability and growth are assured to the extent to which the content of education is based on God's revelation.

The setting for teaching described in this passage includes all those situations in which parents can impress upon their children the commandments of God. There are various occasions when this is to be done: when sitting at home, when walking along the road, when lying down, and when getting up. God's commandments are to be present even as symbols upon people's hands and foreheads, and the doorframes of houses and gates. The whole of life provides situations in which persons can be discipled and nurtured in the ways of God.

The primary focus in Deuteronomy 6 is parents and their essential role in education. Despite the multiplicity of educational influences today, parents are still the primary educators who actively or passively determine what influences their children. The challenge is for the Christian church to equip parents for their roles as ministers and educators in their homes and in the choice of other educational influences in the lives of their children.

In Deuteronomy 6, Moses exhorts the people of Israel to remember and to teach. The context for this teaching is the home, in which persons learn to relate their faith in God to all of life. Because of the contemporary tendency to compartmentalize life, faith is often relegated to those limited occasions when one is involved in church-related activities, typically confined to a few hours on Sunday morning. The Book of Deuteronomy demonstrates that faith in God is related to all of life. Wherever faithful persons interact there is an occasion for Christian education—provided this interaction is deliberate, systematic, and sustained.

Education entails conscious planning, implementing, and evaluating of educational experiences. Intentionality in Christian education involves the effort to share biblical content, to grapple with its implications for life, and to suggest avenues for appropriate response. A similar point is emphasized in James 2:14–17. This approach has recently been advocated by Lawrence O. Richards, whose conceptions have clarified the nonformal and informal aspects of education.[5] Richards is largely dependent upon a socialization or enculturation model for education that focuses on education for life.[6]

Richards assumes that the values of formal education will be implicitly addressed in the Christian community; however, it is clear that these values need to be planned in educational ministries that enable persons to move beyond a community norm, in a prophetic sense, as well as nurturing them in ways of a particular community. Prophetic education calls persons and communities to be accountable to biblical norms and demands at points where sin, injustice, and oppression are evident, where the life of the home or nurturing community is critiqued rather than affirmed. These two foci—affirmation and critique—are patterned after the blessing and warning associated with God's covenant (see Deut. 27–28). These foci are implied in Deuteronomy 6, which emphasizes attentiveness to God's commands and parental instruction.

Affirmation and critique are as essential today as they were in biblical times. Thus, while a family or community may faithfully pass on to the next generation the truth of God through socialization and enculturation processes, it may also at key points need correction and reorientation. Formal education can often serve as a vehicle for correction and reorientation of the efforts of a particular home or community. Likewise, a particular home and community may minister to an agency of formal education. This is the case when parents take an active role in determining the policies and goals of a Sunday, private, or public school.

Deuteronomy 30–32 also provides essential insights for understanding the nature of Christian education. Jesus himself made repeated reference to the Book of Deuteronomy during his wilderness temptations.[7] In the current educational wilderness of a plurality of educational philosophies, Christian educators can likewise gain strength and clarity by considering the insights offered from the following three passages: 30:11–20; 31:9–13; and 31:30–32:4. The education described in these passages comes to its full fruition in the life and ministry of Jesus Christ.

Deuteronomy 30:11–20: Finding Life By way of analogy, Deuteronomy 30:11–20 clarifies some of the issues at stake in current Christian education efforts. This passage records a covenant renewal challenge

5. For a complete discussion of the content-implications-response sequence, see Lawrence O. Richards, *Creative Bible Teaching* (Chicago: Moody, 1970).

6. Richards's conceptions are elaborated in his *A Theology of Christian Education.*

7. See Matthew 4:1–11 and Luke 4:1–13.

given to the people of Israel and describes the curses or warnings that will result from disobedience to God:

> Now what I am commanding you today is not too difficult for you or beyond your reach. It is not up in heaven, so that you have to ask, "Who will ascend into heaven to get it and proclaim it to us so we may obey it?" Nor is it beyond the sea, so that you have to ask, "Who will cross the sea to get it and proclaim it to us so we may obey it?" No, the word is very near you; it is in your mouth and in your heart so you may obey it.
>
> See, I set before you today life and prosperity, death and destruction. For I command you today to love the LORD your God, to walk in his ways, and to keep his commands, decrees and laws; then you will live and increase, and the LORD your God will bless you in the land you are entering to possess.
>
> But if your heart turns away and you are not obedient, and if you are drawn away to bow down to other gods and worship them, I declare to you this day that you will certainly be destroyed. You will not live long in the land you are crossing to enter and possess.
>
> This day I call heaven and earth as witnesses against you that I have set before you life and death, blessings and curses. Now choose life, so that you and your children may live and that you may love the LORD your God, listen to his voice, and hold fast to him. For the LORD is your life, and he will give you many years in the land he swore to give to your fathers, Abraham, Isaac and Jacob.

Christian educators are to make clear God's offer of life or death. Christian education is one of the church's ministries that seeks to encourage persons of all ages to choose life—the spiritual and full life found in Jesus Christ. Choosing life requires loving, listening to, and holding fast to God. This choice is imperative because God is the source of life, a truth echoed in 1 John 5:12: "He who has the Son has life; he who does not have the Son of God does not have life." Christian education entails sharing a knowledge of, and encouraging a response to God that results in life.

Deuteronomy 31:9–13: The Word of God and Human Response Deuteronomy 31:9–13 emphasizes the importance of reading and hearing God's Law. This passage records the sabbatical legal renewal of God's covenant with God's people:

> So Moses wrote down this law and gave it to the priests, the sons of Levi, who carried the ark of the covenant of the LORD, and to all the elders of Israel. Then Moses commanded them: "At the end of every seven years, in the year for canceling debts, during the Feast of Tabernacles, when all Israel comes to appear before the LORD your God at the place he will

choose, you shall read this law before them in their hearing. Assemble the people—men, women, and children, and the aliens living in your towns—so they can listen and learn to fear the LORD your God and follow carefully all the words of this law. Their children, who do not know this law, must hear it and learn to fear the LORD your God as long as you live in the land you are crossing the Jordan to possess."

Those addressed are to listen, to learn to fear God, and to follow carefully in God's ways. God's Law is a trust, a heritage that is to be shared not only with adults but also with children and youth in the community of faith. These formal and legal arrangements are finally fulfilled and transcended in the new covenant. From the perspective of the New Testament, the importance of God's Law is extended to all of Scripture (2 Tim. 3:14–17). God's Word provides the essential content for teaching. Christian education can be further distinguished by its focus on God's revelation as expressed in the Old and New Testaments. God's Word is to be passed on from generation to generation with the intent of fostering a response of faithfulness on the part of the hearers. The authority of God's Word is understood within the community of faith, the church of the living God, which is described as the "pillar and foundation of the truth" (1 Tim. 3:14–16). With this understanding, educators must submit any private interpretations of Scripture to the shared wisdom of the church in both its historical and present expressions.

Deuteronomy 31:30–32:4: Fostering Liberation and Facilitating Worship Deuteronomy 31:30–32:4 provides a description of education in Old Testament times. This passage is an unusual introduction to a long poetic curse upon the nation that is followed by the promise of restoration.

And Moses recited the words of this song from beginning to end in the hearing of the whole assembly of Israel: "Listen, O heavens, and I will speak; hear, O earth, the words of my mouth. Let my teaching fall like rain and my words descend like dew, like showers on new grass, like abundant rain on tender plants. I will proclaim the name of the LORD. Oh, praise the greatness of our God! He is the Rock, his works are perfect, and all his ways are just" (Deut. 32:1–4a).

This passage describes an education that liberates persons to grow and be refreshed in God. It is also an education that encourages people to celebrate, to attribute worth to God. It liberates in the sense of enabling persons to be and become all that God has intended them to be as God's creatures and as members of the covenant community. The threat of curse as well as the anticipation of blessing provide opportunities for learning. Such a liberating education requires the effectual working of God to restore persons and groups so they can reflect God's image in their lives, just as rain and dew restore and renew plant life in a desert. Liberation is the empowerment to be and become all that God has intended persons to be by the Creator's continual action in transforming and caring for individuals, groups, and societies.[8] This liberation includes the denouncement of sin along with the announcement of forgiveness. Christian education is characterized by teaching/learning that results in the liberation of persons. Jesus affirms this emphasis in John 8:31b, 32: "If you hold to my teaching, you are really my disciples. Then you will know the truth, and the truth will set you free."

The education described in Deuteronomy 31:30–32:4 also entails celebration. It is celebration in the sense of encouraging participants to praise God. God is praised for God's gracious activity, care, providence, judgment, justice, and righteousness. Participants in this educational event are called by Moses to recognize their utter dependence upon God and to respond with obedience to divine demands in all spheres of human activity. Therefore, in addition to liberation, celebration is an outcome of education that is biblical in character.

The life and ministry of Jesus is the fullest expression of the nature of education that is described in these passages from Deuteronomy. Jesus Christ is the life, the Word Incarnate, and the ultimate source for liberation and celebration. Jesus Christ is the life (John 14:6), the bread of life (John 6:35), and the resurrection and the life (John 11:25). He comes to offer everlasting life to all who believe in him (John 3:16, 36; 1 John 5:12). Jesus Christ as the Word Incarnate (John 1:1–18) fulfills God's Law (Matt. 5:17–20). In Christ there is the fullest realization of liberation (John 8:31–36) and the occasion for celebration (John 15:9–11). His discipling ministry with the twelve disciples provides a model for the kind of education that affects the total life of participants.[9] More than just imparting content as revealed truth, Jesus shared his very life with his disciples as the Word Incarnate.

What possible educational implications can be drawn from consideration of these biblical foundations from the Book of Deuteronomy? Several can be suggested in relation to the need for reform in local church education using the categories suggested above. Other implica-

8. See Exodus 6:6–8 for a description of liberation as God worked in the life experience of the nation of Israel.

9. For an insightful description of Jesus' teaching ministry, see the classic works, A. B. Bruce, *The Training of the Twelve* (Grand Rapids: Kregel, 1971); and Herman H. Horne, *The Teaching Techniques of Jesus* (Grand Rapids: Kregel, 1920). A more recent work is Joseph A. Grassi, *Teaching the Way: Jesus, the Early Church, and Today* (Washington, D.C.: University Press of America, 1982).

tions might be suggested in relation to education in various settings, but our focus is on the implications as they relate to the local church.

From Deuteronomy 30:11–20—"Finding Life"—the following implications can be suggested:

1. Reemphasize the evangelistic functions of the Sunday school and other educational programs of the local church.
2. Train Sunday school teachers and adult participants in areas of evangelization and follow-up.
3. Explore the possibilities of classes and Bible study groups geared to those inquiring about the Christian faith.
4. Pray for and anticipate decisions for a life commitment to Jesus Christ as Sovereign and Savior.

From Deuteronomy 31:9–13—"The Word of God and Human Response"—the following implications emerge:

1. Develop and work toward goals of biblical literacy for all age groups.
2. Evaluate and select curriculum that is Bible-centered and comprehensive in dealing with the whole counsel of God.
3. Relate biblical themes to contemporary life and help students in all educational programs to grapple with the implications of biblical truth for their response in the modern world.

Deuteronomy 31:30–32:4—"Fostering Liberation and Facilitating Worship"—suggests the following implications:

1. Maximize the active participation of all persons in educational programs. Complement action with time for serious thought and reflection in dialogue with others.
2. Raise questions concerning distinctive Christian life-styles in a pluralistic society. What does it mean to affirm Christ's lordship in various areas of life?
3. Consciously rely on the renewing work of the Holy Spirit in the lives of individuals, groups, and structures.
4. Work toward the coordination of education programs with the themes and emphases of weekly corporate worship.
5. Prepare children and youth for and expose them to corporate worship. Provide helps for parents in this area of preparation.
6. Allow for spontaneous and planned occasions of worship during education events.
7. Inquire about the spiritual growth of persons in education programs.

Psalm 78

Psalm 78:1–8 is another key Old Testament passage providing insights for understanding the setting for Christian education. This passage speaks about the attention given to God's activities in history on behalf of God's creation and the redeemed community:

O my people, hear my teaching;
listen to the words of my mouth.
I will open my mouth in parables,
I will utter hidden things, things
from of old—
what we have heard and known,
what our fathers have told us.
We will not hide them from their
children;
we will tell the next generation
the praiseworthy deeds of the LORD,
his power, and the wonders he
has done.
He decreed statutes for Jacob
and established the law in Israel,
which he commanded our forefathers
to teach their children,
so the next generation would know
them,
even the children yet to be born,
and they in turn would tell their
children.
Then they would put their trust in
God
and would not forget his deeds
but would keep his commands.
They would not be like their
forefathers—
a stubborn and rebellious
generation, whose
hearts were not loyal to God,
whose spirits were not faithful
to him.

Wherever God's words and deeds are passed on to succeeding generations forms a context for Christian education. By necessity intergenerational relationships must be present for this to occur. Both the Old and New Testament communities have a shared memory or history. In rehearsing the accounts of God's activities in both distant and recent history, the meaning and purpose of life in God are shared. Followers of the living God are not to forget, but rather to learn from the victories and failures of persons in the past. God's community is called to reflect upon God's covenant and the responses of persons, groups, and communities that have resulted in both blessing and curse. Where this reflection and dialogue are facilitated is the place where the covenant can be renewed.

In Old Testament times, the family was the primary setting for education. The efforts of the family were supplemented and complemented by instruction in the covenant community as it gathered. In exilic and postexilic times the agencies of education also included both synagogues and schools.[10] Even with these developments the extended family continued to be important in education.

In the New Testament the church functions as the extended family of God. It is the responsibility of those so gifted and experienced to pass on to the next generation accounts of the acts, the power, and the wonders of God in the past and present. Those who are gifted and experienced have responsibilities as stewards to transmit this life-giving message to new members of the faith community. This transmission is crucial if persons are to gain a sense of rootedness and identity in relation to the faith community. Constant diligence is necessary to sustain this faithful transmission.

Nehemiah 8:1–18

Following the return of the exiles from captivity, Ezra reads the Law to the people (Neh. 8:1–18). Ezra's ministry is an instrument for renewal in the life of the community; those able to understand are assembled to hear God's Word.[11] The hearing and heeding of God's Word issues in the restoration of life and worship. The uniquely educational aspect of this event is the Levites' instruction of the people. They clarify the words of God so that the people can understand. When the people clearly see the implications of biblical teachings, then they can respond in ways that are pleasing to God. The tasks of education include enabling others to come to an understanding of God, divine revelation, and expectations for personal and corporate human life.

The responsibilities of educators or teachers include: (1) *proclamation*, that is, the reading, speaking, or sharing of God's Word; (2) *exposition*, that is, the translation and explanation or opening up of the meaning of God's Word; and (3) *exhortation*, that is, the suggestion of direct appli-

10. For a full description of education in Old Testament times, see William Barclay, *Train Up a Child: Educational Ideals in the Ancient World* (Philadelphia: Westminster, 1959), 11–48.
11. Cf. Romans 10:14–18.

cation and response for those who hear. The responsibilities of the hearers or students include the following: (1) *knowing* God's Word by listening attentively to its proclamation; (2) *understanding* God's Word by responding to its exposition; (3) *obeying* God's Word by responding wholeheartedly to its exhortation; and (4) *worshiping* God who is encountered through the proclaimed Word and celebrating the restoration realized in personal and corporate life.

In general, hearers or students are expected to have reverence for God's Word (the people stand while Ezra reads the Book of the Law) and to respond at several levels, including thoughts, decisions, and affections. A response includes the intellect in terms of understanding, the will in terms of obedience, and the emotions in terms of repentance and worship. A call is made to set one's mind, will, heart, and affections upon God. Ezra's instruction is an example of education that goes beyond the immediate family situation to include the whole nation.

Wisdom Literature

Crucial in understanding education from the perspective of the Old Testament is the concept of wisdom and, in particular, its embodiment in wisdom literature. In the Hebrew world view wisdom was intensely practical, resulted in successful living, and applied to the heart. A special group of persons was endowed with the gift of wisdom and had the responsibility of sharing their advice with others. Their task was to develop workable plans, to prescribe advice for successful living (Jer. 18:18). But wisdom in its fullest sense was only to be understood in relation to its source, namely God.[12] David H. Hubbard provides helpful insights in his description of wisdom:

> Wisdom in the fullest sense belongs to God alone (Job 12:13ff; Isa. 31:2; Dan. 2:20–23). His wisdom is not only completeness of knowledge pervading every realm of life (Job 10:4, 26:6; Prov. 5:21; 15:3) but also consists in his irresistible fulfillment of what he has in mind (J. Pedersen, *Israel: Its Life and Culture,* I–II, page 198). The universe (Prov. 3:19f.; 8:22–31; Jer. 10:12) and man (Job 10:8ff; Ps. 104:24; Prov. 14:31; 22:2) are products of His creative wisdom. Natural (Isa. 28:23–29) and historical (Isa. 31:2) processes are governed by his wisdom, which includes an infallible discrimination between good and evil and is the basis for the just rewards and punishments which are the lot of the righteous and the wicked (Pss. 1, 37, 73; Prov. 10:3; 11:4; 12:2). Such wisdom is inscrutable (Job 28:12–21). God in his grace must reveal it if man is going to grasp it at all (Job 28:23, 28). Even wisdom derived from natural abilities or

12. David H. Hubbard, "Wisdom," in *The New Bible Dictionary,* ed. J. D. Douglas (Grand Rapids: Wm. B. Eerdmans, 1962), 1333.

distilled from experience is a gracious gift, because God's creative activity makes such wisdom possible.

Biblical wisdom is both religious and practical. Stemming from the fear of the Lord (Job 28:28; Ps. 111:10; Prov. 1:7; 9:10), it branches out to touch all of life. . . . Wisdom takes insights gleaned from the knowledge of God's ways and applies them in the daily walk. This combination of insight and obedience (and all insight must issue in obedience) relates wisdom to the prophetic emphasis on the knowledge (i.e., the cordial love and obedience) of God (e.g., Hos. 2:20; 4:1, 6; 6:6; Jer. 4:22; 9:3, 6; and especially Prov. 9:10).[13]

What implications emerge from this Old Testament understanding of education? First, God imparts wisdom and people are dependent upon God's grace for any claim to wisdom. Therefore, wisdom that is apart from or inconsistent with the truths of God's revelation must be suspect and questioned. Education at its best must be God-centered, seeing God as the source. Educators are called to integrate all areas of knowledge with God's revelation.

A second implication is that education should have an impact upon people's lives and should enable them to grapple with the practical consequences of those truths studied or discerned. Therefore, the appeal to a strictly theoretical or academic agenda that addresses the mind divorced from affections and actions cannot claim to be faithful to the biblical tradition. Questions of character, ethics, and life-style are appropriate, along with how truth and commitment relate to all areas of life. Herein is the need for a wholistic and integrated perspective on education that affects the head, heart, and hands of both teachers and students.

A third implication for education is that those who are identified as teachers must be evaluated in terms of the extent to which they give evidence of having received the gift of wisdom from God. Teachers are ultimately responsible to God for the use of their gifts and responsible to students in sharing the fruit of their insights. Approaches to education which emphasize facilitation of student-directed learning may not provide adequate times when a teacher's wisdom can be shared.

The New Testament

Matthew: Sharing Vision, Mission, and Memory

In the New Testament, the Old Testament patterns of education persist, but the followers of Jesus are provided with a new agenda for their educational efforts. This agenda is most explicit in Matthew 28:18–20.

13. Ibid.

The purpose of the disciples' ministry is to enable others to become obedient disciples of Jesus Christ.

It is a difficult task to teach obedience. Those who have taught others can appreciate this difficulty. Yet there is the promise that Christ's very presence, as well as his authority, will empower his disciples to disciple others, be it in the home, the church, or the classroom. The purpose of making disciples is totally dependent upon sharing the content of Jesus' own teachings, those truths revealed by God with direct implications for life. The challenge posed for current efforts in Christian education is this: Are obedient disciples of Jesus Christ being nurtured and taught all that Jesus taught? If so, there is a basis for affirmation and continued reliance upon God's gracious undertaking. If not, there is a challenge for careful evaluation and renewed efforts.

In addition to this educational commission, the whole pattern of instruction of Matthew's Gospel shows how teaching was conducted in the early church. Matthew's Gospel is a teaching manual for discipling Christians. The five major sections of instruction include the following: 5:1–7:27; 10:1–42; 13:1–52; 18:1–35; and 23:1–25:46. These sections comprehensively address major areas of the Christian life.[14] They can be categorized in terms of three elements that a Christian community shares with its members: a vision, a mission, and a memory.

The first teaching section is the Sermon on the Mount (Matt. 5:1–7:27). This passage contains Jesus' teaching on the personal and social ethics of the kingdom. It provides a vision for participation in God's kingdom.

Matthew 10:1–42 records Jesus' charge to the twelve disciples, outlining his teaching on mission. Jesus sends out his disciples as an extension of his own ministry with specific directives to guide their ministries.

The third teaching section, Matthew 13:1–52, includes the parables of the kingdom in which Jesus teaches about redemptive history and provides insights for discerning the nature of the kingdom itself. The kingdom has small beginnings, but grows in the midst of an evil world. This history of the kingdom provides a framework for understanding past, current, and future developments in the mission of the kingdom.

Matthew 18:1–35 contains Jesus' discourse on church discipline in which he describes the nature of his disciples' commitments to one another in love and truth. This passage addresses the area of mission as related to a local body of disciples who are called to model a community of love, healing reconciliation, and justice.

14. Glenn W. Barker, William L. Lane, and J. Ramsey Michaels, *The New Testament Speaks* (New York: Harper & Row, 1969), 264–66.

The final section, Matthew 23:1–25:4, contains Jesus' teaching on eschatology. The happenings at the end of the present age with the in-breaking of the coming age of God's kingdom fulfilled on earth are described. Thus the focus is again on vision.

The New Testament model for Christian teaching, then, centers upon the shared Christian vision, mission, and memory, as the followers of Jesus Christ seek to be faithful to God's calling in the world.

In relation to current educational efforts, Christians are called to evaluate the extent to which the Christian vision, the Christian mission, and the Christian memory are effectively shared. Such criteria provide standards for evaluating Christian education today. As with Deuteronomy 30–32, several educational implications can be suggested for local church educational efforts based upon the consideration of Matthew's teaching model.

From the first element of education—sharing vision—the following implications emerge:

1. Educational leaders in the local church, including the pastor, are to explicitly state, preferably in written form, their vision for God's work in their specific locality.
2. Provide an extended period of time, perhaps in a retreat format, when persons involved in educational ministries can study biblical insights for education and can share their vision for ministry.
3. Periodically devote time to evaluate the implementation of a vision for a specific ministry and to reorient efforts.

From the second element of education—sharing mission—the following implications can be suggested:

1. Develop a statement of mission to guide educational work that identifies specific purposes and goals for long- and short-term time periods.
2. Consider needs both within and outside of the immediate Christian community and biblical demands concerning mission. (Challenges in home and foreign missions cannot be neglected in focusing on local concerns.)
3. Delegate specific responsibilities and establish avenues of accountability for various components of mission implementation.
4. Evaluate existing programs and efforts in terms of an agreed upon mission statement.
5. Periodically reconsider the mission statement in the light of new challenges and changing situations.

The third element of education—sharing memory—suggests the following implications:

1. Plan times when the history of God's work in a particular local church and/or denomination can be recounted and celebrated.
2. Relate local history to the advance of God's kingdom over the centuries.
3. Identify specific points of continuity and discontinuity with the past in relation to the present and future of the local church.
4. Include children, youth, and adults in exploring historical roots.

These implications are suggestive and serve to illustrate the value of exploring foundations for the actual practice of education in the setting of the local church. Other factors must be considered, but biblical models can be reappropriated and reinterpreted to provide helpful frameworks in which to conceive of and practice Christian education. This approach is an alternative to the uncritical appropriation of dominant models current in society which nevertheless can be considered for secondary insights.

Luke: Methods from the Master Teacher

Another passage of particular significance for a discussion of education, and of methods in particular, is Luke 24:13–35, in which Jesus talks with two disciples on the road to Emmaus.

> Now that same day two of them were going to a village called Emmaus, about seven miles from Jerusalem. They were talking with each other about everything that had happened. As they talked and discussed these things with each other, Jesus himself came up and walked along with them; but they were kept from recognizing him.
> He asked them, "What are you discussing together as you walk along?"
> They stood still, their faces downcast. One of them, named Cleopas, asked him, "Are you only a visitor to Jerusalem and do not know the things that have happened there in these days?"
> "What things?" he asked.
> "About Jesus of Nazareth," they replied. "He was a prophet, powerful in word and deed before God and all the people. The chief priests and our rulers handed him over to be sentenced to death, and they crucified him; but we had hoped that he was the one who was going to redeem Israel. And what is more, it is the third day since all this took place. In addition, some of our women amazed us. They went to the tomb early this morning but didn't find his body. They came and told us that they had seen a vision of angels, who said he was alive. Then some of our

companions went to the tomb and found it just as the women had said, but him they did not see."

He said to them, "How foolish you are, and how slow of heart to believe all that the prophets have spoken! Did not the Christ have to suffer these things and then enter his glory?" And beginning with Moses and all the Prophets, he explained to them what was said in all the Scriptures concerning himself.

As they approached the village to which they were going, Jesus acted as if he were going farther. But they urged him strongly, "Stay with us, for it is nearly evening; the day is almost over." So he went in to stay with them.

When he was at the table with them, he took bread, gave thanks, broke it and began to give it to them. Then their eyes were opened and they recognized him, and he disappeared from their sight. They asked each other, "Were not our hearts burning within us while he talked with us on the road and opened the Scriptures to us?"

They got up and returned at once to Jerusalem. There they found the Eleven and those with them, assembled together and saying, "It is true! The Lord has risen and has appeared to Simon." Then the two told what had happened on the way, and how Jesus was recognized by them when he broke bread.

Key components of this teaching episode are discussion (v. 14), open inquiry (v. 17), correction and clarification (vv. 25–27), role modeling (vv. 30–31), and the need for response (vv. 33–35). Whereas this educational encounter includes the dimension of declaration as evidenced in Jesus' exposition of the Scriptures, it also includes the dimension of dialogue that enables the disciples to be engaged not only at the level of their minds, but also includes their affections, wills, and actions. Here is an educational encounter that calls for a head, heart, and hand response to the good news declared by Jesus.

Jesus' approach in interacting with these disciples includes three noteworthy elements. First, Jesus asks them questions (vv. 17–19). The Master Teacher knows the answers to these questions, yet he wants his students to think for themselves. Second, Jesus listens. He hears their response to the questions he asks. Teachers often fail to listen to students and to allow adequate time for thought. Third, it is only after questioning and listening that Jesus both exhorts these disciples and opens the Scriptures, explaining their meaning. Jesus explains the truths discussed by Moses and the prophets through his interpretation of the texts. In response to Jesus' teaching, these disciples describe their encounter as one in which both their eyes and the Scriptures were opened. The word for "open" here is the same word used to describe how a womb is opened at the birth of a child. There is a sense of joy and the burning of the heart that parallels a birth experience in terms of its personal impact. The joy associated with such a disclosure is a desperately needed dimension in each and every Christian education endeavor. It is interesting to note that these three same elements—asking questions, listening, and sharing one's understanding—are present in the description of the twelve-year-old Jesus at the temple in Jerusalem (Luke 2:41–52).

In addition to this account of Jesus' teaching, the Gospels provide examples of the wide variety of methods which Jesus used in his teaching ministry.[15] James Stewart identifies some general principles and particular features of Jesus' methodology. The general principles: Jesus' teaching was authoritative; Jesus trusted in the power of truth to convince his hearers; Jesus sought to have persons think for themselves; Jesus lived what he taught; and Jesus loved those he taught. The particular features: Jesus' teaching was oral instruction; it was occasional in nature, elicited by quite casual events; it was adapted to his audience; and it included figurative elements such as illustrations, epigrams, paradoxes, and parables.[16] Christian educators are not limited to the oral instruction which Jesus employed but have access to a wide variety of media and methodologies. Nevertheless, the example of Jesus as the Master Teacher needs to be studied if one is to effectively and faithfully minister. In this study one must recognize the unique role and mission of Jesus' teaching.

1 Corinthians 2:6–16: Wisdom from the Holy Spirit

Christian educators need to consider the extensive teaching ministry of Paul in the first century. Paul's focus is wisdom from God, a wisdom whose source is the Holy Spirit. Paul teaches in words taught by the Spirit, expressing spiritual truths in spiritual words. The reception of these words also requires the work of the Holy Spirit in the lives of the hearers. A person without the Spirit does not accept the things that come from the Spirit. Paul reflects the words of Jesus to his disciples: "But the Counselor, the Holy Spirit, whom the Father will send in my name, will teach you all things and will remind you of everything I have said to you" (John 14:26); "But when he, the Spirit of Truth, comes, he will guide you into all truth. He will not speak on his own; he will speak only what he hears, and he will tell you what is yet to come" (John 16:13). The Holy Spirit, who is responsible to teach the disciples of Christ all things and to remind them of Jesus' teachings, equips the

15. Robert H. Stein, *The Method and Message of Jesus' Teachings* (Philadelphia: Westminster, 1978), provides a helpful categorization of the forms of Jesus' teaching. He points out that three important considerations in teaching include what is taught, who the teacher is, and how the teacher teaches.

16. James D. Stewart, *The Life and Teaching of Jesus Christ* (Nashville: Abingdon, n.d.), 64–71.

Christian teacher to effectively minister and releases the creativity necessary to appropriately understand and share Christian truths.

Effective teaching and learning require the continuing presence and work of the Holy Spirit. Teaching itself is described as one of the gifts bestowed upon the church by Christ through the Holy Spirit (Rom. 12:3–8; 1 Cor. 12:27–31; Eph. 4:7–13; 1 Peter 4:10–11). Teaching is not only a Spirit-endowed and -motivated gift, but teaching also requires that the teacher be continually filled and guided by the Holy Spirit in the process of teaching (Eph. 4:29–32; 5:15–20) The spiritual dimensions of education are foundational in a New Testament perspective.

The wisdom from the Holy Spirit is in contrast to the knowledge or wisdom from the world. This distinction is also explicit in James 3:13–18. In 1 Corinthians Paul describes a "wisdom of this age" (2:6) and a knowledge that puffs up (8:1–3). In comparison, "spirited" knowledge and wisdom are characterized by a love which builds up or edifies. Knowledge easily breeds conceit, provides glib answers, and at best is incomplete. What matters more is spiritual wisdom that is expressed in a love that promotes the good of others and glorifies God. Paul prays that the Ephesians might know the love of Christ that surpasses knowledge (3:19). Paul does not denounce knowledge but sees it being transcended through the work of the Holy Spirit making the love of Christ a reality.

From the experience of teaching an active group of twelve to fifteen junior high boys in East Harlem, New York City, the author can testify to the essential dimension of love shared both within and outside of the classroom. Beyond any knowledge shared in the lessons, students have commented over the years on the glimpses of God's love seen during Saturday outings and service projects.

Ephesians: Pattern and Purposes

A general pattern of Paul's ministry reflected in the Book of Ephesians, but also in his other writings, is one that incorporates instruction, intercession, and exhortation.[17] Instruction consists of a focus upon the content of Christian faith, upon what God has done. Intercession is prayer for those instructed with a conscious dependence upon God and the work of the Holy Spirit. The third element of the pattern is exhortation. Paul specifies what believers are to be and do in light of God's activities and revelation in Christ.

In addition to this general pattern, Ephesians 4:7–16 provides specific insights for discerning the purposes of the teaching or educational ministries of the church. Teaching is a spiritual gift. The immediate purpose

17. John Stott, *God's New Society: The Message of Ephesians* (Downers Grove, Ill.: Inter-Varsity, 1979), 146.

of teaching is the preparation of God's people for works of service within the church and world. A truth of particular significance for the Christian church in the twentieth century is the ministry of all believers. The sixteenth-century church affirmed the priesthood of all believers which is now being understood in terms of a ministry that each believer possesses. All of God's people must be equipped, taught, and trained for their varied ministries, making use of the gifts God has bestowed upon a covenant people.

Beyond this immediate purpose of preparation for works of service, there is an ultimate purpose for teaching, for educating. This ultimate purpose is the edification of the church. The gift of teaching is given so that the body of Christ, the church, might be built up. Whereas sanctification centers upon the personal spiritual growth of an individual, edification centers upon corporate spiritual growth that is by necessity mutual, collaborative, and cooperative. The church is Christ's body and his headship and lordship are essential if edification is to occur. This edification is in the areas of unity and maturity. Unity is a unity in the faith and knowledge of the Son of God and it is a unity in the truth. Maturity is in terms of the fullness of Christ. The church grows into this maturity by truth and love. Speaking the truth in love involves maintaining, living, and doing the truth within relationships of love.

Edification requires the corresponding work of sanctification; both processes are mutually supportive. Thus the purposes of education must include both corporate and personal dimensions of growth in the Christian faith. In addition, the immediate purpose of preparation for service must be seen in relationship to the ultimate purpose of edification. It is through actual opportunities for service that the body of Christ is built up. Therefore, education in the Christian faith that does not issue in service can be questioned as being inadequate in the same way that the Book of James questions a faith that is devoid of deeds (James 2:14–26).

Colossians and Philippians

Wisdom in Christ   In Colossians 1:9–14 Paul prays that God will fill the Colossian Christians with a knowledge of God's will through all spiritual wisdom and understanding. He prays this in order that these Christians might live their lives worthy of the Lord, pleasing God in every way. Paul specifies ways in which this worthiness might be expressed: bearing fruit in every good work; growing in the knowledge of God; being strengthened with all power according to God's glorious might; and joyfully giving thanks to God. In other words, service, spiritual growth and empowerment, and worship are evidences of the application of Christian knowledge and wisdom to life.

Paul goes on to emphasize the supremacy of Christ in creation and his centrality in the experience of Christians. It is in Christ that Christians have redemption, the forgiveness of sins (1:14). It is in Christ that Christians must center their education. Paul describes his purpose in ministering that fellow believers "may have the full riches of complete understanding, in order that they may know the mystery of God, namely, Christ, in whom are hidden all the treasures of wisdom and knowledge" (2:2–3). It is in Christ that integration and wholeness in education can be found because in him are all the treasures of wisdom and knowledge. Reality itself is found in him (2:17). Paul warns of hollow and deceptive philosophy, which depends on human tradition and the basic principles of this world, rather than on Christ (2:8). It is essential that the christocentric character of Christian education be recognized and affirmed at its roots. Christ himself is at the center of all of life from a Christian world and life view.

In relation to the centrality of Christ and the treasures of wisdom and knowledge in him, the Christian is called to a rigorous task in the area of education. This task is suggested by Paul's exhortations to the Christians in Philippi. In Philippians 4:8–9, Paul shares a vast agenda for Christian educators at all levels of society:

> Finally, brothers, whatever is true, whatever is noble, whatever is right, whatever is pure, whatever is lovely, whatever is admirable—if anything is excellent or praiseworthy—think about such things. Whatever you have learned or received or heard from me, or seen in me—put it into practice. And the God of peace will be with you.

This is an agenda that encompasses all the areas of human intellectual endeavor and study. In relation to these areas, Christians are to think about such things, are to take such things into account. They are to allow this valuable knowledge to shape their attitudes and lives. But the obligation does not end with mere thought or reflection. Whatever the Philippian Christians had learned, received, or heard from Paul, or had seen in him, was to be put into practice. Thought without practice is incomplete. It is also helpful to note that Paul's influence was not only direct and intentional through what was learned, received, and heard, but it was also unintentional and indirect. Paul himself served as a model so that what was seen in his life was also instructive. This is the dimension of teaching that is more caught than taught through the teacher's relationships with students.

Supremacy of Relationships   With an emphasis upon wisdom and knowledge, Christian educators must also be aware of the dimension of interpersonal relationships which the New Testament addresses. Christian education centers on relationships with the triune God and with other persons. Various biblical texts could be cited that deal with relationships among persons as they are to be patterned after the foundational relationship with God. One passage of particular significance is John 15:12–17, which presents Jesus' new commandment to love others as he himself has loved his disciples. This is overwhelming and yet foundational for all interpersonal interactions in Christian education.

Also of significance is the nature of Jesus' relationship, as the Master Teacher, with his disciples, his students. Jesus shared his very life by laying it down for his disciples. They were not just viewed as servants, but most significantly as friends. Wherever possible, teachers are called upon to foster friendship with students and to give of themselves sacrificially following the model of Jesus. Sacrificial giving can include such efforts as being available both before and after scheduled teaching times for interaction and active listening with students.

Paul describes his relationship to his Thessalonian disciples as one that includes both maternal and paternal dimensions (1 Thess. 2:7–12). In verse 8, Paul says that not only were the ministers and teachers delighted to share the gospel of God, but their lives as well. The maternal dimension included care and nurture while the paternal dimension included encouraging, comforting, and urging others to live lives worthy of God. The challenge is for Christian teachers to be open to a level of servanthood that places the teacher in a position of risk and vulnerability in loving and interacting with students. This interaction requires the sharing of one's very life and the willingness to serve as an example in guiding others. Being an example does not mean that the teacher is a complete and sinless person, but one who with others is in need of forgiveness and yet still seeks to be faithful.

Complementing the focus upon love in relationships is the dimension of truth. Ephesians 4:15, 2 John 1, and 1 Peter 1:22 link the virtues of love and truth in encouraging Christians to speak or maintain the truth in love or to love in truth. There needs to be a standard of truth. For the Christian educator, this is provided in the Scriptures and consummately in the person of Jesus Christ. There is the assurance that all truth, wherever discerned, is God's truth for God alone is its source. Truth without love results in harshness; and love without truth results in compromise. The Christian gospel maintains both of these virtues together in a creative complementarity.[18] A constant challenge posed in every educational setting is to balance love and truth.

18. See Thom Hopler, *A World of Difference: Following Christ Beyond Our Cultural Walls* (Downers Grove, Ill.: Inter-Varsity, 1981), 185–95, for a helpful general discussion of these themes.

An additional responsibility for teachers is suggested by the admonition in 2 Timothy 2:2. Teachers are called to duplicate their efforts through the teaching ministries of their students. Persons taught are to be prepared and equipped to teach others. Thus the Christian teacher is to be sensitive to opportunities to disciple others. In order to fulfill this obligation, the Christian teacher is dependent upon the work and presence of God the Creator, Redeemer, and Sustainer.

Hebrews: A Question of Readiness

Hebrews 5:11–6:3 provides insights for the important question of readiness prior to and during teaching interactions:

> We have much to say about this, but it is hard to explain because you are slow to learn. In fact, though by this time you ought to be teachers, you need someone to teach you the elementary truths of God's Word all over again. You need milk, not solid food! Anyone who lives on milk, being still an infant, is not acquainted with the teaching about righteousness. But solid food is for the mature, who by constant use have trained themselves to distinguish good from evil.
>
> Therefore let us leave the elementary teachings about Christ and go on to maturity, not laying again the foundation of repentance from acts that lead to death, and of faith in God, instruction about baptisms, the laying on of hands, the resurrection of the dead, and eternal judgment. And God permitting, we will do so.

The writer to the Hebrews warns against those who may fall away from the faith and explains that some need to be retaught the elementary truths of God's Word. This is the case because they had not understood, accepted, or exemplified these truths in their lives. These particular persons are slow to learn. Using the metaphor of food, the writer notes that some persons need the milk of elementary teaching because they cannot handle the solid food of teachings for the mature. Other passages also describe various levels of maturity (1 Cor. 2:6–3:4; 9:19–23; Titus 2:1–15; 1 Peter 5:1–7) that need to be assessed and considered in any teaching endeavor. Christian educators are called to have discernment in adjusting their teaching to the spiritual, social, cultural, economic, and political characteristics of their hearers in the effort to address participants at appropriate levels of understanding and readiness.

The issue of adequately assessing the readiness of participants in Christian education efforts is complex and can be overwhelming when one considers the wide variety of variables that influence persons individually, corporately, and contextually. Yet there is a resource person who is available to Christian educators for this task. That person is the Holy Spirit. But in discussing the ministry of the Holy Spirit, who assists Christian teachers in assessing the readiness of participants and planning appropriately for it, teachers must realize that their readiness also is an issue. Educators are reminded of the warning in James 3:1: "Not many of you should presume to be teachers, my brothers, because you know that we who teach will be judged more strictly." Part of that judgment involves the discernment that one in fact has the gift of teaching. Confirmation of that gift involves active service and a genuine openness to the feedback of others and to the improvement of one's skills.

An Integrated Model

Based upon the biblical foundations for Christian education, it is possible to suggest a model to guide current thought and practice. E. V. Hill uses the image of a softball or baseball diamond to suggest the tasks of the contemporary Christian church.[19] But moving beyond the confines of a baseball diamond, a network or web of education can be proposed for the church's tasks. These tasks have direct implications for the purposes of Christian education (see fig. 2).

In this model, one base represents education for evangelism (*kerygma*) that seeks to enable persons to consider their personal commitment to Jesus Christ. By necessity this purpose includes sharing the basic content of the Christian faith. It also includes teaching about the need for personal response, about the need to make a decision regarding

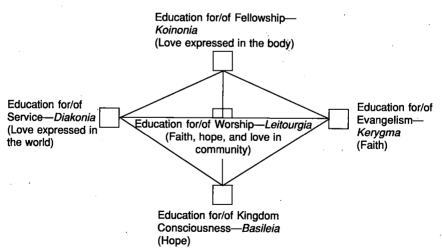

FIGURE 2   The Educational Tasks of the Church

19. Edward V. Hill, "A Congregation's Response," lecture presented at Gordon-Conwell Theological Seminary, South Hamilton, Mass., 21 January 1976.

the new life offered in Jesus Christ. Persons are not educated into God's kingdom, but educational ministries are opportunities for persons to explore the dimensions of faith in response to the gospel. The Christian virtue most closely, but not exclusively, associated with this thrust in Christian education is faith.[20]

Faith can be viewed as including the dimensions of *notitia* (intellectual affirmation), *assensus* (affective affirmation), and *fiducia* (intentional affirmation) as persons respond to God's activities and revelation in Jesus Christ. Education for evangelism focuses upon enabling persons to explore and grapple with these dimensions of faith and encouraging their response. This response includes an initial personal response and then efforts to share the Christian faith with others. The proclamation of the *kerygma* is crucial in this process (Rom. 10:17), with educational encounters providing for dialogue on the issues of faith in addition to the proclamation of the gospel. This base centers upon faith which is most often related to the temporal dimension of the past with an assurance based upon Christ's completed work in history.

In addition to education for evangelism with its explicit and active emphasis upon *kerygma* or proclamation, this base also represents the education of evangelism. The education of evangelism denotes the more receptive and implicit teaching and learning that occur through the witness of the Christian faith in word and deed. Education for evangelism includes encouraging the response of non-Christians to the claims of Christ and training Christians for their witness in formal settings. Education of evangelism includes the nonformal and informal learning that occur when Christians personally and corporately own their commitments to Christ and the implications of such commitments before the world in various ways. For example, a local church's advocacy and/or outreach to single parents and their participation in church life, or a church's commitment to honesty and integrity in its economic and political life can be a proclamation of the gospel.

A second base represents education for fellowship (*koinonia*)—fellowship with God and with other Christians. It includes the processes of training, instruction, and nurture which enable persons to grow and mature in their faith.[21] Maturation and growth, given the nature of

20. Christian virtues or values become important in Christian education because who and what persons are and are becoming in Christ are central concerns. See, for example, 1 Timothy 4:12–16.

21. *Training* can be defined as education that deals with predictable, replicable situations. Training is a conserving element of education that emphasizes continuities with the past and the passing on of an unchanging heritage. *Instruction* can be defined as education that deals with unpredictable situations. Instruction is a transforming element of education that emphasizes renewal and change in response to changing situations in

Christian community and fellowship, include not only personal sanctification, but also corporate or mutual edification. For the purpose of analysis, it is possible to distinguish training, instruction, and nurture, and to include both personal and corporate dimensions. But in actuality, these various elements should complement each other and foster an integration of biblical content and experience, of faith and life. The Christian virtue most closely, but again, not exclusively, associated with education for fellowship is that of love as it is expressed within the body for others. Love as a virtue relates most closely to the temporal dimension of the present, with a focus on maximizing the potential of each current situation and interaction.

Paralleling the active and receptive models of the first base described, this second base can also be seen as encompassing two facets. The education of fellowship includes those learnings and implied insights and values which are communicated through the shared life of the faith community. For example, church dinners that seek to include everybody and perhaps share various ethnic, cultural, and racial dishes communicate and teach values and attitudes beyond formal training and instruction. Lessons more caught than taught comprise the elements of education of fellowship, and each faith community, group, family, or school must ask itself what in fact is being nurtured during times together.

A third base represents education for service (*diakonia*)—service to God, to other persons, and to the world. Christian educators are called to equip Christians for the task of service within the local church and the task of incarnating their faith in life through social action. In terms of the wider society, Christians are called to a prophetic ministry, to be vehicles for Christ's transforming power that can be effective at several different levels. Christians are called to be salt and light in various organizations and institutions, to work for justice and righteousness in various economic, political, social, educational, and ecclesiastical structures. The church order outlined in Ephesians 4:7–13 points up the need to work for the ministry of all believers, each serving and ministering in the contexts of their homes, work places, communities, societies, and world.

Christ's transforming power is also operative in the intentional and ideational realms, where knowledge and meanings are produced and distributed. A Christian world and life view is crucial for realizing mean-

society and a consideration of the discontinuities with the past. It envisions new possibilities and calls for the personal and corporate responses of Christians. *Nurture* involves love, nourishment, and spiritual direction. Nurture, by its very nature, requires a vital and intimate relationship and interaction with others.

ing, purpose, and integration in life, and the call is to bring every thought captive in obedience to Christ (2 Cor. 10:5), recognizing that it is the Lord who gives wisdom and that from his mouth come knowledge and understanding (Prov. 2:6).

This renewing power of Christ is also needed in the realm of culture with its various values, beliefs, and attitudes. Christ seeks to preserve, redeem, and transform cultures. Christians need spiritual discernment in exploring how the Christian faith interacts with surrounding cultures. The Christian virtue most closely associated with this third base, as is the case with second base, is love. But in this instance, love is primarily focused upon the world and expressed in deed and word through service. As with the second base, the temporal focus is on the present.

This third base includes a receptive mode to complement the active stance of education for service. Advocacy for various persons, groups, and causes, along with actual deeds of service, provide occasions when others can learn from both Christians and non-Christians. Christians, for example, can learn the real human costs of certain political, social, and economic policies through ministries with the poor and in the process be spiritually enriched through contacts with disadvantaged Christians. On the other hand, non-Christians can gain insights about the Christian faith from the sacrificial service of Christians in the world as they serve as living epistles to the transforming power of Jesus Christ.

The fourth base signifies education for kingdom consciousness (basileia). Christians are called to realize that their hope is in God and God's reign in history. Human efforts in ministries must be evaluated in terms of kingdom values. Outcomes must be evaluated in terms of God's creative and redemptive purposes for all humankind, which include concerns for justice, peace, and righteousness. God's purpose is "to bring all things in heaven and on earth together under one head, even Christ" (Eph. 1:10). All of creation awaits the future glory that God will bring to fruition in the completed adoption of God's children and the redemption of their bodies (Rom. 8:18–27). There will be a new heaven and a new earth which will be the home of righteousness as God has promised (2 Peter 3:13). John speaks of God's future in Revelation 21:1–5:

> Then I saw a new heaven and a new earth, for the first heaven and the first earth had passed away, and there was no longer any sea. I saw the Holy City, the new Jerusalem, coming down out of heaven from God, prepared as a bride beautifully dressed for her husband. And I heard a loud voice from the throne saying, "Now the dwelling of God is with men, and he will live with them. They will be his people, and God himself will be with them and be their God. He will wipe every tear from their eyes. There will be no more death or mourning or crying or pain, for the old order of things has passed away."

He who was seated on the throne said, "I am making everything new!" Then he said, "Write this down, for these words are trustworthy and true."

This perspective of God's future kingdom does not negate an appreciation of the past, nor an active working in the present to cooperate with God's purposes within the church and within the world. Education for kingdom consciousness encourages Christians to gain this perspective on the future and God's purposes. The Christian virtue logically associated with this fourth base is hope, which envisions God's future and human participation in that future.

Education for/of kingdom consciousness includes both acculturation and disenculturation. Acculturation is a process which affirms the place of a particular Christian culture and becoming a responsible member of a community in which that culture is affirmed. In contrast with acculturation, disenculturation is a process which places the values of God's kingdom above any given cultural expression and community of the Christian faith. Both processes are interdependent and necessary, for as Leslie Newbigin has aptly observed, "the gospel provides the stance from which all culture is to be evaluated; but the gospel . . . is always embodied in some cultural form."[22]

Education for kingdom consciousness can be seen as acculturation into the vision of God's future as embodied and expressed in a particular community with its proximate purposes for God's reign. Education of kingdom consciousness involves a receptive stance which enables a critical consciousness of proximate purposes in the light of the ultimate purposes of God's reign. A particular Christian community, for example, may emphasize the need for its participants to use the most updated media and technological resources to equip children and youth for the challenges of influencing modern Western culture. This can be viewed as an appropriate proximate purpose. But from the perspective of the kingdom values of shalom for all and stewardship of global resources, the tremendous outlay of capital to secure such media and technology may be questioned in terms of ultimate purposes.

The emphasis that centers and integrates educational efforts at each of the four bases is education for worship (*leitourgia*), located at the center of the diamond network. In educational ministries, persons are to be encouraged to see the sovereign God as Lord of all and therefore worthy of worship, honor, glory, and praise. Education for worship encourages persons to celebrate the presence of God in all areas of life and

22. Leslie Newbigin, *Foolishness to the Greeks: The Gospel and Western Culture* (Grand Rapids: Wm. B. Eerdmans, 1986), 21.

to respond with the sacrifice of their very lives (Rom. 12:1, 2). Abraham Heschel is one religious educator who has spoken directly to this need. Heschel points out that the Greeks learned in order to comprehend, the modern person learns in order to use, but the Hebrews learned in order to revere. Heschel reminds Christian educators of the need to encourage students to revere, to sense wonder and awe in response to God and to God's multifaceted creation.[23]

Christian educators have not adequately addressed education for worship. Instead, models of education emphasizing production and efficiency have been perpetuated. Alternative models based upon biblical sources can provide opportunities for persons to reflect upon the majesty and wonder of God and God's workings. They can tap the creative potential of persons that find expression in praise of God. The chief end and purpose of education, as of life, can thus be seen in terms of the glorification and enjoyment of God. William Temple said: "To worship is to quicken the conscience by the holiness of God, to feed the mind with the truth of God, to purge the imagination by the beauty of God, to open the heart to the love of God, to devote the will to the purpose of God."[24] Christian education at its best will enable persons to worship the one true God in all of God's fullness and grandeur.

In addition to education for worship, the education of worship must be noted. Worship is active participation in the liturgy of the faith community which attributes honor, glory, praise, and worth to God. This active participation can result in receptivity to new insights regarding God, self, others, or the world. Such receptivity can include cognitive, aesthetic, emotional, intuitive, volitional, and spiritual insights and bring a greater sense of wholeness and integration to life.

Beyond the particulars of each base, educators must be aware of the interconnections among the bases to form a network. The first base of *kerygma* primarily emphasizes knowing and its complement at the third base of *diakonia* emphasizes doing. For effective educational ministry, both knowing and doing of the faith must be addressed along this first axis. The second basis of *koinonia* emphasizes feeling at one or being reconciled with God, others, and all of creation while being in the world. The complement of this second base is the fourth base of *basileia*, which stresses not so much feeling at one as feeling distinct or being not of the world in relation to values of God's kingdom. As with the first axis, understanding educational ministry along this second axis requires bal-

23. Abraham J. Heschel, *Between God and Man: An Interpretation of Judaism from the Writings of Abraham Heschel*, ed. Fritz A. Rothschild (New York: Free Press, 1959), 35–54.

24. William Temple, *The Hope of a New World* (London: Student Christian Movement Press, 1941), 30.

ancing the Christian vocation of being in, but not of the world, balancing the reconciliation of the already present blessings of God with the anticipation of the "not yet." The fifth and central base of *leitourgia* serves as the nexus of the two axes, where the challenges of knowing, feeling, and doing are brought into perspective in relation to discerning the eternal purposes of God and orienting all of life to God's glory. It is upon these bases that the educational ministry of the Christian church is to be founded.

The biblical foundations for Christian education are multiple but can be woven together to provide an impressive tapestry of ministry in the service of Jesus Christ. The warp and woof of that tapestry are the efforts of the sovereign and triune God and those of God's adopted family who have been gifted and equipped for educational ministry.

The perspective of Scripture provides the essential basis for educational ministries. In their various efforts, Christian educators may well take to heart Peter's exhortation:

> Each one should use whatever gift he has received to serve others, faithfully administering God's grace in its various forms. If anyone speaks, he should do it as one speaking the very words of God. If anyone serves, he should do it with the strength God provides, so that in all things God may be praised through Jesus Christ. To him be the glory and the power for ever and ever. Amen. (1 Peter 4:10–11)

Table 1 summarizes some of the foundational passages and major insights suggested in this chapter. Other portions of Scripture could be cited which provide additional insights and potential models. These are noted only to provide an initial basis for discussion and dialogue in grappling with biblical foundations. Further expansion with critical, canonical, and contextual studies is necessary. In considering these foundations, Christian educators need to evaluate their theological commitments, which raises issues to be explored in the following chapter.

Table 1 **Biblical Foundations for Christian Education**

Passage	Audience/Focus	Insight	Implication/Question
Deut. 6:1–9	Family/Parents	God's commands foster loving obedience.	Formal and nonformal instruction must be deliberate.
Deut. 30:11–20	Nation	A decision for life as offered by God is crucial.	The priority of education emphasizing personal response must be seen.

Deut. 31:9–13	Faith Community	God's Word must be shared.	Focus on the Word of God must include opportunities for response.
Deut. 31:30–32:4	Nation	Liberation and celebration are purposes for teaching.	Does our teaching empower and issue in worship and joy?
Ps. 78	Intergenerations	The stories/ accounts of God must be passed on.	Intergenerational sharing is indispensable.
Neh. 8:1–18	Nation	Teachers must foster under- standing and obedience.	A wholistic response to God's Word can bring personal and communal renewal.
Wisdom Literature	Teaching Relationships	Wisdom must be shared.	Biblical wisdom is practical.
Matt.	Jesus' Disciples	Jesus suggests a new educational agenda.	Obedient disciples are nurtured by sharing vision, memory, and mission.
Luke 24:13–35	Disciples	A teacher must be attentive to students.	Dialogue and listening are valuable for disclosure.
1 Cor. 2:6–16	Faith Community	Spiritual wisdom is distinct.	How can one foster the message and work of the Holy Spirit in teaching?
Eph.	Church	Equipping and training for ministry is the purpose of education.	Mutual edification requires active commitment and service.
Col./Phil.	Christian Wisdom	We must use our minds for Christ.	The pursuit of truth requires diligence in thought and practice.
John 15:12–17	Christian Relationships	Love and truth are both needed.	Interpersonal relationships require attention.
1 Thes. 2:7–12	Discipling Relationships	Teachers share their life and message in teaching.	Female and male dimensions of nurture must be affirmed.
Heb. 5:11–6:3	Teaching Relationships	A varied diet may be necessary.	Consider readiness in teaching.

2

Theological Foundations

In emphasizing the final authority of Scripture as divine revelation, evangelicals have been predisposed to grapple seriously with biblical sources in all areas of faith and practice. Therefore, in dealing with education, both as a theoretical and practical endeavor, evangelicals have turned to Scripture and to biblical theology in considering various principles. In general, evangelicals have had a predisposition to emphasize a theological approach in education over against one that highlights the social sciences. Specifically, evangelicals have tended to emphasize propositional theology over against process, liberation, existential, neoorthodox, natural, or other theologies in their educational efforts. Thus evangelicals have had a preference for the term *Christian education* as compared with *religious education* to denote an emphasis upon Christian and evangelical distinctives of theology that guide thought and practice. This preference for Christian distinctives has occasionally resulted in limited dialogue with those who identify the academic community of religious educators with a more pluralistic and diverse effort.

Four Theological Distinctives

An evangelical approach to religious education emphasizes four distinctives that are primarily theological in nature: biblical authority, the

49

necessity of conversion, the redemptive work of Jesus Christ, and personal piety. Each of these distinctives can be viewed as a gift that God has graciously bestowed upon the church for the advance of God's work in the world. But in relation to each of these distinctives or graces, a potential danger exists: each distinctive must be related to the greater revelation of God's truth that holds each grace in proper balance with other graces. This is the case in individual experience as well as in the corporate experience of evangelicalism.

An individual's strength can potentially become a weakness if it limits his or her awareness of other dimensions of life, truth, or relationships. For example, a person can so emphasize his or her physical development that mental, social, psychological, or spiritual development is inappropriately ignored. Likewise, one may be so consumed with a particular aspect of personal spiritual growth, that responsibilities to others are largely unfulfilled. With the need for balance in the whole of the Christian life, evangelical educators can appreciate their distinctives while being aware of potential dangers that result from overemphasis, imbalance, and lack of sensitivity.

Biblical Authority

Evangelical educators consciously grapple with biblical revelation and claim to be "under the Word of God." The written Word of God is Scripture in its entirety and variety, and evangelicals are to teach the whole counsel of God. This stance does not imply a mindless literalism, but appropriation of the plain or commonsense meaning of Scripture as normative for thought and practice. The Scriptures are viewed as divinely inspired and believers are called to discern a biblical agenda in the area of Christian education, as in all areas of thought and practice. The Scriptures function as the final authority and serve as the grid through which all other truths are examined for their consistency with a Christian world and life view.

As compared with a relatively greater emphasis in other traditions upon persons reading the Bible to discern truths that relate to their experience, evangelicals emphasize that the Bible itself "reads" or confronts persons and proposes a world and life view which they are to appropriate and to live. Certainly, the evangelical educator does not exclude the practice of reading the Bible, but emphasizes that final authority resides in biblical revelation over against reason, tradition, or experience, which are secondary sources for understanding. Scripture functions as the Word of God. Thus evangelicals must carefully attend to the biblical foundations cited in chapter 1 to guide their educational programs.

The danger of such a distinctive is that it can lead to a dead orthodoxy, a literalism or biblicism emphasizing biblical propositions divorced from life. It can also result in an educational practice which imposes truths upon persons without enabling them to think seriously about and grapple with the implications of affirming such truths. Such an imposition is manipulative indoctrination, and does not result in personal appropriation, internalization, and the transfer of learning to other situations. Such an authoritarian stance in education demands mindless compliance and obedience at the loss of personal integrity and rationality. It reduces the response of loving obedience to God to a superficial conformity contrary to a biblical understanding of persons. A mindless and spiritless focus upon the written Word may not result in vital contact with the living Word, Jesus Christ.

The Necessity of Conversion

Evangelism and conversion are issues at stake in evangelical education which complement a focus upon catechesis and nurture. Catechesis is instruction that fosters the integration of Christian truth with life. Nurture is the interpersonal sharing among Christians characterized by love and spiritual nourishment. Both catechesis and nurture presume that the teacher, parent, model, or discipler is a committed Christian and that the student is either a Christian or one who is and will be seriously considering a commitment to Christ as Lord and Savior.

Through educational efforts the basic truths of biblical faith are shared, namely, the great saving acts of God in the birth, life, death, and resurrection of Jesus Christ. But in sharing these basic truths, a constant emphasis is made upon personal response and the need for commitment. In his letter to the Thessalonians, Paul thanks God for the faith response of these Christians to his ministry among them. Their response evidences the new life that they found in their conversion to the living and true God:

> For we know, brothers loved by God, that he has chosen you, because our gospel came to you not simply with words, but also with power, with the Holy Spirit and with deep conviction. You know how we lived among you for your sake. You became imitators of us and of the Lord; in spite of severe suffering, you welcomed the message with the joy given by the Holy Spirit. And so you became a model to all the believers in Macedonia and Achaia. The Lord's message rang out from you not only in Macedonia and Achaia—your faith in God has become known everywhere. Therefore we do not need to say anything about it, for they themselves report what kind of reception you gave us. They tell how you turned to God from idols to serve the living and true God, and to wait for his Son from heaven, whom he raised from the dead—Jesus, who rescues us from the coming wrath (1 Thess. 1:4–10).

Paul provides a similar description of the experience of salvation, of being made alive in Christ, in Ephesians 2:1–9:

> As for you, you were dead in your transgressions and sins, in which you used to live when you followed the ways of this world and of the ruler of the kingdom of the air, the spirit who is now at work in those who are disobedient. All of us also lived among them at one time, gratifying the cravings of our sinful nature and following its desires and thoughts. Like the rest, we were by nature objects of wrath. But because of his great love for us, God, who is rich in mercy, made us alive with Christ even when we were dead in transgressions—it is by grace you have been saved. And God raised us up with Christ and seated us with him in the heavenly realms in Christ Jesus, in order that in the coming ages he might show the incomparable riches of his grace, expressed in his kindness to us in Christ Jesus. For it is by grace you have been saved, through faith—and this not from yourselves, it is the gift of God—not by works, so that no one can boast. For we are God's workmanship, created in Christ Jesus to do good works, which God prepared in advance for us to do.

This matter of conversion is also made explicit by John in 1 John 5:9–12, in which faith in the Son of God is essential:

> We accept man's testimony, but God's testimony is greater because it is the testimony of God, which he has given about his Son. Anyone who believes in the Son of God has this testimony in his heart. Anyone who does not believe in God has made him out to be a liar, because he has not believed the testimony God has given about his Son. And this is the testimony: God has given us eternal life, and this life is in his Son. He who has the Son has life; he who does not have the Son of God does not have life.

It is absolutely essential that evangelism be a key purpose of the educational ministry of the church. Evangelism can be defined as the presentation of Jesus Christ in the power of the Holy Spirit that enables persons to place their faith in God through Christ, to accept Christ as their Savior, and to serve their King in the fellowship of his church.[1]

Evangelism is not simply "soul winning," because the Christian faith, as Harold Mason has pointed out, is concerned with Christian intelligence, Christian nurture, Christian culture, and personal choice.[2] Edu-

1. This definition is adopted from that of William Temple, cited in Michael Green, *Evangelism Now and Then* (Leicester, England: Inter-Varsity, 1979), 13–14.

2. Harold Mason, *The Teaching Task of the Local Church* (Winona Lake, Ind.: Light & Life Press, 1960), 173.

cational evangelism, then, can be defined as reaching and guiding persons in the direction of a personal experience of Christ as Lord and Savior, which does not replace either personal or mass evangelism.[3]

In relation to the three dimensions of saving faith mentioned in chapter 1 (*notitia, assenus,* and *fiducia*), educational evangelism primarily focuses upon *notitia,* the intellectual dimension of faith. Education generally appeals to reason and deals with intellectual content. Although it does not exclude the dimensions of *assensus* and *fiducia,* which emphasize the emotional and volitional dimensions of faith, by its essential nature education shares those *indicia* or facts about the faith that support an intellectual grappling with the person and work of Jesus Christ.

What impact does this distinctive have upon practice? Mason suggests some helpful corollaries for this emphasis on educational evangelism:

1. The student must know the moral law and the implications of the Christian ethic for morally responsible persons.
2. The teacher/evangelist must herself or himself have experienced that which she or he teaches to others, that is, must be a Christian.
3. The teacher must devote time and care to young Christians who must be nurtured in the faith and grow in grace.
4. Educational evangelism involves a knowledge of basic principles of Christian theology.
5. One of the functions of the church's educational ministry is enlistment or recruitment of new participants.
6. One of the evangelistic functions of any Christian education program, such as the Sunday school, is to encourage students to hear the preaching of God's Word.
7. United prayer for those considering Christian commitment should be a regular component of preparation for teaching.
8. Parents in Christian homes must be supported in their efforts to make the Christian faith significant in their personal lives and in the lives of their children and youth.[4]

The danger of such a distinctive is that it may lead to easy believism, shallow discipleship, and "soul winning" devoid of substance in the effort to encourage a personal faith response to Jesus Christ. Dietrich Bonhoeffer poignantly warns of a cheap grace that ignores the costs of discipleship and the implications of affirming Christ as Lord as well as Savior.[5] Educational evangelism, therefore, must be explicit about the

3. Ibid.
4. Ibid., 173–83.
5. See Dietrich Bonhoeffer, *The Cost of Discipleship,* rev. ed. (New York: Macmillan, 1959).

costs and responsibilities of faith in Christ. Such evangelism must also evidence a concern for whole persons and not merely their souls or spirits. Educational programs that teach a spiritual gospel which ignores physical and social needs and neglects discipleship are shallow and abortive.

There is a real danger inherent in an educational evangelism that fails to be representative of the whole gospel:

Your Holiness and My Loneliness

I was hungry and you held meetings to discuss my hunger.

I was imprisoned and you crept off quietly to pray for my release.

I was persecuted and you explained to me how Christ was persecuted.

I was sick and you knelt down and thanked God for your health.

I was homeless and you preached to me of the spiritual shelter of the love of God.

I was lonely and you left me alone to pray for me.

You seem so holy and I'm still very lonely.*

Evangelicals must likewise beware of a social involvement that ignores the proclamation of the gospel and the vital place of evangelism.

The Redemptive Work of Jesus Christ

Carl F. Henry observes that evangelical Christians "affirm the fundamental doctrines of the gospel, including the incarnation and virgin birth of Christ, his sinless life, substitutionary atonement, and bodily resurrection as the ground of God's forgiveness of sinners, justification by faith alone, and the spiritual regeneration of all who trust in the redemptive work of Jesus Christ."[6]

Evangelical educators affirm these fundamental doctrines because they provide the essential framework in which the Christian faith has been historically defined. Frank Gaebelein clarifies how these doctrines function for the evangelical:

> It is these that make up the framework of our Christian world view. What are they? They are the facts upon which Christianity rests. Included in them are the existence of the living God, the Maker of heaven

---

*This poem was discovered by Michael Green on the door of a chaplain's office at a hospital in Africa. It was recounted in his lecture series, "Foundations for Evangelism from the New Testament Churches" (Miami, Fla.: Mobile Media, 1978).

6. Carl F. H. Henry, "Evangelical," in *The New International Dictionary of the Christian Church*, ed. J. D. Douglas, rev. ed. (Grand Rapids: Zondervan, 1978), 358–59.

and earth; man's creation in the image of God, an image ruined through the fall beyond human power to repair, but not beyond God's power to regenerate; the incarnation of God the Son and His redemption of lost humanity; the activity of God the Holy Spirit in calling out of this present world a community of believers which is Christ's Body, the Church; and, finally, the end of earthly history through the "glorious appearing of the great God and our Saviour Jesus Christ."

Let us understand once and for all that there is nothing sectarian about these truths; they are common to all branches of the Christian church. Granted that in many quarters they have been and are today being watered down through concessions and reservations, or obscured through man-made tradition and dogma, the fact remains that such truths as these stand as both the foundation and frame of reference for a Christian world view. It is upon them that Christian education must build; it is within them that it must work.[7]

In dealing with the actual impact of these beliefs upon the thought and practice of education, it is appropriate for the educator to consider some possible implications. For example, if one affirms God as Creator, what is the proper attitude to the use of the land and resources as an outworking of ecological responsibilities?

Whereas this distinctive enables clarity of belief and continuity with biblical revelation, it may lead to a static and uncritical stance that fails to address the need for contextualization. Contextualization is the continual process by which truth is applied to and emerges from concrete historical situations. This process grapples with the implications of the gospel's values for the actual transformation of realities and with commitments to that transformation. This process also raises questions about cultural impositions that distort the radical demands of the New Testament.

A faithfulness to Christ requires scrutiny in relation to various personal, cultural, political, economic, and social realities. These realities may be affirmed, rejected, or transformed in relation to the demands of affirming Christ as Lord and working for the advance of his kingdom in the world. God's sovereign rule in the person of Jesus Christ and allegiance to Christ requires the Christian to live out the good news as well as believe it. Evangelicals may be reluctant to address such realities and opt for a "ghettoized" existence that fails to struggle with how Christ relates to various cultures and societal issues. This is done under the peril of denial of the Christian faith and its power. A theological certainty that eliminates the need for contextualization denies God's creative and providential works in history and in the present world.

7. Frank E. Gaebelein, *The Pattern of God's Truth: Problems of Integration in Christian Education* (New York: Oxford University Press, 1954), 34–35.

A crucial issue is the relationship of theology to Christian education. Sara Little suggests the following possibilities:

1. Theology is the content to be taught in Christian education.
2. Theology is the point of reference for what is to be taught and for methodology, and functions as the norm for the critical work of analysis and evaluation of all Christian education.
3. Theology is irrelevant to the task of Christian education; Christian education is autonomous.
4. "Doing theology" or theologizing is Christian education in the sense of enabling persons to reflect on their current experiences and perspectives in the light of the Christian faith and revelation.
5. Theology and Christian education are separate disciplines that are engaged mutually and collegially in the advance of God's kingdom.

Little also points out that no one alternative is the only way to relate Christian education and theology.[8]

While being aware of the danger of positing one definitive relationship, evangelical educators can explore the implications of their theology in the resolution of this issue. The basic perspectives of evangelical theology would affirm Little's first two alternatives, neither of which is mutually exclusive. Theology can be viewed as both content and norm. Yet transmission does not have to be imposed or communicated in an authoritarian manner, but can be done with a sensitivity to persons and their needs. Nevertheless, truths essential for faith and practice must be taught. Without the communication of such essential truths, teaching that claims to be Christian can be unorthodox.

The third possibility Little mentions—theology as irrelevant to Christian education—is not an option for the evangelical educator who seeks to be consistent with his or her faith. An affirmation of Christ as Lord assumes the significance of theology, defined most simply as the study of God, for all of life. Theology grapples with the implications of faith as mediated through the experience of God's revelation. Such implications must deal with the thought and practice of education. Thus theology is indispensable for the task of Christian education.

The fourth possibility in Little's scheme poses unique challenges for the evangelical educator. Religious educators have emphasized the need for education to encourage the process in which persons become more skilled at using their faith to reflect upon contemporary experience and using their contemporary experience to reflect upon faith. This reflec-

8. Sara Little, "Theology and Religious Education," in *Foundations for Christian Education in an Era of Change*, ed. Marvin J. Taylor (Nashville: Abingdon, 1976), 31–33.

tion seeks to discern the action of God in history as it is being written, and to examine inherited religious conceptions for their adequacy in confronting global realities and problems. "Theologizing" or "doing theology" is the term applied to this process of reflection.[9] Evangelicals generally affirm the need for critical reflection and for addressing global realities. But evangelicals are extremely cautious in using contemporary experience to reflect upon faith. Their emphasis upon biblical authority resists the tendency to place experience as a higher authority than Scripture. Evangelicals are not reluctant to discuss or use personal experience. But experience functions as an evidence of faith, not as a judgment of faith for the evangelical.

Little's fifth possibility—theology in dialogue with Christian education—poses additional challenges. Christian educators can shape the reflection that characterizes the study of God in theology by raising essential questions. These questions have been posed by Thomas H. Groome in *Christian Religious Education.* Groome poses six questions that can be phrased with the interrogative pronouns *what, why, where, how, when,* and *who:*

1. *What* is the nature of Christian education? (nature and content)
2. *Why* is Christian education essential? (purposes)
3. *Where* is Christian education undertaken? (context)
4. *How* is Christian education conducted? (methods)
5. *When* is it appropriate to share particular Christian truths and experiences? (readiness)
6. *Who* is interacting in Christian education? (relationships)[10]

By addressing these six essential questions, Christian educators deal with theological issues in the areas of ecclesiology, soteriology, eschatology, anthropology, Christology, and the doctrine of God and Scripture as they affect education. Christian education at its best is an area of practical theology. It also explores the place of theology in the formation of persons who can mature in the Christian faith.

As Christian education can contribute to the tasks of theology, so theology can contribute to Christian education. Theology can be a tool for reflecting upon the thought and practice of Christian education. Theology can also inform the faithful practice of education by raising questions regarding consistency in relation to biblical values. A dialectical

9. See Norma Thompson's discussion of theology in "Current Issues in Religious Education," *Religious Education* 73 (November–December 1978):617.

10. Thomas H. Groome, *Christian Religious Education: Sharing Our Story and Vision* (San Francisco: Harper & Row, 1980), xiv.

interaction between theology and Christian education as separate disciplines can be established that enables the actualization of faithful Christian living within the church and the world. Thus cooperative dialogue can enhance the effectual and creative work of each discipline.

Personal Piety

As was the case with the second distinctive, evangelicals stress the need to personally appropriate the Christian faith and to grow in one's devotion to and walk with Christ. Because of this distinctive, evangelicals have historically fostered the development of spiritual affections and disciplines. This has not been done to the necessary exclusion of a reasoned faith, but rather as a complement to intellectual devotion to Christ. In some instances this has led to a religion of the heart devoid of a religion of the mind, but a balance of both emotional and intellectual dimensions of the faith is an ideal that is an element of the evangelical educational agenda. This distinctive is one that has been more covert or implicit than publicly affirmed and promoted.

The danger in this distinctive is a piety devoid of social consciousness given its personal and introspective preoccupation. A blatant disregard of social sins and a corresponding social passivism that condones the status quo can too readily emerge. A conservative theology can also imply a stance with regard to all of life that fails to be sensitive to God's continued activity in the historical process and God's giving the church new wineskins for the advance of God's kingdom in the world. A shallow piety can also result in the proposal of easy solutions to complex social problems and an insensitivity that divorces the Christian from cultural concerns.

The matter of culture raises an important question in relation to the place of culture from the standpoint of the Christian faith and Christian education. H. Richard Niebuhr proposes five possible relationships between Christ and culture[11] (see fig. 3):

1. *Christ against culture.* Christ is the sole authority; the claims of culture are to be rejected.
2. *Christ of culture.* The Christian system is not different from culture in kind but only in quality; the best culture should be selected to conform to Christ.
3. *Christ above culture.* The reception of grace perfects and completes culture though there is not a "smooth curve or continuous line" between them.

11. See H. Richard Niebuhr, *Christ and Culture* (New York: Harper & Row, 1956).

FIGURE 3* Christ and Culture

Type I Christ *Against* Culture	Type IV Christ and Culture in *Paradox*	Type V Christ the *Transformer* of Culture	Type III Christ *Above* Culture	Type II Christ *of* Culture	(The World of the Non-Christian: Rejection of Christ)
Tolstoy Tertullian John (1 John)	Paul Luther	John (Gospel of) Augustine F. D. Maurice	Clement of Alexandria Aquinas	Gnostics Abelard Ritschl	
Radical Christians	Dualists	Conversionists	Synthesists	Cultural Christians	

"The Church of the Center"

*Taken from David J. Hesselgrave, *Communicating Christ Cross-Culturally* (Grand Rapids: Zondervan, 1978), 81. Used by permission.

4. *Christ and culture in paradox.* Both are authorities to be obeyed; the believer, therefore, lives with this tension.
5. *Christ the transformer of culture.* Culture reflects the fallen state of persons; in Christ, persons are redeemed and culture can be renewed so as to glorify God and promote God's purposes.[12]

David J. Hesselgrave notes that from a biblical perspective there seems to be some value in emphases that fall under types 1, 4, and 5, and possibly, 3.[13] The danger of an emphasis on personal piety is that evangelical Christians may opt exclusively for type 1 or type 2 and thereby be unaware of either the impact of culture upon Christians or the potential influence of Christians upon culture. Evangelical Christians have generally opted for types 1, 4, and 5 in their educational thought and practice at various times and in various contexts.[14] A type 1 response results in a countercultural posture with the isolation of the Christian community from the wider culture. A type 4 response opts for a posture in which the church and wider society are viewed as complementary

12. David J. Hesselgrave, *Communicating Christ Cross-Culturally* (Grand Rapids: Zondervan, 1979) 79–80.
13. Ibid., 80.
14. A further discussion of culture is found in chapter 5.

and the status quo is maintained. A type 5 response assumes a proactive stance in working for renewal and reform at all levels of society.

An Orthodox Foundation

Beyond these four theological distinctives, it is possible to outline the theological foundations of evangelical education by referring to the Apostles' Creed. The Apostles' Creed provides a helpful framework for exploring questions of theology with affirmations regarding Scripture.[15] Each affirmation has implications for Christian education. In relation to these major theological doctrines of the orthodox or evangelical faith, some implications are provided that have direct relevance to the biblical foundations explored in chapter 1. It is possible to consider these implications even if one is not from a creedal tradition.

God the Creator

Because God is the Creator of the world and of humankind, God is the source of life and persons are responsible to God. God has in fact established a creative covenant with persons. A God-centered educational approach that is dependent upon divine revelation and that encourages persons to find meaning in the life that is in God is essential. Persons need to be instructed in their responsibilities as creatures of God. The status of creaturehood undermines an exclusive emphasis on human autonomy. Such an emphasis on autonomy ignores a dependency upon God and an interdependency with other persons and the created world. God has initiated efforts to be in communion with persons, and educational efforts should foster the response of persons to God. Persons are adopted as members of God's family with all the resulting privileges and responsibilities.

Because God is the redeemer-liberator of persons, groups, and societies, God is the source of righteousness, justice, and freedom; the one on whom persons must depend for fulfillment; and the initiator of a redemptive covenant. Human understanding and efforts in the areas of righteousness, justice, and freedom, therefore, must be subject to the divine agenda for actualization. This does not relieve human responsibility but subjects it to God's sovereignty.

Christian educators are called upon to raise the consciousness of persons in issues that relate to righteousness, justice, and freedom as components of God's continuing activity in the world. Given the realities of

15. For a further discussion of the place of the Apostle's Creed, see James D. Smart, *The Creed in Christian Teaching* (Philadelphia: Westminster, 1962); and Bernard L. Marthaler, *The Creed* (Mystic, Conn.: Twenty-Third Publications, 1987).

sin and its effects in personal and corporate life, persons are dependent upon God for redemption to realize fulfillment and freedom. The realities of sin and human fallenness must be addressed in Christian education. The need for structure, discipline, forgiveness, and reconciliation applies to educational interactions in which persons confront one another. The place of evangelism in Christian education is to be recognized; the outworkings of God's redemptive work in all human endeavors must be explored.

Jesus Christ

Jesus Christ is the Son of God, Lord and Savior, Son of Man, and King. Since Jesus Christ is the giver of life, Christian education must strive to be christocentric, enabling persons to know the living Word and to mature in him. Christian educators are called upon to help persons grapple with the implications of Christ's lordship personally and corporately. The reality of a new creation in Christ provides hope for educators and students alike in their joint efforts. As Son of Man, Jesus Christ is sensitive to the needs and dilemmas of human existence and actively intercedes for those who are committed to him. The example or model of Jesus Christ in his earthly life and teaching ministry is instructive for both teachers and students. Those who identify with Christ and his kingdom have obligations in relation to that kingdom. Teaching and learning can be seen as activities that glorify the name of Christ and extend his kingdom.

The Holy Spirit

The Holy Spirit is the activator and sustainer of life, the Spirit of truth, and the transformer of persons. Christian teachers, parents, administrators, and students must be sensitive to the work of the Spirit in motivating persons and pray for the Spirit's effectual working in their lives. The Holy Spirit applies, complements, and corrects human teaching. The human quest for truth in education must be seen in relation to God being the source of all truth. The Holy Spirit enlightens the minds of persons to discern truth in special and general revelation. The Spirit also enables persons to live in accordance with the truths disclosed or discovered. The Holy Spirit is the agent working for personal and social transformation among persons in the world. Christian educators must, therefore, be sensitive to the workings of the Holy Spirit in the areas of renewal and transformation. Ways of cooperating with the Holy Spirit both within and outside of the educational encounter must be explored. Recognition of transformation and renewal becomes a basis for thanksgiving and celebration.

The Written Word of God

The Bible is the basis for authority and is God's revelation and source of truth for all of life. The Bible functions as the final authority or screen through which all truths are evaluated. The authority of teachers and others who educate is derivative. It must be judged in terms of its consistency with God's revealed and discovered truth. The Bible is the essential, though not exclusive, content of Christian education. It provides a sufficient, though not exhaustive, guide for faith and life. Biblical truths must be integrated with all areas of educational thought and practice, with all subject areas and disciplines.

The Holy Catholic Church

The church is the body of Christ. It is holy by virtue of Christ's righteousness, and it is catholic in that it includes persons from all cultures, nations, and tribes across the ages. In the church, a variety of ministries parallels the various New Testament descriptions. The educational mission of the church has manifold expressions. A diversity of gifts for teaching and a diversity of insights from learning can be celebrated by the church. The church is both an organization and an organism and concerns for both structures and relationships are appropriate.

The Communion of Saints

Christian persons form the Christian family or community of faith. Those involved in education are called to maintain positive relationships that balance concerns for truth and love. Relationships are to bring honor to the name of Christ.

The Forgiveness of Sins

Christians are in need of reconciliation and healing in their relationships with God and with others. Personal and corporate sins must be addresssed as part of the agenda in educational encounters. The ministry of reconciliation must be operative at all levels of personal, interpersonal, and intergroup interactions in Christian education.

The Resurrection of the Body

The biblical view of persons is wholistic. Christian educators are challenged to correct an overemphasis on the body/soul dualism and theory/practical dichotomies which confront educational efforts, and work for integration. Christians in the West have much to learn from Christians in non-Western contexts in this area. Western cultures, while emphasizing intellectual analysis, have fostered the fragmentation of human personality and the disembodiment of life.

Life Everlasting

The various efforts of persons in Christian education must be evaluated in terms of God's ultimate plan for creation and the redeemed community. The efforts of students and teachers are conditioned by God's purposes in history.

A Reforming View of Education

Beyond this orthodox foundation, it is possible to explore theological foundations by considering the example of the Reformed wing of the Christian church which represents just one tradition. The author is most familiar with this tradition which nevertheless has insights for other communities.

Reformed educators generally emphasize three distinctive theological tenets that guide their view of education: the covenant of creation, the fall, and the covenant of redemption.

From the covenant of creation, Reformed educators emphasize that all persons are God's image bearers and therefore must be taught to show forth the glory of God. As image bearers, persons are responsible to build the kingdom of God and need to be prepared for this end.[16] Educators must be mindful of ecological responsibilities toward nature, religious responsibilities with respect to God, and political, aesthetic, and intellectual responsibilities in relation to other persons and oneself.[17] The task of educators is to encourage persons to fulfill their responsibilities, ultimately with respect to the Creator God. In serving and worshiping the Creator, Christians are to recognize the unity of culture and the unity of the human race which implies a sensitivity to the world and society.[18] The kingdom of God in this perspective is defined as the rule or reign of God that extends beyond a spiritual and otherworldly domain to include the created world and human society. Therefore, Reformed education at its best seeks to enable students to grapple with the implications of a Christian view for all of life.

The second tenet of a Reformed view of education considers the fall. People freely revolted against God and refused to live in trustful obedience, preferring instead to act as if they were self-normed. As a result they became confused about their responsibilities and in many ways denied them. They mutilated the earth, victimized other persons, squan-

16. Cornelius Van Til, *Essays on Christian Education* (Nutley, N.J.: Presbyterian & Reformed, 1977), 78–80.
17. Nicholas Wolterstorff, *Educating for Responsible Action* (Grand Rapids: Wm. B. Eerdmans, 1980), 9, 33.
18. Van Til, *Essays*, 83–85.

dered abilities, and set up surrogate gods.[19] This tenet eliminates the possibility of viewing persons as having free will and autonomy in any ultimate sense. Thus, any educational strategy that views autonomy as the highest developmental stage or goal must be questioned. Recognizing the reality and extent of sin, Reformed educators emphasize the demands of divine standards and warnings that issue from rebellion against God.[20]

The third tenet, the covenant of redemption, provides hope for humankind and creation in God's provision for recreation and renewal in Jesus Christ. Out of God's great love, God acted so that persons can again live in joyful fulfillment with themselves, their neighbors, nature, and God.[21] Persons must accept their cultural task and opportunity anew in Christ through the regenerating power of the Holy Spirit. Christians have by grace repented from sin and are called to contribute positively to the coming of God's kingdom through their cultural efforts.[22] The task of Christian education is to equip persons in this vital area of renewal through presenting Christ and encouraging response to him as Savior and Lord of all. In fact, all of life becomes the subject matter of Christian education given the multifaceted dimensions of the cultural task in relation to God's creation.

Whereas these three tenets are foundational for a thoroughgoing Reformed view of education, they may not be of sufficient breadth to address some of the challenges that confront the church of Jesus Christ today. A Reformed view of education has generally emphasized theological distinctives that emerged during the Reformation. In selecting this focus, Reformed educators have often failed to be adequately sensitive to historical developments prior and subsequent to the Reformation. Rather than a Reformed view of education, the need is for a reforming view which affirms the theological distinctives of a biblical view, but then builds upon them in addressing the current historical context.

A reforming view maintains that God is still active in history and that the church is gaining a greater understanding of the implications of God's revelation in Scripture and in Jesus Christ. In addition, a reforming view or perspective recognizes the contextualized nature of theology which is a continuing and ongoing task, rather than one that has been set definitively at the time of the Reformation. God has chosen Christians to address the needs of their time in categories that necessitate a continual renewal. This renewal entails the sensitivity to new wineskins

19. Wolterstorff, *Educating for Responsible Action*, 9, 10.
20. Van Til, *Essays*, 86.
21. Wolterstorff, *Educating for Responsible Action*, 10.
22. Van Til, *Essays*, 87–91.

with which God is blessing the church for sharing the new wine of the gospel in the modern world. A reforming view emphasizes the phrase *semper reformanda*, "always reforming."

In proposing a reforming view of education, a danger of adulteration in the gospel certainly exists. Nevertheless, while maintaining the orthodox faith, Christian educators can gain insights from other theologies to the extent to which they remain faithful to biblical revelation. One truth regarding the creation affirms that persons are rational and creative by virtue of creation and have the responsibility of glorifying God through their thought. In addition, the Holy Spirit is alive and active, and provides continued illumination regarding the application of God's truth to the world.

In the development of a reforming view, insights from liberation theology as they relate to the tasks of education are helpful. A reforming view has implications for all traditions in the Christian church beyond Reformed communities. A Reformed view of education can be identified as a received perspective and a liberation view as a reflexive perspective (see table 2).

Table 2 **Reformed, Reforming, and Liberation Perspectives**

Received Reformed Perspective	Restructuring Reforming Perspective	Reflexive Liberation Perspective
Closed	Both	Open
Traditional-Culture Taking	Both	Futuristic-Culture Making
Determined	Both	Innovative
Conservation	Both	Change
Absolutism	Both	Relativism
Determinism	Both	Voluntarism

A Reformed view emphasizes a relatively closed system of thought relative to first and essential principles of theology. It is traditional in the sense of affirming or taking a religious culture and thought system as developed during the Reformation and passing it on to the next generations. It assumes a transmissive form of communication. The basic structure of Reformed theology has largely been accepted and any elaboration occurs within that structure. In addition, this view is characterized by conservation, absolutism, and determinism in doctrine and life. In its extreme form, a Reformed view as a received perspective fails to adequately account for differences or deviations from an existing pattern in the structures of relationships between God and persons, among persons, and between persons and the entire creation.

By comparison, a liberation view is a relatively open system of thought and understanding with regard to first and essential principles of theology. It is futuristic in the sense of emphasizing an open future in which persons must assume responsibility for the development of a religious culture and thought system for the present and next generation. It assumes a dialogical and interactive form of communication. The basic structure of liberation theology is innovative in the development of new categories to fit changing situations. In addition, this view is characterized by an emphasis on change, relativism, and voluntarism in doctrine and life. Change is taken to the extremes of radical revolution if warranted by the context. In its extreme form as a reflexive perspective, a liberation view fails to account for regularities, similarities, continuities, and absolutes.[23]

A reforming view or a restructuring perspective is one in which both received and reflexive perspectives can be brought together as two related modes of understanding both the theological truths in the Scriptures and the possibilities of change in relating those truths to different cultures and historical situations.[24] It mediates between the two extremes of a strict Reformed view and a liberation view. Such a view affirms the need for the conservation of biblical and theological essentials of the Christian faith while recognizing the need for innovation in relating those essentials to changing needs, forms, and structures. A reforming view stresses both the need for stability, authority, and reliability and the need for critical inquiry and creativity in theological reflection.

The question that remains to be addressed is how liberation theology affects a reforming view of education. This question can be explored by reconsidering the dangers of each of the theological distinctives of an evangelical approach and how a liberation view can help at these very points of potential weakness. The choice of liberation theology is based upon the truths it reveals which have been too readily forgotten in evangelical communities.

Liberation theology emphasizes the place of praxis, the interaction between reflection and action in life. Such an emphasis in Christian education can address the danger of a mere verbalism that neglects the implications of biblical truth for life. The clarion call of those who espouse a liberation perspective is the need for active engagement with the world. Serious questions can be raised as to the nature of that engagement in relation to the biblical agenda; nevertheless, the avoidance of a spectator and passive stance in relation to Christian commitments can be wholeheartedly affirmed. The concerns for active participation

23. See John Eggleston, *The Sociology of the School Curriculum* (London: Routledge & Kegan Paul, 1977), 52–92, for a discussion of received and reflexive perspectives.
24. Ibid., 71.

are also distinctives of a liberation view that are a necessary corrective for a dead orthodoxy. A danger inherent in the liberation view is that of an activism which fails to adequately address the biblical sources of the Christian faith in favor of an exclusive preoccupation with the current historical context.

Liberation theology also attempts to seriously grapple with what it means to follow Christ and carry out God's agenda in concrete historical contexts. Liberationists do not ignore the physical and social needs of persons while sharing the gospel. They take a stand with those who have suffered various forms of oppression. Liberationists have not only stressed the costs of discipleship, but have modeled a willingness to sacrifice for their cause. Unfortunately for some, this has included an identification of the oppressed with God's people irrespective of a personal response to Christ as Lord and Savior.

One hallmark of the liberation view has been its emphasis on the contextual nature of theology. It calls for an unambiguous commitment to reality in its historical concreteness. This concrete rootedness issues in the call for contextualization, for a theology which does not stop with mere reflection on the world in its particular setting, but rather tries to be part of the process through which the world is transformed. Faith becomes incarnated in the historical process in the effort to understand and liberate various cultures in light of gospel demands. Such a perspective demands careful listening as well as an active and incisive critique of those perspectives and practices that embody ideologies contrary to the gospel. The danger in a liberation view is allowing the historical context to set an agenda which is contrary to biblical faith and the embodiment of a revolutionary agenda as an alternative gospel.

Liberation theology also maintains a stance that is so committed to social issues and activism that concerns for personal piety and an appropriate affirmation of the status quo may be ignored. Liberationists have sought to raise the consciousness of persons regarding the extent of social sins and the need for corrective action.

A reforming view of education, as has been proposed, enables the evangelical educator to incorporate those insights from a liberation view that are faithful to the biblical and theological distinctives of the Christian faith. The inherent dangers of an evangelical approach to religious education can be addressed through active dialogue and interaction with those who grapple with the implications of liberation theology for Christian education. The God of the Bible is a God of liberation, who brings full liberation in the person and work of Jesus Christ. Yet the implications of the gospel of Jesus Christ extend to all areas of personal and corporate life. God speaks through Moses to the Israelite people, promising deliverance from their bondange in Egypt:

Therefore, say to the Israelites: 'I am the LORD and I will bring you out from under the yoke of the Egyptians. I will free you from being slaves to them and will redeem you with an outstretched arm and with mighty acts of judgment. I will take you as my own people, and I will be your God. Then you will know that I am the LORD your God, who brought you out from under the yoke of the Egyptians. And I will bring you to the land I swore with uplifted hand to give to Abraham, to Isaac and to Jacob. I will give it to you as a possession. I am the LORD' (Exod. 6:6–8).

Our God still brings deliverance from spiritual and physical bondage. God's reign embodies redemption of whole persons in this life and in the life to come.

Insights from Paulo Freire

The implications of a reforming view of education can be further explored by considering the work of Paulo Freire, a Brazilian educational philosopher and social educator who is an advocate of a liberation education. Freire's thought will be analyzed in terms of various affirmations and criticisms from the perspective of a reforming view.

Paulo Freire was born in 1921 into a middle-class family. Due to financial reverses caused by the American stock market crash in 1929 he experienced poverty. He was dedicated to the education and advancement of the poor and oppressed of Brazil and to the transformation of society. As a result of his revolutionary work, Freire was imprisoned and later exiled by the Brazilian government after the military coup of 1964. After his exile he first moved to Chile, then migrated to the United States, and later worked as an educational consultant at Harvard University. Since the 1970s he has worked with the Office of Education of the World Council of Churches in Geneva, Switzerland and subsequently has returned to Brazil where he is serving as a professor.

Freire's religious background is Roman Catholic. He has also been influenced by various philosophies, including phenomenology, personalism, existentialism, and Marxism. Freire refers to himself as a Christian humanist and describes his educational philosophy as humanistic. For Freire, humanization is the goal of every valued educational and social activity. Dehumanization is destructive of true human nature and dignity.[25]

Freire describes his own educational theory in *Cultural Action for Freedom:*

25. John Elias provides a detailed description of Freire's work in "Paulo Freire: Religious Educator," *Religious Education* 71 (January–February 1976):40–56.

> Our pedagogy cannot do without a vision of man and his world. It for-
> mulates a scientific humanist conception which finds its expression in
> a dialogical praxis in which teachers and learners, together, in the act of
> analyzing a dehumanizing reality, denounce it while announcing its
> transformation in the name of the liberation of man.[26]

Freire affirms persons as reflective and free, created by God to expand
continually the potentialities of their being by living out relationships
with God and other persons. This is full humanity and the goal of
education.

Freire maintains that learners need to be liberated from the oppression
of the traditional teacher who limits the activity and power of students.
His solution is to develop a style of teaching which is intrinsically liberating in the sense of enabling persons to become more aware of and
responsible for themselves and their world. This occurs through a process of reflection followed by action and further reflection (praxis).

Freire's main contribution to education lies in his concept of "conscientization," a word originally coined to describe the arousing of a
person's positive self-concept in relation to the environment and society.
Because this term is no longer used by Freire given its misuse by persons
in the West who disassociate action from knowledge, the term *transformation* is substituted here. Transformation is a liberating education
that treats learners as subjects, as active agents, and not as objects or
passive recepients of shared wisdom. Students are thus viewed as active,
creative subjects with the capacity to examine critically, interact with,
and transform their world. Transformation is also described as problem-
posing education that encourages freedom for students in cooperative
dialogue with the teacher and other students.[27] In contrast with transformation is banking or problem-solving education which imposes
knowledge upon passive students. In banking education, the teacher assumes an authoritarian role, prescribing what the students are to learn
and how they are to think and behave.[28]

26. Paulo Freire, *Cultural Action for Freedom* (Cambridge: Harvard Educational Review and the Center for the Study of Development and Social Change, 1970), 20.
27. Lyra Srinivasan, *Perspectives on Nonformal Adult Learning* (New York: World
Education, 1977), 2–7. For a discussion of conscientization, see Freire, *Cultural Action
for Freedom*, 27–52; and Paulo Freire, *Education for Critical Consciousness* (New York:
Seabury, 1973). Freire ceased using the term *conscientization* when he realized that
persons did not relate this term to action as indispensible to their knowing and learning.
Critical consciousness for him implies a total life response to new understandings and
perspectives gained through education. This perspective is also encountered in a Hebraic
understanding of knowledge as a total life response to that which is known.
28. Paulo Freire, *Pedagogy of the Oppressed*, trans. Myra Bergman Ramos (New
York: Seabury, 1970), 58–74.

Freire's theology represents a redefinition of traditional theological understandings in line with the insights of various liberation theologies. God is seen as the Creator who seeks a relationship of liberation with humanity. God is the active and dynamic God of the Hebrews and the human person of Jesus who acts to save persons. God is involved in the ongoing process of creating persons and the world with the cooperation of persons. This cooperative, interactive process is one which Freire seeks to replicate in education with teachers and students cooperatively working together.

Jesus is viewed as the radical critic of oppressive institutions and experiences who offers the possibility of redemption and salvation. Redemption is redefined in terms of a Christian's willingness to undergo death by struggling for new life and freedom for oppressed peoples and not remaining neutral in political struggles. Thus sin is viewed as oppression as it is exercised against persons and against God. Salvation is not viewed so much in terms of individuals, but in terms of the process of bringing persons and societies to true freedom (humanization). The Christian gospel is the proclamation of the radical reordering of society in which persons are oppressed.[29]

Freire's theology is problematic:

1. His use of a situational hermeneutic can lead to a distorted interpretation of Scripture; political analysis takes priority over biblical theology. Freire does not consider Scripture as a primary frame of reference.
2. In Freire's Christology, the absence of the doctrine of the Holy Spirit is apparent. We can encounter antichrist in our neighbor, in the oppressed. Christ is not mediated through persons alone.
3. Freire's anthropological theology does not consider the extent of sin. He views the oppressed as the people of God—not just potentially, but actually. God is thus dependent upon persons and loses transcendence. The God of the Bible makes demands upon humanity and is revealed through the living, created, and written Word.
4. Since Freire holds to a qualitatively defined salvation, there is a truncated view of salvation. Freire forgets that salvation is not appropriated automatically in joining a struggle for liberation, but through an *act of faith* in God and Jesus Christ as Lord and Savior which results in works of faith.
5. In Freire's theology, little appreciation exists of the church's role as the proclaimer of the gospel of Jesus Christ. The kerygma is to

29. Elias, "Paulo Freire," 42–46.

be declared in word and action. Little appreciation exists of the church's mission: enabling persons to place their faith in Christ. No evangelism as historically understood exists for Freire.

6. Finally, a vagueness is present in an unqualified open future. Hope emerges only out of the present and is defined in terms of God's ultimate plans for the creation as revealed in Scripture.[30]

In relation to the implementation of Freire's theory, Bennie Goodwin's critique provides additional insights. Goodwin's insights are particularly helpful in that he represents the black church, a community that has and is experiencing oppression in the United States.

1. Opting for a godless theology is the result of a dependence upon humanism and personalism. The loss of a biblical or theological base for educational efforts is apparent and limits the value of Freire's theory for Christian educators.
2. Open implementation of an avowedly revolutionary strategy results in a great deal of resistance and hostility which may not be necessary to realize renewal in all contexts.
3. Liberation in the social, political, and economic spheres, falling short of violent revolution, requires the assistance and cooperation of at least some of those who are in power. There is the need to work for the conscientization of oppressors as well as the oppressed. Freire chooses the level of ideas and values in making his appeal to the oppressed and ignores the need to address oppressors. Jesus' gospel calls both oppressed and oppressors to reconciliation with God, each other, and the creation.
4. Freire's theory, epistemology, and axiology are not fully developed.[31]

In spite of these criticisms, several commendations of Freire's work can be made:

1. It addresses the concrete historical situation of persons. It is concerned to contextualize education and theology by drawing out the implications of faith and the need for response.
2. It emphasizes a service-oriented salvation and education.

30. For discussion of these criticisms, see Orlando Costas, *The Church and Its Mission: A Shattering Critique from the Third World* (Wheaton, Ill.: Tyndale, 1974), 219–64; and Clark H. Pinnock, "Liberation Theology: The Gains and Gaps," *Christianity Today* (16 January 1976):13–15.

31. Bennie Goodwin, *Reflections on Education* (Atlanta: Goodpatrick Publishers, 1978), 86–92.

3. It provides insights for Christian educators in how to educate for social action and how to raise the consciousness of Christians to the realities and needs of persons in other cultural contexts.
4. It takes seriously the need to demonstrate an incarnational theology, one that is lived out. It seeks to relate faith to life.
5. It affirms the biblical emphasis upon the poor and oppressed in Christ's ministry (Luke 4:18–19), recognizing the challenges of Marxist ideology.
6. It focuses on the humanity of Christ in reaction to an exclusive emphasis upon his deity.
7. It encourages a critical awareness that the Western world is part of the global problem of oppression and injustice.
8. It emphasizes that Christian education is prophetic education, challenging oppressive social structures by: questioning those programs and techniques of education which neither consider the social and corporate implications of the gospel nor question the status quo; and developing Christian consciousness of the global context of oppression while leading Christians in constructing new and faithful life-styles.
9. It stresses the need for structural and social transformation as well as personal transformation/redemption inherent in the gospel.
10. It confronts the myth of a life of better "things" and forces an examination of the tension between professed or stated intentions and values (ideas and ideals) and revealed preferences (reality).

Much can be gained through critical interaction with educators such as Freire because his insights address areas of weakness and have plagued evangelical educators. It is essential that Christian educators critically examine received traditions and conceptions and grapple with what God is saying to the church of Jesus Christ in our time.

The theological foundations explored in this chapter provide an essential ground for relating biblical directives and principles to Christian education in the modern world. A reforming view is one possible contemporary formulation that seeks to build upon the Reformed tradition in theology and Christian education along with the insights of liberation theologies. Certainly Lutheran, Anglican, Pietist, Arminian, charismatic, and other formulations also build upon a common evangelical heritage and are equally faithful to the Christian faith. It is essential that Christian educators explore and rediscover those theological sources that provide beacon lights in the stormy waters of educational thought and practice in the modern world and thus glorify Jesus Christ in all aspects of life.

Beyond the insights of theology, Christian educators are also called to consider those philosophies which further clarify the universals undergirding their thought and practice. These universals are the givens, the assumptions, the ideals, and the values with which persons function in their lives.

3

Philosophical Foundations

Lhe third foundation for Christian education is philosophy, which in conjunction with biblical and theological foundations provides transcultural and cultural universals to guide thought and practice. Charlotte Mason (1842–1923), a Christian educator and school reformer in England during the nineteenth and early twentieth centuries, wrote, "As a stream can rise no higher than its source, so it is probable that no educational effort can rise above the whole scheme of thought which gives it birth."[1] A philosophy of education attempts to articulate a systematic scheme of thought which can guide practice. This is crucial because, as Mason sensitively implies, education is the fruit of its philosophic roots. The challenge for each Christian educator is to make his or her philosophy of education explicit and consistent with a Christian world view.

General Definitions

It is essential in exploring philosophical foundations to consider basic definitions to guide one's inquiry. A world view can be defined as a

1. Charlotte Mason, *Home School Education*, vol. 8 of the *Home Education Series*, 6th ed. (Oxford: Scrivener, 1953), ix.

collection of underlying presuppositions from which one's thoughts and actions stem. A Christian world view is comprised of those fundamental Christian beliefs that most adequately describe the God-creation distinction and relationship.[2] Arthur Holmes, a Christian philosopher, suggests that an overall world view has the following characteristics: (1) it has a *wholistic* goal, trying to see every area of life and thought in an integrated fashion; (2) it is a *perspectival* approach, coming at things from a previously adopted point of view which now provides an integrative framework; (3) it is an *exploratory* process, probing the relationship of one area after another to a unifying perspective; (4) it is *pluralistic* in that the same basic perspective can be articulated in somewhat different ways; and (5) it has *action outcomes* for what we think, what we value, and what we do.[3]

Thus a preliminary task for the Christian educator is to formulate a Christian world view which will then have direct implications and action outcomes for education. The means of developing such an overall world view is the discipline of philosophy.

Philosophy can be literally defined as "the love of wisdom." The Christian is reminded in Scripture that it is the Lord who gives wisdom and that from his mouth come knowledge and understanding (Prov. 2:6), that the fear of the Lord is the beginning of knowledge or wisdom (Prov. 1:7; 9:10). Indeed, in Christ are hidden all the treasures of wisdom and knowledge (Col. 2:3). As an academic discipline, philosophy seeks a coherent organization of all knowledge and addresses human concerns to discern the true, the good, the right, the real, and the valuable. These very concerns are those which Paul encouraged the Christians at Philippi to think about and practice (Phil. 4:8, 9).

Whereas philosophy in general is an intellectual discipline concerned with the nature of reality and the investigation of the general principles of knowledge, existence, and truth, Christian philosophy is concerned with the reality and truth of God. For the Christian, God is the source of all truth and reality. In the final analysis, the subject matter of Christian philosophy is the human relationship with the Creator/Redeemer God.[4] Thus the challenge for the Christian is to think "Christianly" and rightly in all areas of human endeavor. One such area of endeavor is education and the challenge for Christians is to think about and realize an education that is in fact Christian.

2. See Arthur F. Holmes, *Contours of a World View* (Grand Rapids: Wm. B. Eerdmans, 1983) for a discussion of this perspective.
3. Arthur F. Holmes, ed., *The Making of a Christian Mind: A Christian World View and the Academic Enterprise* (Downers Grove, Ill.: Inter-Varsity, 1985), 17.
4. Colin Brown, *Philosophy and the Christian Faith* (London: Inter-Varsity, [1969] 1973), 288.

A philosophy of Christian education or a Christian philosophy of education can therefore be defined as "an attempt to arrange systematically some thoughts on education as they are given their meaning by the biblical teachings that constitute the orthodox Christian faith."[5] For the evangelical educator, this poses the challenge of rethinking education biblically given prior commitment to biblical authority.

FIGURE 4   A Range of Definitions

	Formal Education		Nonformal/Informal Education	
Definitions	Schooling	Intentional Educating	Socialization	Life or Experience

Definition of Education

The definition of the essential terms *education* and *Christian education* poses a unique challenge given the plurality of educational philosophies in the modern world and the preparadigmatic nature of education.[6] Various definitions of education have been suggested which can be placed on a continuum (see fig. 4), whose poles are formal and nonformal/informal education.[7]

Formal education can be defined as education that is "conventional, given in an orderly, logical, planned, and systematic manner."[8] Formal education is associated most directly with the institution of the school and the actual classroom experience. Generally a formal understanding confines education to the experiences of persons within the classroom with little or no reference to the students' incidental and varied experiences outside the classroom.[9] This is a limited definition of education in comparison to that of the Bible, which did not envision the primary place of the school.

5. Norman DeJong, *Education in the Truth* (Nutley, N.J.: Presbyterian & Reformed, 1974), 16.

6. See the introduction for a discussion of the "preparadigmatic" state of education as a discipline. A Christian world view certainly provides the outline of a paradigm for Christians which is nevertheless pluralistic and is, in the final analysis, "preparadigmatic" in Kuhn's terms.

7. Fayette Veverka describes these various definitions in an unpublished work, "Matters of Definition and Perspective" (Boston College, Chestnut Hill, Mass., 1983).

8. Carter V. Good, ed., *Dictionary of Education* (New York: McGraw-Hill, 1945), 175. I am indebted to Douglas M. Sloan, Professor of History and Education at Teachers College, Columbia University, for his analysis.

9. Ibid.

At the other end of the continuum is nonformal/informal education that defines education in terms of life. Nonformal education is education that occurs through shared identity and experience. Nonformal education occurs in settings other than the school and classroom.[10] This definition of education views all of life and experience as education. It views informal and unintentional interactions as occasions in which learning can occur. This definition is perhaps too broad in that all experience is not education, but may be in fact miseducation if one considers questions of value.

A caution with regard to this definition is warranted given the truths implied by the following proverbs: "experience is the best teacher, but is the school of a fool"; "experience is a dear school, but fools will learn in no other." Experience is not sufficient for education. Having recognized this warning regarding experience without opportunities for serious reflection in schools or other settings, the Christian educator can affirm the reality that God can use all of life's experiences to instruct persons. But in terms of a definition, education that includes all of life and experience must be distinct in some ways from other activities in life.

Given these extreme definitions, one too narrow and the other too broad, alternatives must be explored. In 1960, Bernard Bailyn, an educational historian, proposed a definition to solve this dilemma. In considering developments in colonial America, Bailyn defined education as "the entire process by which a culture transmits itself across the generations."[11] He explored various educational agencies and persons that passed on their understanding to the next generation, and proposed that history revealed four great axles or agencies of society involved in education: the family, the church, the community, and the economy. Bailyn's definition shifted focus from formal education in the school to the vast processes of socialization and enculturation.

The Bible reveals the impact of these agencies in the formation of persons according to the principles of faith and Jewish culture. Many of the educational responsibilities outlined in Scripture are addressed to parents as representatives of the faith community. They are to pass on faith in God to the next generation (Deut. 6:4–9; Ps. 78:1–8; Eph. 6:1–4). Socialization is the process that enables persons to become responsible

10. For an extensive discussion of formal, nonformal, and informal aspects of education, see Lawrence O. Richards, *A Theology of Christian Education* (Grand Rapids: Zondervan, 1975), 144, 236–39, 317–19.
11. Bernard Bailyn, *Education in the Forming of American Society* (New York: W. W. Norton, 1960), 14.

and contributing members of a community. For Israel and the New Testament church, socialization was to enable persons to become responsible members of the faith community. In this perspective, education is equated with socialization. But as was the case with the definition of education as life, this may still be too broad a focus.

As persons grow within a community or family, some or perhaps most learning experiences are not intentionally planned. The dilemma is again posed as to what makes education distinct or unique. An additional problem emerges if education is equated with socialization. This entails the limitation of reformation or renewal in the community because it is not only a community which shapes or educates an individual, but an individual can shape or educate a community. In addition, biblical faith includes the process of disenculturation or prophetic education, in which a community norm or standard is seriously questioned or critiqued in the light of biblical values. The realization of these values often transcends the processes of socialization and enculturation. The very structure of covenantal faith assumes a place for blessing and warning, for affirmation and critique that would limit the exclusive association of education with socialization. A biblical perspective affirms the place of socialization to the extent to which the models are consistent with the model of Jesus Christ (1 Cor. 11:1). Scripture provides numerous examples of the disobedience and unfaithfulness of communities and parents in their efforts to model a righteous life.

What becomes apparent is that education includes formal schooling, life experiences, and socialization. But what unique characteristic of education combines these various aspects? Lawrence Cremin, another educational historian, defines education as "the deliberate, systematic, and sustained effort to transmit, evoke, or acquire knowledge, attitudes, values, skills, or sensibilities, as well as any outcomes of that effort."[12] Cremin's definition includes educational agencies beyond the school while maintaining the deliberate, systematic, and sustained character of education. Education is deliberate in the sense of being intentional and planned. It is systematic in terms of sequential exposure and sensitivity to the readiness of participants. In addition, education is sustained over time, implying a continuity of exposure and interaction along with a continuing relationship between students and teachers. This definition includes transmission, discovery, and self-education and expands the limited focus on knowledge that has characterized some schooling efforts. While emphasizing the intentional dimension of education that

12. Lawrence A. Cremin, *Traditions of American Education* (New York: Basic Books, 1977), 134ff.

implies responsibility and accountability, Cremin recognizes the unintentional aspects of education by including "any outcomes of the effort" to educate in his definition.

While recognizing the strengths of Cremin's definition, Christian educators must also identify potential weaknesses. Cremin's definition is so broad and inclusive that it fails to deal with the normative dimensions of education. There is no way to distinguish miseducation from education that is appropriate and helpful for students. In dealing with education, educators must address fundamental value judgments. For the evangelical educator, that which is in accord with a Christian world view and scriptural revelation is proper education, and that which is not in accord with these foundations is miseducation.[13] In order to adequately define and determine education, Christian educators must determine those values and desired goals which will guide the entire process. Such values and goals require the clear identification of ultimate foundations. In relation to these ultimate foundations, the words of C. S. Lewis are particularly instructive in a pluralistic society: "An open mind, in questions that are not ultimate, is useful. But an open mind about the ultimate foundations either of Theoretical or of practical Reason is idiocy."[14]

Definition of Christian Education

Given the importance of normative dimensions for defining education, evangelicals are called upon to propose a definition of Christian education that can guide their efforts. Several possibilities follow:

1. Christian education is a Bible-based, Holy Spirit-empowered (Christ-centered) teaching-learning process. It seeks to guide individuals at all levels of growth through contemporary teaching means toward knowing and experiencing God's purpose and plan through Christ in every aspect of living. It also equips people for effective ministry, with the overall focus on Christ the Master Educator's example and his command to make mature disciples. (Werner Graendorf)[15]

13. Cornelius Van Til, *Essays on Christian Education* (Nutley, N.J.: Presbyterian & Reformed, 1977), 81.

14. C. S. Lewis, *The Abolition of Man* (New York: Macmillan, 1947), 60.

15. Werner C. Graendorf, ed., *Introduction to Biblical Christian Education* (Chicago: Moody, 1981), 16.

2. Christian education is the Christ-centered, Bible-based, pupil-related process of communicating God's written Word through the power of the Holy Spirit for the purpose of leading others to Christ and building them up in Christ. (Roy Zuck)[16]

3. Education is the recreation and development of the true relationship between God and man, man and fellow man, and man and the physical universe. (Norman DeJong)[17]

4. Education is the divinely instigated and humanly cooperative process whereby persons grow and develop in life, that is, in godly knowledge, faith, hope, and love through Christ. (Norman DeJong)[18]

5. Christian education is the deliberate, systematic, and sustained divine and human effort to share or appropriate the knowledge, values, attitudes, skills, sensitivities, and behaviors that comprise or are consistent with the Christian faith. It fosters the change, renewal, and reformation of persons, groups, and structures by the power of the Holy Spirit to conform to the revealed will of God as expressed in the Old and New Testaments and preeminently in the person of Jesus Christ, as well as any outcomes of that effort. (Robert Pazmiño)[19]

A viable definition combines the descriptive dimensions of Cremin's suggestions with the normative dimensions fundamental to the Christian faith. While such a definition stresses intentionality, it recognizes that learning can take place in situations in which human intentionality is not present.[20] Divine effort or agency is essential as well as human agency. This is the case because God is the author and finisher of the Christian faith. God is not in need of appropriating the faith as is the case with human persons.

This definition views education as a process more limited than socialization or enculturation, though it includes these aspects. It allows for personal study as well as interpersonal instruction, thereby embracing self-education. It envisions interactions across the generations, with adults teaching children or children teaching adults; with the intragenerational education of peers within or across families and cultures; and

16. Roy B. Zuck, *Spiritual Power in Your Teaching*, rev. ed. (Chicago: Moody, 1972), 9.
17. DeJong, *Education in the Truth*, 118.
18. Ibid.
19. I am indebted to Lawrence Cremin's definition.
20. Cremin, *Traditions*, 134.

with the self-conscious coming of age which persons experience. Finally, this definition expands education beyond the school setting to a vast variety of persons and institutions that educate.[21] Christian education is much more than Sunday or church schooling.

Philosophical Questions

Before exploring the specific dimensions of philosophy, it is helpful to gain some perspective on the dimensions of the task in a larger framework. Norman DeJong suggests a philosophic ladder with corresponding questions that must be addressed in formulating a philosophy of education (see fig. 5):

FIGURE 5   The Philosophical Ladder

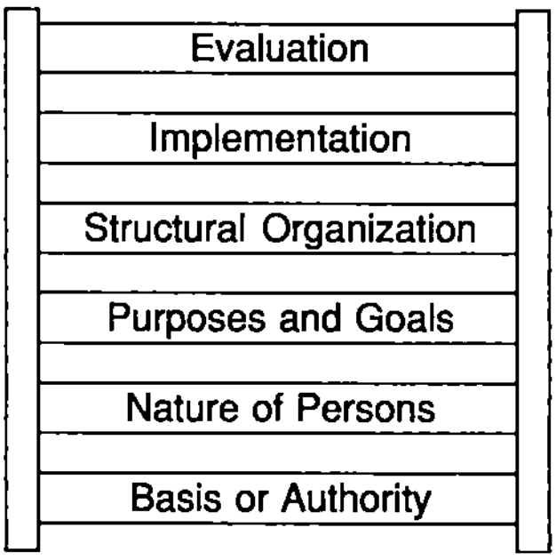

Evaluation
Implementation
Structural Organization
Purposes and Goals
Nature of Persons
Basis or Authority

1. *Basis or authority.* What is the basis upon which all thinking rests?
2. *Nature of persons.* What or who are persons?
3. *Purposes and goals.* What are the purposes and goals in education?
4. *Structural organization.* In what structures and by what agents are these purposes and goals to be realized?
5. *Implementation.* With which resources, tools, and methods will the purposes and goals of education be implemented?
6. *Evaluation.* How well are things being done?

DeJong rightfully contends that these questions must be addressed sequentially from the lowest to the highest rung and that there must be

21. Ibid, 134–36.

a consistency at all points with the underlying basis or authority.[22] Answers to these basic questions vary among Christian educators.

The subject areas of philosophy can be detailed in the following manner. *Metaphysics* is the study of what constitutes the nature of reality and of what reality is constituted. It addresses the question, "What is real?" and includes such disciplines as theology, anthropology, ontology, and cosmology. *Theology* is the study of God which for theistic educators provides the essential foundation, while *anthropology* is the study of persons, societies, and cultures. *Ontology* is the study of being and life itself, and *cosmology* is the study of the world and material being.

A second subject area is *epistemology*. Epistemology, the study of knowledge, addresses the question, "What is true?"

Axiology, the third subject area, is the study of values and addresses the question, "What is of value?" It is concerned with ethics and aesthetics. *Ethics* is the study of value judgments and considers what is good or right. *Aesthetics* is the study of beauty and considers what is beautiful.[23] Each of these subject areas will be briefly considered with their implications for a philosophy of education.

Metaphysics

Metaphysical insights affect each rung of DeJong's ladder, but in unique ways for the evangelical educator. As was suggested in addressing theological foundations, theology has a particular contribution to make when addressing questions of authority, persons, and purposes with implications for questions of structure, implementation, and evaluation. Evangelical theology stresses the authority of Scripture which functions as the essential basis for all inquiry. Theology similarly contributes to understanding the nature of persons as creatures of God and therefore responsible to God. In the case of purposes and goals, theology suggests those purposes and goals which guide persons in all of their efforts including education. Thus theology provides the essential ground or foundation for a thoroughgoing Christian philosophy of education.

Anthropology centers primarily upon the nature of persons. From a Christian world view, persons are viewed as created in God's image and

---

22. DeJong, *Education in the Truth*, 61–63.

23. I am using the outline suggested by George R. Knight in *Philosophy and Education: An Introduction in Christian Perspective* (Berrien Springs, Mich.: Andrews University Press, 1980), 14–37.

therefore having responsibilities and obligations as image bearers. But persons are also viewed as fallen and marred by sin with consequences at the personal and corporate levels of life. Implications that emerge from the created and fallen aspects of persons affect education. For example, persons are to be increasingly encouraged through education to act responsibly in all of their interactions and relationships, thereby glorifying God their Creator. In addition, persons are to be encouraged to give expression to their creative nature as endowed by God. Recognizing the effects of sin, Christian educators must consider structure and discipline as important dimensions in educational planning and implementation. Structure and discipline are complemented by the effort to encourage actions that evidence the redemptive and restorative work of Christ.

Given the created nature of persons, students can be encouraged to be active participants in their own education and to interact with the world as the focus of their lives. Thus the study of anthropology forces consideration of more than individuals and the isolated classroom. Persons must be seen in relation to society and culture. Persons must also be seen in relation to their personal and corporate histories. This forces the evangelical educator to consider interpersonal, intergroup, intercultural, and intersocietal questions beyond a comfortable preoccupation with personal life and piety. In relation to society, various forces, groups, movements, and institutions can be seen as being oppressive and/or liberating in terms of biblical norms and purposes. Likewise, cultures can be seen as reflecting and/or denying God in their various dimensions and Christians can be seen as called to preserve, redeem, or transform cultures at various times in relation to gospel values. In this wider task, Christian educators are required to exercise careful analysis and discernment in enabling others to consider the challenges of being in, but not of the world. This is possible only through the redeeming and renewing work of Christ in the lives of persons and groups.

Ontology poses questions of being and life. Paul declared to the Athenians that it is in God that "we live and move and have our being" (Acts 17:28). The biblical world view maintains that God's being is primary while persons' being is secondary or derivative from divine being. This is a natural consequence of the creation. The purpose of being is for persons to glorify and enjoy God forever. The Christian accomplishes this purpose through being in but not of the world, made possible through God's redemptive work.

The Christian is in the world as an exile and pilgrim, as a member of God's kingdom working for renewal and expressing the fruits of redemption in Jesus Christ. Christians are called to work out their salvation with fear and trembling while recognizing the work of God in them to fulfill God's purposes (Phil. 2:12, 13). As a new creature in Christ, the Christian's vocation is that of being Christ's ambassador, bearing the message of reconciliation (2 Cor. 5:17–21). The Christian's being is one that necessitates the daily indwelling of the Holy Spirit to fulfill God's purposes. Thus ontological inquiry has direct implications for the first two rungs on the philosophic ladder.

Cosmology raises questions concerning the nature of the cosmos, the universe, and the world. The world is perceived as a network of interdependencies that emerge from the creation and God's continuing providence. In relation to these issues the words of David are pertinent:

> The earth is the LORD's, and
>   everything in it,
> the world and all who live in it;
>   for he founded it upon the seas
> and established it upon the waters.
>   (Ps. 24:1, 2)

In relation to education, questions of proper stewardship of the earth and ecology must be raised. Persons must remember that the cosmos has been provided by God and must be cared for and shared. A difficult question is the place of personal property in relation to the needs of others and in light of the unity of creation. Cosmological inquiry explores the nature of persons as inhabitants of the cosmos (rung 2) and the purposes and goals of education (rung 3) in relation to human responsibilities for the cosmos. Howard Snyder suggests a model for the church in the world that develops the idea of kingdom ecology, demonstrates great sensitivity to cosmological issues, and possesses important implications for Christian education.[24]

Epistemology

Questions of epistemology have a direct impact upon one's conception of education in the area of its basis, its view of persons, and its proposed purposes and goals (rungs 1 through 3 of the philosophic ladder). George R. Knight proposes an alternative way of exploring the impact of epistemology and other philosophical questions (see fig. 6).[25]

24. See Howard A. Snyder, *Liberating the Church* (Downers Grove, Ill.: Inter-Varsity, 1983).
25. Knight, *Philosophy and Education*, 35.

Knight indicates that a distinct metaphysical and epistemological viewpoint will affect one's stance on axiological questions. This stance on values, in conjunction with a corresponding view of reality and truth, will determine the choice of purposes and goals in the educational process.[26] Knight's scheme builds upon DeJong's philosophic ladder and illustrates the various contextual factors (political, social, economic, communal, and familial) that influence educational practices beyond philosophy. At any point in this scheme the actual influence varies in strength; there may not be a consistent relationship between one person's or group's position on philosophic issues and actual educational practice.

Cremin helpfully points out that in education as in life, "there is inevitably a gap between aspiration and achievement, and between ideal and reality. And there is frequently a gap between stated intentions and revealed preferences."[27] Nevertheless, the challenge for the Christian educator is to select and develop with discernment those educational practices that are consistent with beliefs and are, concurrently, feasible in their political, social, economic, and communal contexts.[28] Constant

FIGURE 6*   The Relationship of Philosophy to Educational Practice

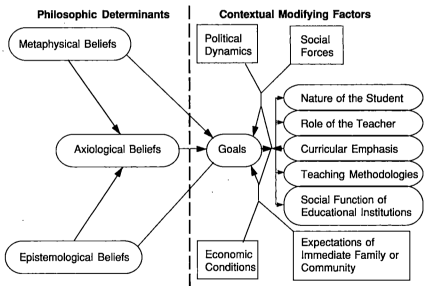

*Taken from George R. Knight, *Philosophy and Education: An Introduction in Christian Perspective* (Berrien Springs, Mich.: Andrews University Press, 1980), 35. Used by permission.

26. Ibid., 34.
27. Lawrence A. Cremin, *Public Education* (New York: Basic Books, 1976), 36.
28. Knight, *Philosophy and Education*, 36.

diligence is necessary if this is to be a possibility along with the continual evaluation of educational practice in the light of stated purposes and goals. The discernment of revealed preferences in relation to such stated intentions requires a predisposition and openness toward reform and renewal. Reform and renewal, in turn, often emerge through the reappropriation of original purposes and goals in the light of changing contextual factors. Therefore, a *reforming* rather than a *Reformed* perspective in education is needed, one that is sensitive to the continuing work of the Holy Spirit in today's world and that addresses contemporary issues.

In relation to substantive questions of epistemology, recent scholarship in the field of religious education has reopened the consideration of the nature of knowing and the validity of various ways of knowing.[29] This inquiry has forced Christian educators to reconsider Scripture as the source for their efforts. The biblical view of knowledge is one that is wholistic in the sense of involving knowledge in the cognitive sense along with feeling and action. Knowledge includes a physical dimension that implies personal commitment and intention to be one with the person or thing known. In the case of knowing God, this knowledge embodies a loving, obedient, and believing response to God and thus a relational/experiential/reflective way of knowing grounded in God's revelation as described in the Scriptures.[30]

Parker Palmer, in his search for a biblical epistemology, suggests that knowledge as understood in our societal context must be related to human interests and passions that are often ignored. In this analysis, Palmer suggests that knowledge can be tied to the three human interests or passions of control, curiosity, and compassion. The knowledge gained through applied empirical and analytical study generally seeks to gain control over a body of information. The knowledge gained through speculative, historical, and hermeneutical study generally seeks to discover knowledge as an end in itself to satisfy curiosity. The knowledge that liberates is one which Palmer finds described in 1 Corinthians 8:1–3: "Now about food sacrificed to idols: We know that we all possess knowledge. Knowledge puffs up, but love builds up. The man who thinks he knows something does not yet know as he ought to know. But the man who loves God is known by God." This knowledge is one associated with compassion or love.[31]

Certainly the New Testament maintains that knowledge or truth

29. An extensive discussion in this area is provided by Thomas H. Groome, *Christian Religious Education: Sharing Our Story and Vision* (San Francisco: Harper & Row, 1980), chaps. 7 and 8.

30. Ibid., 141–45.

31. Parker J. Palmer, *To Know as We Are Known: A Spirituality of Education* (San Francisco: Harper & Row, 1983), 6–10. Also see Jürgen Habermas, *Knowledge and Human Interests* (Boston: Beacon, 1971).

must be related to love (Eph. 4:15; 2 John 1) and that all truth is God's truth for he alone is the source of all knowledge, wisdom, and understanding (Col. 2:2, 3). The problem posed for the Christian educator is how to maintain in creative tension those truths discerned through study in various disciplines with the truths revealed in Scripture while at the same time being guided by love for God, others, and the creation. It is Jesus' prayer that his disciples be sanctified by God's truth, recognizing that God's Word is truth (John 17:17). Christ declares that he incarnates truth (John 14:6).

In relation to this problem Knight suggests six epistemological observations:

1. The biblical perspective is that all truth is God's truth which eliminates the distinction between secular and sacred truth.
2. The truth of Christian revelation is true to what actually exists in the universe so the Christian can pursue truth without the fear of ultimate contradiction.
3. Forces of evil seek to undermine the Bible, distort human reasoning, and lead persons to rely on their own inadequate and fallen selves in the pursuit of truth.
4. The Bible is not concerned with abstract truth, but truth as related to life. Therefore, knowing in the biblical sense is applying perceived knowledge to daily life.
5. The various sources of knowledge available to the Christian (the special revelation of Scripture, the general revelation of the natural world, and reason) are complementary and should be used in the light of the biblical pattern.
6. Given the unity of truth, the acceptance of a Christian epistemology cannot be separated from the acceptance of a Christian metaphysics.[32]

Knight's observations can be explored in relation to the particular challenge posed by contemporary scientism, which maintains that scientific inquiry is the only reliable way of knowing. Scientism, as contrasted with science, denies that truth can be discerned through the revelation of the Christian faith and presupposes that empirically based reason is the only medium for understanding. Huston Smith points out the dangers of the limited epistemology of scientism. Science values control, prediction, objectivity, numbers, and signs while faith values surrender, surprise, subjectivity and objectivity, words, and symbols. Whereas science deals with the instrumental values of utility, useful-

32. Knight, *Philosophy and Education*, 161–62.

ness, service, and control, faith deals with the intrinsic values of wonder, awe, reverence, creativity, imagination, and promise. Whereas becoming is the dominant focus of science, being/becoming is the focus of faith.[33]

The faith perspective of Christianity provides an alternative way of knowing that expands upon, but is not contradictory to the truths of science given that all truth is God's truth. The Christian is free to explore the insights of science discerned or discovered through use of reason and empirical observation in relation to the natural world of God's general revelation. But the Christian must also beware of the potential forces of evil that would seek to exalt science inappropriately.

A Christian view of the physical world and nature maintains that the creation is real and good and thus amenable to experimentation; therefore, empirical science can be affirmed. A Christian view also maintains that nature is ordered and intelligible; therefore theoretical science is appropriate. Finally, a Christian view maintains that history and culture have meaning and purpose. Thus applied science and technology can be fully pursued.[34] But in each of these scientific areas

> a Christian view of the physical world sees nature in the light of Scripture and with a concern for culture. This involves a creative view of nature that recognizes the world as real and good. It includes a critical view of scientific ideas and methods that looks to Scripture for guidance, and for faith in the order and intelligibility revealed in creation. And it attempts a constructive view of culture that finds purpose and meaning in seeking to improve the world for the good of humanity and the glory of God.[35]

From the perspective of a Christian world view and epistemology, it is helpful to see the potentials and dangers of science, as well as the Christian graces that can counter those dangers which emerge in scientism (see table 3).[36]

The first potential of science is that of providing explanations for reality and contributing to human knowledge. But there is the potential danger of a misplaced worship that glorifies the scientific process or the human explanations derived from that process. Christian faith can help to focus worship upon the God of all creation who is revealed to persons

---

33. Huston Smith, "Excluded Knowledge: A Critique of the Modern Mind Set," *Teachers College Record* (February 1979):419–45.

34. Joseph Spradley, "A Christian View of the Physical World," in *The Making of a Christian Mind: A Christian World View and the Academic Enterprise*, ed. Arthur F. Holmes (Downers Grove, Ill.: Inter-Varsity, 1985), 59–69.

35. Ibid, 79.

36. I am indebted to Larry Martin, student at Gordon-Conwell Theological Seminary, for figure 9.

Table 3 **Science and the Christian Graces**

Potentials of Science	Dangers in Scientism	Christian Graces
Explanation (Knowing)	Misplaced worship	Faith
Prediction (Choosing)	Unwarranted expectations	Hope
Control (Changing)	Misuse of power	Love

through the natural order. A second potential of science is that of predicting natural phenomena and contributing to human decision making processes. But an inherent danger is that of unwarranted expectations in relation to future events and human capabilities to determine those events. The grace of a living hope alerts the Christian to God's sovereignty and providential care along with the appropriate place of human responsibility in predicting and choosing the future. The third potential of science, which Palmer also identifies, is that of control and of changing the natural or human condition. The corresponding danger of this potential is the misuse of power, something repeatedly witnessed in history. Complementing this danger is the quintessential Christian grace of love which sets the glory of God and the welfare of others and the creation above the use of power.

This discussion of scientism illustrates the importance of a biblical epistemology and the usefulness of Knight's observations for considering epistemological questions. The truths of science can be integrated with a Christian world view that affirms all truth as God's truth. The Christian can pursue a scientific way of knowing, but one that is subject at all points to biblical revelation. Biblical truth can address the dangers inherent in the misappropriation of science. A Christian epistemology is dependent upon a Christian metaphysics, and in particular a Christian cosmology, that sees the physical world as God's creation and therefore subject to God in all of its variety and unity.

Axiology
Questions of value involve both ethics and aesthetics. Ethics is the study of moral principles and practices. Christian ethics deals with the reality of sin and the Christian calling of service and sacrifice in the world. Aesthetics is the study of beauty and the creative dimensions in life. For the Christian, aesthetics is based upon the fact that God created a world of beauty; this implies a personal responsibility to both appre-

ciate and create beauty.[37] The relationship between axiology and education can be explored by considering different value systems affecting the purposes and goals of education. Both metaphysical and epistemological issues interact with these axiological perspectives.

Paulo Freire emphasizes the need for a clear articulation of values in education and for critical reflection upon and problematization of values.[38] Freire calls for intentionality, integrity, and honesty regarding those values which in fact guide the entire educational process. Such intentionality, integrity, and honesty are fundamental to any educational efforts that claim to be Christian because the standards of truth apply to all levels of conception, planning, and action.

Values are generally conceived as conceptions to which worth, interest, and goodness have been attributed. Values are choices of ultimate concern which by their very nature embody theological considerations for the Christian. They deal with what is desirable, meaningful, and enduring even within a given time span. Values identify those goals, ideals, and ultimate ends of human thought and endeavor which make up the very fabric of everyday life. They inherently involve belief in propositions, belief in the desirability or necessity of those propositions, and commitment to them (personal conviction and full involvement).[39] To educate is to teach at every point the complex web of religious, moral, and intellectual values which ultimately define the arrangements of any community and society.

In dealing with values in education, the struggle is often between that which is viewed as good and that which is viewed as better. This poses the question of priority and preference in values. Values for the educator thereby present the dilemma of choosing commitments involving one's thoughts, efforts, and love. In dealing with the choice of values, Milton Rokeach suggests in an early work that each person holds many values arranged loosely and more or less flexibly in a hierarchy with different value systems having priority.[40]

In contrast with Rokeach's conceptions are those of Lynn White, who describes a changing canon of culture in considering value. According to White, the traditional hierarchy of values has in fact been turned at right angles to become a spectrum of values in which every human activity, including educational activity, embodies the possibility of greatness. No human activities are viewed by nature as being more profitable.

37. Knight, *Philosophy and Education*, 171–77.
38. See Paulo Freire, *Pedagogy of the Oppressed*, trans. Myra Bergman Ramos (New York: Seabury, 1970).
39. Daniel and Laurel N. Tanner, *Curriculum Development: Theory into Practice* (New York: Macmillan, 1975), 127.
40. See Milton Rokeach, *The Nature of Human Values* (New York: Free Press, 1973).

What results is an equality of values. Though values imply a monetary metaphor that is scaled up and down rather than sideways, White suggests that the term *value* must be used in describing this spectrum of choices available to persons.[41] Whereas Christians have traditionally identified value hierarchies, White's insights are helpful because of the problems posed by change in educational planning where values must be reformulated and reapplied to new and varying situations. This is not to support a situation ethics, but to consider the various contextual modifying factors which Knight emphasizes in relating philosophy to educational practice (see p. 86). With a spectrum of values, the Christian educator is called upon to regularly make conscious choices that will direct the actual practice of education.

Whereas with White's conceptions the scope of value choices is broadened and widened in dealing with a pluralistic society, the Christian educator must assert that some value systems better represent the totality of reality. This assertion is possible given the nature of biblical revelation, supernatural realities, reason, and faith experiences. The Christian educator can propose higher values because he or she can answer such questions as: What are persons and their ultimate end? What is the meaning and purpose of human activity? What, or rather, who is God? These questions can be answered with a certainty and surety not possible outside of a revealed faith.

Before identifying specific value systems as they influence thought and practice, it is possible to suggest four implications for Christian educators in this area of axiology. First, Christian educators must be aware of the values undergirding their efforts in teaching, ministry, and life. Christian educators have too readily accommodated themselves to their culture in ways that deny the gospel and kingdom values. Considering values fosters conscious identification and integration of biblical values in teaching and learning. Awareness of such values assumes a personal commitment to them.

Second, Christian educators must translate their values into the actual purposes and goals which guide educational practice. Values must be synthesized with and internalized throughout the actual educational enterprise so that persons can be encouraged to act consistently in accordance with stated values. This second implication assumes that values have prescriptive power and that they both consciously and unconsciously affect educational plans and their implementation.

A third implication that emerges from this emphasis upon values translation is that values must be pursued in communal and institutional contexts because we live in a communal and institutional world.

41. Lynn White, Jr., *Frontiers of Knowledge* (New York: Harper & Bros., 1956), 312.

Values too readily become privatized. A subjective preoccupation with self can plague Christians as a result of the psychologization of evangelicalism (my peace, my joy, my self-esteem, my self-worth, my health, and my. . . .). Consequently, there is relative inattention to the common welfare of all persons, especially those who are disadvantaged or oppressed. Given this situation it is essential that Christian educators translate their values into communal and institutional goals.

A fourth implication is that Christian educators must be aware of the constant need for renewal in relation to their values. Given the nature of persons, communities, institutions, and social structures, Christians must constantly reaffirm basic biblical values in the spiritual battle for the minds and lives of persons. This need for renewal emerges from the reality of sin in its personal and corporate manifestations. Paul Tillich suggests that Christians are called to constantly live in relation to the Protestant principle. This principle maintains that reform and renewal is a constant need in institutions given the changing needs, conditions, and issues of contemporary life. The Christian vocation is to protest against those efforts, forms, and structures that are no longer faithful to the gospel and to suggest alternatives consistent with biblical values.[42] This indeed is the task of Christian educators. While protesting, the Christian recognizes the essential work of the Holy Spirit to actualize effective reform and renewal.

In considering questions of value, Dwayne Huebner suggests five value categories which generally guide the practice of education in various settings. First, *technical valuing* emphasizes the importance of control and efficiency in education. This form of valuing maintains a means-end rationality that approaches an economic model and strives to mobilize material and human resources to produce ends. This valuing focuses on those elements in education which can be conditioned or controlled and therefore effectively manipulated.

Second, *political valuing* addresses questions of power which are usually covert in the process of education. Teachers or educators have a position of power and control over others and can influence them in various ways. Students also possess power to influence teachers and others. Education can be viewed as slow-fuse politics which attempts to either support the status quo or to work for change. Educators and students can raise questions about those ideologies and structures which maintain and legitimate injustice or unrighteousness in the wider society. Students and educators can be viewed as potential or actual change agents in the church and world.

42. Paul Tillich, *The Protestant Era*, trans. James L. Adams (Chicago: University of Chicago Press, 1948), 161–81.

Third, *scientific valuing* emphasizes those efforts in education which produce new knowledge with an empirical base. In this valuing category, scholarship and inquiry are emphasized along with the exploration of various options for meaning.

Fourth, *aesthetic valuing* focuses on activities having a symbolic or aesthetic meaning. Imagination, creativity, and dealing with the unconditioned or open-ended aspects of life are involved in this educational category.

Fifth, *ethical valuing* considers the encounter among persons with education contributing to the realization of moral life. In this category, the teacher is called upon to influence students with their responsibility (or "response-ability") in various areas of life. This valuing generally emphasizes the need for conversation and for sharing a vision of a moral community among persons both within and outside of the educational encounter.[43]

Huebner does point out that education is seldom valued from within only one of these categories, but that all five influence the actual process of valuing in education.[44] But in relation to these five categories, Christian educators might suggest a sixth category, "spiritual valuing," that would include a concern for freeing persons from the power of sin to live righteously and justly before God as God's adopted children. It would emphasize understanding and living in accordance with God's Word while encouraging a sense of wonder, awe, and worship in all of life. It would then be possible to view spiritual valuing at the apex of a hierarchy or pyramid of values that in turn would influence the other valuing categories (see fig. 7).

Spiritual values, being the highest of values for the Christian, need to influence the other value options. In figure 7, spiritual valuing serves as the foundation as well as the apex of a values hierarchy given the need for a clearly articulated, authoritative basis for value decisions in educational questions which is provided by a Christian world view.

While these portrayals are real options, a reforming perspective on education suggests another alternative which might be diagrammed with ethical, aesthetic, scientific, political, and technical values as adjacent blocks encapsulated in the larger block of spiritual valuing (see fig. 8). Spiritual valuing is the entire domain in which educational values must be considered. Rather than seeing spiritual valuing as a sixth valuing

43. See Dwayne Huebner, "Curriculum Language and Classroom Meanings," in *Curriculum Theorizing: The Reconceptualists*, ed. William Pinar (Berkeley: McCutchan, 1975), 215–28.
44. Ibid., 228.

FIGURE 7   Hierarchy of Values

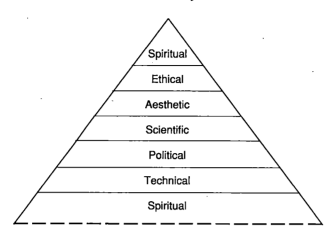

Spiritual

Ethical

Aesthetic

Scientific

Political

Technical

Spiritual

FIGURE 8   A Reforming Alternative

Spiritual Valuing (Reforming)				
Ethical	Aesthetic	Scientific	Political	Technical

category, spiritual values must impinge upon each of the valuing categories suggested by Huebner, reforming them in five ways.

First, *technical valuing,* which emphasizes control and efficiency, can be reformed or renewed to emphasize the stewardship of God's resources. The life portrayed and values communicated in education can be seen in relation to God's ordered creation, reflecting God's harmony, providence, and sovereignty.

Second, *political valuing,* which emphasizes power and legitimation of that power, can be reformed in education to value the effort to free and empower others. This occurs as others are humbled before God and through redemption in Jesus Christ become vehicles of his transforming power in society. Being light and salt in the world and experiencing daily the resurrection power of Jesus Christ in one's personal and social life are then the focus of this valuing in education (Matt. 5:13–16; Phil. 3:10). There is power in the ministry of reconciliation, power in modeling love and service to others, and power in obeying God's will which mitigates human powers.

Third, *scientific valuing,* with its concern for empirical knowledge, can be reformed to focus on knowing God as the basis for better knowing God's creation. The challenge in all scientific inquiry is to take captive every thought to make it obedient to Christ (2 Cor. 10:5), seeing in him all the treasures of wisdom and knowledge (Col. 2:2, 3). This provides the essential perspective for integrating the discoveries of all scientific disciplines. The challenge is to have the very mind of Christ as his thoughts relate to the natural and supernatural worlds.

Fourth, *aesthetic valuing* addresses concerns for freedom, creativity, and beauty. This category can be reformed to emphasize in education the disclosure of the beauty of Christ as revealed in creation and in humanity's creative expression and potential. Persons can give glory to God through all creative arts and see the beauty of God in the common things of life. There is a need in education to enable persons to better image their God given freedom within the structures and forms of God's creation.

Fifth, *ethical valuing* can be reformed in education to encourage persons to consider and actualize responsible action—first in relation to God, and then in relation to creation, others, and oneself. This necessitates grappling with the dimensions of a Christian life-style and ethical decisions in all areas of human endeavor. The Christian educator is challenged with the call for an integrity which addresses the contradictions of personal and social sin. This challenge must also be posed for students.

Specifics of an Educational Philosophy

The exploration of axiology has served to indicate the essential role of Christian values for decisions regarding the purposes and goals of education. A further consideration involves metaphysical, epistemological, and axiological concerns and how they affect a stated philosophy of education that strives to be Christian. In order to consider this issue, the Christian educator must adopt a model that identifies the key elements of an educational philosophy per se. Harold Burgess suggests such a scheme that includes purposes and goals, content, teacher, student, environment, and evaluation.[45] There are direct parallels between these categories and those of Knight: (nature of the student, role of the teacher, curricular emphasis, teaching methodologies, and the social function of educational institutions). The "content" in Burgess's school can be equated with Knight's "curricular emphasis," and Burgess's "environment" category mirrors Knight's "teaching methodologies" and "social function of educational institutions." Burgess and Knight provide a comprehensive framework for an educational philosophy.

45. Burgess's areas are standard for considering an educational philosophy or theory. See Harold William Burgess, *An Invitation to Religious Education* (Mishawaka, Ind.: Religious Education Press, 1975), 12, 13, 167.

Purposes and Goals How do evangelism, fellowship, service, kingdom consciousness, and worship relate to the purposes of Christian education or education in general? The model described in chapter 1 suggests a direct relationship between the purposes of the church and those of Christian education. This perspective does not equate Christian education with church education, but views the church as existing in a multiplicity of settings and relationships. Nonetheless, it assumes that in homes, schools, communities, work places, relationships, and individual places of study a unity of purpose in Christian education should exist.

Some may raise serious questions regarding the dissolution of what traditionally has been viewed as a gap between the purposes of Christian education per se and secular education, and the participation of Christians in both spheres. What purposes can a Christian have in the area of vocational training in a public school? Others may maintain that the acquisition of knowledge, values, skills, sensitivities, and behaviors are ends in and of themselves. The additional purposes or goals of evangelism, fellowship, service, and the like reveal a utilitarian or pragmatic emphasis that is foreign to the tasks of education in its purest and highest form. Why then suggest any additional purposes? A third area of concern may be raised by Christians who emphasize other scriptural foundations than those cited, or by those who place a greater emphasis upon experience or reason in the formulation of a Christian philosophy. Such alternative decisions at key points would make for a difference in what purposes and goals are identified. The need for clarity and consistency in the definition and implementation of whatever purposes and goals are selected obviates such questions.

In *Objectives in Religious Education* (1930), Paul H. Vieth suggested a list of seven goals derived from the thought of leaders in the field at that time: [46]

1. Seek to foster a consciousness of God as a reality in human experience, and a sense of personal relationship to God through Jesus Christ.
2. Seek to develop an understanding and appreciation of the personality, life, and teachings of Jesus so as to lead persons to experience him as Lord and Savior, and to follow him loyally and obediently in daily life and conduct.
3. Seek to nurture a progressive and continuous development of Christlike character through the work of the Holy Spirit.

46. Paul H. Vieth, *Objectives in Religious Education* (New York: Harper & Bros., 1930), 70–78.

4. Seek to develop the ability and disposition to participate in and respond to the spiritual and social outworkings of the gospel, being about God's work in the world while not being of it.
5. Seek to develop the ability and disposition to responsibly participate in the Christian family when appropriate, and the extended Christian family which is the church.
6. Seek to encourage the development of a Christian world view that is contextualized in the life of each person.
7. Seek to educate Christians in the whole counsel of God as recorded preeminently in Scripture which is the authoritative guide for all faith and life.[47]

Although the relative emphasis on each of these seven goals may vary with the actual teaching context, their general thrust has an enduring quality. The careful articulation of such purposes and goals is the key element of an educational philosophy. The following general purpose for Christian education can be proposed:

The general purpose of the church's educational ministry is that all persons know of, and develop a dynamic and growing personal relationship with God (John 17:3) and God's creation. This knowledge and relationship is to be grounded in God's revelation and self-disclosure in Scripture and centered completely and decisively in Jesus Christ as Lord and Savior (John 14:6; 17:7; 2 Tim. 3:16). Persons of all ages are to be enabled by the Holy Spirit to respond in faith, love, and obedience such that each person is continually growing as a member of the Christian community and living in the world as a representative of Christ, while abiding in the hope of his second coming. The goal of educational ministry is that persons become obedient disciples of Jesus Christ (Matt. 28:18–20), prepared for works of service and conformed increasingly to the image of Christ (Eph. 4:11–16).

Content   Although the place of the Bible in Christian education has been emphasized thus far, Lois LeBar suggests an expanded perspective in which Christian education centers on both the living Word of God (Christ) and the written Word of God (the Bible).[48] This suggestion counters the danger of an emphasis upon the Bible that fails to relate biblical content to the living Christ and to the lives of persons. Evangelical educators have been particularly prone to this temptation. Another issue at stake is the place of the students' experiences and needs

47. Ibid.
48. Lois E. LeBar, *Education That Is Christian*, rev. ed. (Old Tappan, N.J.: Fleming H. Revell, 1981), 212–15.

in the choice of content. Some suggest that student needs, problems, and interests should have priority, while others suggest that the logical and sequential order of the content should be the primary guide. Others, in addition, emphasize the place of social or communal responsibilities. Each of these three options are explored in the discussion of person, society, and subject-centered approaches.[49]

In a societal situation that evidences an overwhelming preoccupation with human needs, evangelical educators must exercise discernment to distinguish the nature of those needs. This is the case because one dictum of the common wisdom of the age is that student needs should be the primary determinant of educational content. A distinction must be made between persons' felt needs and their real needs. A corollary of the above dictum is that the educator should initiate his or her efforts by addressing felt needs, and then eventually disclose and address the real needs of students. Following such common wisdom may result in serious inattention to the demands of God upon persons in various areas of responsibility. Abraham Heschel has described this scenario as the tyranny of needs.[50] Christian educators must evaluate human needs making use of scriptural categories because a society or culture can actually distort perceptions of need.

One example of this problem is the tendency to define the better life through education in terms of progress measured by the increased accumulation of material resources. Thus the constant need is for increased possession and consumption of material goods of greater worth. Such a materialistic view fails to adequately critique those areas of need as perceived through a particular culture which may conflict with a Christian world view. This is the case because of human sinfulness. In fact, the educational task may be to challenge perceived needs with divine demands which suggest alternative values beyond materialism. (This does not, of course, negate addressing appropriate or genuine human need as discerned from biblical categories.)

Another issue is the relationship between experience or action and content or reflection in education. Some educators who emphasize the transmission of accumulated wisdom suggest that content or reflection is primary and that experience or action is secondary. Thus the agenda for educational efforts is to share content and subsequently to address how that content can issue in action or affect experience. Other educators who emphasize the experiential dimensions of life suggest that

49. See pages 111–13.

50. Abraham J. Heschel, *Between God and Man: An Interpretation of Judaism from the Writings of Abraham Heschel*, ed. Fritz A. Rothschild (New York: Free Press, 1959), 129–51.

effective integration in education occurs where experience is primary. Shared experiences or actions are subsequently reflected upon and evaluated in the effort to gain insights.

The first approach can be identified as a deductive agenda that moves from generalized and abstract knowledge to that which is particular and owned by individuals in the immediate context. The second approach can be identified as an inductive agenda that moves from particular and experienced knowledge to that which is perhaps generalized and connected with other experiences through reflection. In many ways, both approaches can be viewed as complementary, but relative differences in emphasis imply a separate agenda in educational content.

The Teacher   Wilbert J. McKeachie suggests that teachers assume six roles, each of which has corresponding goals. These roles and goals are expanded upon in a reforming perspective.

1. *Expert/neophyte.* As an expert, the teacher is to transmit information—the concepts and perspectives of the field or subject— while recognizing areas of inadequate expertise.
2. *Formal authority/subject.* As a formal authority, the teacher is to set goals and procedures for reaching goals and as a subject be open to students' suggestions where appropriate.
3. *Socializing/socialized agent.* As a socializing agent, the teacher is to clarify goals and options beyond the class or course and to prepare students for these. As socialized agent, the teacher is to be open to the suggestions and influence of students and others within and beyond the teaching setting.
4. *Facilitator.* As a facilitator, the teacher is to promote creativity and growth in students' own terms and to help them overcome obstacles to learning. The teacher is to be sensitive to his or her own creativity and growth.
5. *Ego ideal in process.* As an ego ideal, the teacher is to convey the excitement and value of educational inquiry in given areas and recognize areas where ideals and practice are lacking.
6. *Person.* As a person, the teacher is to convey the full range of human needs and skills relevant to and sustained by one's educating activity, to be validated as a human being, and to validate the students as persons.[51]

In relation to McKeachie's six roles, the Christian educator must ask herself or himself the extent to which these roles can be affirmed or

51. Wilbert J. McKeachie, *Teaching Tips: A Guidebook for the Beginning College Teacher,* 7th ed. (Lexington, Mass.: D. C. Heath, 1978), 81–82.

revised. The Christian teacher is called upon to transmit biblical information and the concepts and perspectives of the Christian faith. In addition, she or he may be sharing additional insights from any number of fields and subjects, with the proviso that they are either consistent with a biblical world view or that they help students to grapple with possible inconsistencies. This poses the problem of integration for the Christian teacher and accountability in terms of the Christian heritage. The Christian teacher is an expert to the extent to which he or she manifests faithfulness to God and his or her discipline.

In relation to McKeachie's second role, the Christian teacher is the formal or nonformal authority, but the final authority is always God. Thus the Christian teacher is ultimately and finally accountable to God in all areas of endeavor. Second, the Christian teacher is accountable to a host of persons, groups, and institutions for her or his exercise of authority. The nature of the teacher's formal or nonformal authority is derivative, and the higher calling is to so exercise this derived authority that God is glorified. This perspective does not at all diminish the appropriate role of the teacher in setting goals and procedures for reaching those goals. The Christian teacher is also subject to insights offered by students where they are true and appropriate.

The Christian teacher's role as a socializing agent must be seen in relation to the complementary roles of parents, churches, communities, and governments in various areas of human life. In certain situations, the Christian teacher may also be a resocializing agent, depending upon the nature of other socializing forces in the lives of students. This additional responsibility as a potential "resocializer" requires careful discernment in relation to biblical values and the proper place of disenculturation. Postman and Weingartner allude to this role in their discussion of teaching as a subversive activity—one which poses questions and presents options for students to gain awareness of inappropriate socialization.[52] Postman has also discussed teaching as a conserving activity that affirms the teacher's roles as a socializing agent in terms of cultural and societal norms.[53] The Christian teacher is also socialized by students through their interactions.

As a facilitator, the Christian teacher does indeed promote creativity and growth but not exclusively in the students' own terms. While recognizing McKeachie's focus upon college students, the Christian teacher's perspective is informed by God's terms for understanding creativity and growth. This may not present a standard radically different from that of the students, but in many cases it will. This is the case because human

52. Neil Postman and Charles Weingartner, *Teaching as Subversive Activity* (New York: Delacorte, 1969).
53. Neil Postman, *Teaching as Conserving Activity* (New York: Dell, 1980).

creativity, growth, and freedom must be understood in relation to God's order, structure, and form for life. Within that order there is a tremendous potential for creativity and genuine growth, but also an equal potential for the manifestation of human sin with accompanying illusion and delusion. The Christian teacher must also be aware of his or her own need for continued growth and creativity.

In terms of McKeachie's fifth role, the Christian teacher is only a model the extent to which Christ is a living reality in her or his life (1 Cor. 11:1). The excitement and value of Christian inquiry in all areas of life must be shared by Christian teachers. Too much of Christian teaching has settled for the mundane, lacking excitement and color.

An additional challenge is posed by the sixth role of being a person. Too many efforts in Christian education have denied the essential personhood of the teacher as created by God. The biblical model of teaching stresses a personal relationship and an appropriation of truth that results in sharing both doctrine and life as they reinforce each other.

Properly balancing these roles is a difficult task to accomplish in various teaching settings. The need for competence and excellence in each of these roles is necessitated by the demand for Christian integrity in a world in need of teachers who reflect the glory of the Master Teacher. Further insights can be drawn for the role of the teacher through a careful study of the teaching ministry of Jesus Christ.

From a Christian perspective, teachers are fellow persons with students. They are fellow creatures of God with unique strengths and weaknesses and affected by the fall. In general education, they may be believers in Christ or they may not be, but nevertheless they can be instruments used by God to teach students. Scriptural standards for teachers include the following: (1) a believer in Christ (1 Cor. 12:27–28); (2) called by God and gifted for the teaching ministry (Rom. 12:7; 1 Cor. 12:28; Eph. 4:11–12); (3) faithful to true doctrine (1 Tim. 1:3–7; 2 Tim. 2:2); (4) a servant, an authority, and a mature and maturing disciple of Christ (1 Tim. 3:1–7; James 3:1); and (5) responsible before God for both life and teaching (Matt. 23:10; 1 Tim. 4:12–16; James 3:1).[54]

The Student   If one were to develop McKeachie's roles in terms of the student, the following could be suggested:

1. *Neophyte/expert.* As a neophyte, the student is to receive the information, concepts, and perspectives of the teacher and offer insights in areas of expertise.

54. Al Edeker, "A Philosophy of Christian Education" (Gordon-Conwell Theological Seminary, 1985), 5.

2. *Formal subject.* As subject to the teacher's authority, the student is to accept the goals and procedures set by the teacher, and/or suggest alternative goals and procedures in negotiation with the teacher.

3. *Socialized/socializing agent.* As a socialized agent, the student is to actively participate in the task of clarifying goals and options beyond the classroom in cooperation with the teacher. The student can also be a socializing agent by suggesting goals and options for the transfer of learning.

4. *Fellow facilitator.* As a fellow facilitator, the student is to identify areas for creativity and growth and work to overcome obstacles to learning in cooperation with the teacher.

5. *Ego ideal in process.* As an ego ideal in process, the student is to share in the excitement and value of the educational inquiry and recognize areas where ideals are lacking.

6. *Person.* As a person, the student is to convey the full range of human needs and skills relevant to and sustained by one's educating activity, to be validated as a human being, and to validate other students and teachers as persons.

In describing the roles of the student, we must move beyond an understanding of the student as exclusively passive or receptive and investigate areas for active participation. The extent of student participation and shared responsibility is dependent upon the maturity and experience of the students, but wherever possible this is worth emphasizing given the nature of persons as created by God for total life responses. As suggested by Harold Burgess, "even though Protestant traditional theorists do give some consideration to the student and to the teacher-learning process, they appear to place little reliance upon these factors in their actual theorizing."[55]

Students are co-partners with teachers in the educational effort and any attempt to co-opt their active participation is a denial of their created humanity. Christian truth must be taught to persons, and to neglect persons ignores half of the equation. A reforming perspective recognizes the unique differences among individual students and encourages the place of dialogue, not to deny the need for teachers to share authoritative content and direct teaching, but to enable the active appropriation of truth in the lives of students. Otherwise, evangelical educators are perpetuating rote forms of learning that neither transfer beyond the educational setting nor aid the process of integrating life in terms of a

55. Burgess, *Invitation to Religious Education,* 49.

Christian world view. Edeker suggests the following insights in understanding the student from a biblical perspective:

> The view of the student within a Christian philosophy of education suggests several points. One is that the student is a creation of God and is created in the image of God. The student therefore has value in God's eyes. This means that the student him or herself and others should value and respect the student. The student is not a second class citizen or an empty container to be filled, but he/she is a person of value and potential.
>
> A second point is that the student like all of mankind is fallen. Therefore, the student has limitations, faults, and destructive behavior which affect their growth and interaction with others.
>
> Third, every human is potentially a child of God or is a child of God. This potential is realized in Christ.
>
> Fourth, the student is capable of change and growth. The Christian view suggests that through the work of the Holy Spirit the destructive traits and behaviors of the student can be corrected or nullified through daily sanctification.
>
> Fifth, the student is responsible before God for his or her actions, sinfulness, and response before God.
>
> This view of the student reflects both his/her potential and responsibility. The following roles suggest the possible response of the student of Christ. The student's ability to perform these roles may vary depending upon the student's age and maturity in Christ.

1. The student should strive to grow into the likeness of Christ.
2. The Christian student should worship and glorify God through his/her learning and the application of that learning.
3. The student is to be a good steward of his/her talents.
4. The student should be diligent in all that their hands find to do.
5. The student should test all knowledge with scripture and test spirits and teacher.
6. The student should apply his/her learning, being not only hearers but doers (James 1:22–25).
7. He or she should remain open to the work of the Holy Spirit.
8. He or she should value all of creation.
9. He or she should be in community and encourage others. (Heb. 10:24–25)[56]

The Environment   Various factors in the environment, context, or settings for education must be considered. D. Campbell Wyckoff has insightfully named three interacting aspects of the environment.

The first factor is the *natural aspect.* This aspect entails the physical factors and material resources of the classroom, including room arrange-

56. Edeker, "Philosophy of Christian Education," 6.

ment, decoration, aesthetics, and resource display, along with factors that affect visibility, mobility, and comfort.

The *human aspect* is the second factor. It focuses upon the teacher(s) and student(s) and other human resources and factors. In addition, the nature of commitments, interactions, and personal or shared concerns which are present overtly or covertly in the educational interaction are involved in this aspect.

The last factor is the *divine aspect*. The Holy Spirit is the determinative environmental presence in Christian education and the challenge is to create those conditions in which the Spirit of God can work most fruitfully in the lives of persons.[57]

All three aspects require attention and intention in Christian education. The need is for an approach that considers all three aspects of the environment, giving clear priority to the divine aspect. Every setting for education—formal, nonformal, or informal—involves these three aspects in varying degrees of consciousness and intentionality. The demands of a practical theology are reflected in the need to contextualize efforts of Christian education by carefully assessing these and other aspects of the environment. Knight's analysis suggests the need to consider the human aspects in terms of political, economic, social, communal, and familial forces.[58] The dimension of cultural factors must also be recognized. These various forces will be considered in later chapters. But a perennial question for the Christian educator is how the three aspects of the environment interact and facilitate the most effective learning.

Evaluation   The element of evaluation reintroduces the question of values because it is out of the identification of values that one *e-value-ates*. In evaluation the Christian educator assesses formally and informally the extent to which stated or perhaps unstated purposes and goals have been addressed in actual practice. In evaluation the call is for responsibility and accountability. To a certain extent, the outcomes of Christian education can be observed in terms of the change in knowledge, values, attitudes, skills, sensitivities, and behaviors manifested by both students and teachers. Evaluation is ultimately subject to divine assessment, yet Christian educators must devote the necessary time and energy to carefully observe and assess the results of their efforts and those of their students. The effectiveness of evaluation is largely dependent upon the prior careful articulation of purposes and goals that can be reconsidered and measured after regular periods of time. Evaluation

57. D. Campbell Wyckoff, *The Task of Christian Education* (Philadelphia: Westminster, 1955), 104.

58. See page 86.

strives to combine both objective and subjective criteria for judgment with an openness to the unintended and unexpected results of teaching.

Modern Philosophies of Education

Having considered the specifics of an educational philosophy, we now survey a number of modern philosophies to identify their distinctives. Burgess's first five categories (goals, content, teacher, student, and environment) will be used to outline the distinctives of each philosophy. The sixth category (evaluation) will be used to critique each philosophy. The following educational philosophies will be considered: perennialism, essentialism, behaviorism, progressivism, reconstructionism, romantic naturalism, and existentialism.[59] Some of these philosophies can be viewed as complementary in actual practice, but for the purpose of description they will be viewed as distinct.

Perennialism

Perennialism emphasizes the cultivation of rational powers along with academic excellence. It affirms intellectual, spiritual, and ethical purposes in education in guiding the individual to the truth. Goals include the transmission and assimilation of a prescribed body of classical subject matter. Classical advocates of this philosophy include Aristotle and Thomas Aquinas and more recently Robert Hutchins, Mortimer Adler, and Jacques Maritain.[60]

The content of perennialist education includes *Great Books of the Western World*, the classics, and the traditional liberal arts. The mind and reason are emphasized in exposing students to the great works of the Western intellectual past. The curriculum is subject centered, with a stress on mental discipline and literary analysis.

Teachers are viewed as academic scholars, philosophers par excellence who have a grasp of vast areas of knowledge and wisdom. Corresponding to the teacher's role, students are viewed as rational beings who are to be guided by the first principles revealed in the classics and liberal arts.

For perennialism, the primary settings for learning include the classroom or lecture hall, the study, and the library where the classical heritage can be shared.

Perennialism can be affirmed for its sensitivity to the past, for its concern for rationality, and for its emphasis on excellence. This philosophy maintains that absolute truth exists and that human nature is

59. See Knight, *Philosophy and Education*, 90–126, for a detailed description of these philosophies and theories.
60. Ibid., 102–8.

consistent. Perennialists recognize the intellectual, spiritual, and ethical purposes of education. Perennialism can be criticized for its preoccupation with the past and its tendency toward rationalism. Its curricular uniformity may squelch creativity and its totally intellectual and teacher-directed approach may not recognize the whole character of persons and the limits of human reason.

Essentialism

Essentialist educators stress academic excellence, the cultivation of the intellect, and the transmission and assimilation of a prescribed body of subject matter. The primary advocates of this position are Arthur Bestor and Admiral Hyman G. Rickover.[61]

The content of essentialist education includes the fundamental academic disciplines and the mastery of basic and advanced knowledge. Its curriculum stresses mental discipline. Distinct from perennialism, essentialism considers modern scientific and experimental inquiry in addition to classical studies. Essentialism stresses a movement in education back to the basics along with the mastery of those basics broadly defined.

For essentialism, the model teacher is the person of letters and sciences who is in touch with the modern world and has achieved the level of an expert in the area of her or his competence. Students are viewed as rational beings who are to gain command of essential facts and skills that undergird the intellectual disciplines in adjusting to the physical and social environment.

Like perennialism, essentialism centers upon the primary settings of the classroom and library, but also emphasizes the research laboratory.

Essentialism can be affirmed for its emphasis on the mastery of basic learning skills and its recognition of the need for hard work and discipline in learning. This philosophy also recognizes the intellectual, spiritual, and ethical purposes of education. But distinct from perennialism, essentialism is not totally intellectual and manifests a greater concern for individual adjustment to the physical and social environment. Criticisms can be raised in relation to essentialism's teacher-directedness and its possible tendency toward rationalism. It can lead to exclusivism if the needs of exceptional persons are ignored.

Behaviorism

Behaviorists strive to form persons who function with efficiency, economy, precision, and objectivity. Education serves to shape persons in prescribed behaviors and responses as determined by the educators. The person most closely associated with behaviorism is B. F. Skinner.[62]

61. Ibid., 108–12.
62. Ibid., 118–23.

A behaviorist philosophy incorporates a behavioral modification sequence for desired student responses and skills, using appropriate rein-
forcement. Clear and precise behavioral objectives are stated and students
are exposed to a rewarding environment with the possible use of pro-
grammed instruction and other instructional technologies.

Teachers are viewed as skilled technicians, sculptors of both persons
and environments. A behaviorist approach strives to develop students as
well-sculptured, conditioned persons who are responsive to a societal
ideal. Students are viewed as highly maleable beings in need of clear and
definitive direction.

The appropriate setting for learning is a carefully controlled instructional environment where peripheral stimulation can be eliminated or
unattended.

Behaviorism can be affirmed for its careful consideration of action
and behaviors along with its conscious attention to environmental influences. This educational philosophy has been effective with some student populations and with certain discrete behaviors. The major criticism
of behaviorism is its reductionistic conception of persons and its exclusive and limited focus on behavior. Persons are more than well-conditioned animals. Freedom and dignity have a place in a Christian view
of persons, and transformation beyond the realms of conditioning is
possible in God.

Progressivism

Progressivism fosters the development of reflective thinking for social
problem solving, democratic relationships, and growth. Progressive educators strive to enable students to learn how to learn in order to adapt
to a changing world. Life adjustment in terms of societal expectations
is a key goal in this perspective. Progressive thinkers in education include John Dewey, William Kirkpatrick, Boyd H. Bode, and John L.
Childs.[63]

The content of education for progressivism is a comprehensive, unified exposure to problem-focused studies. Curriculum centers on social
problem solving through the reflective thinking of the scientific method
and the use of democratic processes. Cooperative learning is stressed
with priority given to students' needs and interests. Wherever possible
freedom of choice is given to students.

The teacher is not an authoritative classroom director as is the case
for perennialism, essentialism, and behaviorism. Rather, the teacher is
a person concerned for progress, committed to society and democratic
ideals, and sensitive to the growth of students. Thus the teacher is a

63. Ibid., 91–97.

fellow learner, traveler, and guide who facilitates the group learning process. For progressives, students are autonomously thinking and socially responsible individuals who are called to work democratically and cooperatively with others. Persons are viewed as organisms in ecological continuity with others and their social environment. Students are to be actively engaged in their own learning and that of others.

The preferred setting is the democratic classroom which is sensitive to and reflective of the wider society. In a real sense, the educational setting for progressivism is the world because the learning experience is part of life, not a preparation for life.

Progressivism can be affirmed for its concern for persons, who are viewed as active participants in the learning process. This philosophy encourages a sensitivity to student experiences, needs, and interests, along with a concern for cooperative learning. It deals with issues of everyday life and breaks the dichotomy between academic formality and daily experience. Progressivism can be criticized for its optimistic perspective of persons which does not recognize the effects of sin. Persons cannot solve their own problems without God. Progressivism also evidences relativist tendencies in terms of truth and values and an antisupernatural bias.

Reconstructionism

A reconstructionist educational philosophy holds the goal of building an ideal and just social order. Efforts are directed toward the establishment of a practical utopia where persons are liberated to be and become all they are intended to be. Reconstructionists include Theodore Brameld, George C. Counts, and Paulo Freire.[64]

The content of reconstructionist education centers upon social problems and the development of corrective programs scientifically determined for collective action. Critical analysis is made of social flaws in the effort to expose problems for consideration.

Teachers are viewed as subversive educators, social critics, and community organizers who seek to raise the consciousness of others in the direction of needed change. Students are viewed as potential change agents committed to and involved in constructive social redirection and renewal.

The settings for teaching are varied and include the classroom, the small cell or group meeting, the community center, the streets, and the fields.

Reconstructionism can be affirmed for its critical examination of current social, political, and economic orders and for its concern for social

64. Ibid., 112–16.

needs. Reconstructionists seriously grapple with human responsibility in the corporate and social realms. They recognize problems in current society and see possibilities for reform and change. Educators in this perspective are viewed as primary instruments for social change. Reconstructionists, while recognizing social sins, may ignore the realities of personal sin in the liberators and the oppressed as well as in the oppressors. Their preoccupation with the social order may result in ignoring personal responsibilities and their emphasis upon change may fail to see the need for continuity in personal and corporate life.

Romantic Naturalism

Romantic naturalism values individual freedom to develop one's potentials with the goal of self-actualization. Self-fulfillment and realization are to be fostered through the various growth processes of education. Those who have advocated this perspective include John Holt, Ivan Illich, A. S. Neill, and Carl Rogers.[65]

Learning activities are based upon a person's felt and real needs which are identified with the help of others. The curriculum provides for a free learning environment with the maximization of artistic self-expression and creativity.

Teachers are viewed as visionaries who provide the space for self-discovery and exploration by others. Teachers are sufficiently permissive and supportive to allow others freedom in learning. Students are perceived like unfolding flowers unencumbered by societal limitations. They are encouraged to learn in a variety of modes which best suit their individual dispositions.

The ideal settings for education include the free school, the open classroom, the open world, and the home, where students may be free from intense competition, harsh discipline, and the fear of failure. Such settings could be described as laissez faire in climate or "deschooled," where schooling is associated with rigidity and imposition.

Romantic naturalism can be affirmed for its concern for individuals, human freedom, aesthetics, and creativity. It can be criticized for its negation of the teacher's responsibility and authority to share necessary wisdom and direction. Romantics can deny the realities of human sin with a stress upon freedom and can negate the need for social responsiveness and discipline.

Existentialism

Existentialism as an educational philosophy emphasizes the inner search for meaning for one's own existence in the realization of authen-

---

65. Ibid., 76–84.

tic personhood. Advocates of existentialism in education include Maxine Greene, Martin Buber, and Carl Rogers.[66]

The content for an existentialist education centers upon the themes of the human condition with learning activities free of rational constraints. These activities are designed to free the individual to find her or his own being. The curriculum would include opportunities for introspection and reflection in a free learning environment open to change.

Teachers are viewed as fellow inquirers with students and fellow travelers in the quest for meaning. Teachers are viewed as authentic persons who are mature and deep in their understanding of life. Students are persons in search of the meaning of their own existence and open to inquiry and exploration.

The ideal setting for this in-depth learning should allow for the personal encounter which explores the inner world. A classroom where reflection and introspection are valued provide one such setting, but others can be imagined.

Existentialism as an educational philosophy can be affirmed for its concern for the individual and the place of personal choice. It values authenticity and integrity, emphasizes personal responsibilities, and encourages both the creativity and discovery of students. Existentialism revolts against the materialist and conformist tendencies of modern society and acknowledges the presence of alienation. But existentialism can be criticized in that a focus on individuals diminishes the authority of the teacher. It can lead to a stance that is overly introspective, reducing realities to experiential and relative categories devoid of absolutes or universals. The existential focus on personal existence and choice as primary may diminish the place of God's existence and choice. Truth may be ever expanding and changing in this philosophy with little possibility for continuity in life or in the Christian heritage.

The Choice of Philosophies

A blending of the various philosophies described above best contributes to educational practice. This can be appreciated by locating these philosophies or approaches within a framework suggested by Hollis Caswell, educator and curriculum theorist (see fig. 9).

Caswell's framework distinguishes three different foci for education: student interests, social functions, and organized knowledge.[67] In other words, educational philosophies may center on persons, communities or

66. Ibid.
67. Hollis L. Caswell and Doak S. Campbell, *Curriculum Development* (New York: American Book Co., 1935), 141–89.

societies, or content as their primary focus while recognizing the place of the other two foci. Thus perennialism and essentialism can be seen as philosophies which are content-centered. Behaviorism and reconstructionism can be seen as philosophies which focus largely upon the society or community and are society-centered. Romantic naturalism and existentialism are primarily person-centered. Progressivism can be seen as emphasizing both the society and its democratic processes and persons in need of growth, but its primary emphasis can be seen as society-centered.

With these various foci or centers, educators are challenged with the need for a choice. But as John Dewey asserts in *The School and Society* and *The Child and the Curriculum*, education embodies teaching content to persons in the context of their community and society; extremes of any approach are limiting to a wholistic perspective.[68]

The three approaches to education—person-centered, content-centered, and society-centered—might be roughly compared with the considerations in the preparation of a meal. The content-centered advocate is primarily concerned with the detailed preparation and serving of the food itself. The society-centered advocate is primarily concerned with the choice of the food in relation to the group assembled and the nutritional content of the menu in terms of preparing the guests for the activities during and following the meal. The person-centered advocate desires to please and is sensitive to the individual tastes of each of the guests and their unique needs. Hollis Caswell contends that the educator can act like a chemist, processing the various elements of students' interests, social functions, and organized knowledge in effective teaching.

Using Caswell's framework, it is possible to conceive of various combinations of emphases involving the three centers. It is also possible to conceive of a change in emphases within a particular class or group over time. Given the possible variation and combination of emphases, the educator's problem is how to maintain an adequate balance in his or her class, curriculum, or educational program. Evangelical educators have proposed that a God-centered education offers an alternative and that a

FIGURE 9   The Foci of Education

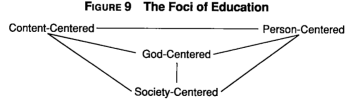

68. See Martin S. Dworkin, *Dewey on Education: Selections* (New York: Teachers College Press, 1959), 33–111.

Christian life view provides distinctives with which to guide the entire educational process. What, then, is a God-centered approach to education, and how is it related to Caswell's framework?

A God-centered approach establishes as its starting point the authority of God as revealed through Scripture and illumined by the Holy Spirit. From the Bible, viewed as the guide for Christian faith and practice, essential principles are derived for educational efforts. One such guiding principle is the affirmation that all truth is God's truth which implies a unity in truth and a correspondence between scriptural truth and reality. This principle calls for the joyful acceptance of truths in Scripture without a rigid literalism.

As was previously stated, the evangelical is not exempt from the tasks of hermeneutics and the challenge to contextualize biblical truths in contemporary settings. A God-centered approach subjects all truth claims to scriptural scrutiny while recognizing that the Bible is not an exhaustive source of truth and knowledge. Thus, any truth claims are initially judged in terms of their consistency with a Christian world and life view. A God-centered approach, with its recognition of the primacy of biblical authority, does not neglect knowledge discerned through nature, rationality, tradition, history, intuition, and even imagination. But insights derived from these sources are always subject to Scripture. This approach recognizes that certain educational issues are not resolved by a flippant proof texting or referral to biblical principles that ignores adequate grappling with the questions.

This survey of philosophical foundations has identified essential issues that demand the continuous attention of Christian educators who seek to be diligent in the task of thinking after Christ in the area of Christian education. Careful thought is not anathema to the faithful practice of Christian education, but essential for the challenges of the modern world. All Christian educators, even those most enamored with practice itself, have philosophies or theories with which they operate. Without attention to philosophical foundations, Christian educators have wandered in the deserts of cultural accommodation or cultural irrelevance and have failed to provide that vision necessary to guide their generation and those to come in relating God's truth, in its beauty and wholeness, to the tasks of Christian education. It is no longer possible to affirm this irresponsible approach and claim to be faithful. The call to be faithful also applies to a careful consideration of one's place in history, which is the focus of the next chapter.

4

Historical Foundations

The first three chapters have explored the biblical, theological, and philosophical foundations of Christian education. Through the study of these foundations, Christian educators seek to identify transcultural and cultural universals or principles to guide thought and practice. In investigating historical foundations, educators are forced to consider aspects of education which are more subject to change and various contingencies in different times and places. These aspects, though evidencing points of continuity, can be identified as cultural variables over against the transcultural and cultural universals discerned through biblical, theological, and philosophical study.

Vigilance is necessary to avoid an ahistorical mind set. In dealing with the challenge of educational ministries, Christians can in fact discern lessons from the past that provide insights for current and future needs. The dominant North American culture has valued a presentism and futurism that all too frequently ignores those principles from the past worthy of continued emphasis. In order to remedy this situation, evangelical educators can affirm those educational principles embodied in the orthodox faith and evidenced through the study of history. A consideration of historical foundations can also indicate particular aspects of history that require careful attention if one is to address one's unique time and location.

History and Historical Method

Marc Bloch defines history as "the science of persons over time."[1] History is a science in the sense of being a disciplined inquiry concerned with the analysis of documents and other evidence. History is a science of persons in the sense that it is concerned with individual persons in a concrete sense and with understanding them in their concrete situations. History is a science of persons over time in the sense that historical time is not a mere abstraction, but a concrete and living reality with a constantly changing and developing character. Thus the task of historical understanding is a continuous one as time progresses and provides new perspectives on the past. History focuses upon a concrete and living reality with a constantly changing and developing character.

The historical method in a narrow sense centers on a pursuit of truth based on careful investigation and cross-examination of documentary evidence. The object of history in this sense is to discover and set forth facts. In a broad sense, the historical method involves a methodology that uses the data and facts accumulated through the critical examination of documents to understand the past. Such an understanding requires interpretation, and Christian educators can avail themselves of those insights gained through the historical method in both its narrow and broad senses.

R. G. Collingwood maintains that the historian is concerned to deal with both the outside and inside of an event and to view past actions as a unity of both dimensions.[2] The outside of an event are those facts discovered through investigation. The inside of an event comprises the thoughts, intentions, motives, and beliefs of persons of which actions, institutions, and all other expressions are embodiments. The historian's goal is to understand persons' consciousness, thoughts, values, beliefs, and intentions, and their expressions in time and space. In addition, the historian considers the changes of these dimensions over time and in different contexts. Following Collingwood's perspective, Christian educators can appreciate both the inside and outside of events which are explored through the use of the historical method in its dual sense.

Historians are interested in the unique, the individual, and the particular in the past. All historians seek to maintain an essential tension between the universal and the particular, between the general and the unique. Given this perspective, they are concerned with development and change over time. Aspects of persons' lives which change over time include their ideas, beliefs, intentions, and commitments. As a result of

1. Marc Bloch, *The Historian's Craft*, introduction by Joseph R. Strayer, trans. Peter Putnam (New York: Alfred A. Knopf, 1953), 20–47.
2. R. G. Collingwood, *The Idea of History* (Oxford: Clarendon, 1946), 210–31.

such changes, other dimensions of life are transformed, including laws, institutions, programs, and views of life. Thus the historian has a particular interest in the potentiality, the mutability, and diversity among persons over time. In fact, the claim can be made that to adequately understand anything human, one must recount its history and grasp the particularity revealed in such a recounting.

The historian views the past from an individualizing point of view, rather than from a generalizing point of view. This distinguishes history from the social sciences, though historians have increasingly made use of the social sciences. Social scientists primarily have nomothetic concerns (*nomos* refers to a law or standard) in formulating generalizations, norms, and laws based on abstraction and application to general phenomena. Historians are primarily concerned with an idiographic perspective (i.e., they are concerned to inquire into unique and particular phenomena). The historian assumes the uniqueness of each person and affirms that meaning is context dependent.

Historical understanding is dependent upon specific situations or settings. The historian views the similarities or continuities and points of discontinuity in which the particular stands in relation to the universal, in which the specific stands in relation to the general. For example, the educational historian can make use of a sociology of education and yet not be dependent upon sociological explanations that tend to reduce the complexities of persons and human interactions to corporate relationships. Rather than being limited to a sociological perspective, the educational historian views realities not readily observable from a scientific viewpoint. The historian considers the pervasive spirit of a particular age or culture, and the varied intentions and interests of persons, groups, and institutions.

History and Education

History cannot serve as a search for quick and easy solutions to present and future problems. History does not disclose particular and concrete answers for the dilemmas in the field of education. Rather, history provides an awareness of both the possibilities and complexities of education. It also helps persons to discern the continuity or carryover of the past into the present and future along with points of discontinuity.[3] From historical inquiry it is possible to discern the persistent and recurring interests, concerns, problems, and issues in the field of education.

But discerning vestiges of the past requires a critical appropriation

3. Arno A. Bellack, "History of Curriculum Thought and Practice," Review of Educational Research 39(June 1969):291.

because of the greater "search for the usable past."[4] Vestiges include physical objects such as textbooks and school architecture, but also mental attitudes, values, institutional structures, and ideologies. A danger in discerning such vestiges is that persons will tend to absolutely reject the tradition represented by such vestiges. Such a response may fail to recognize the stability of tradition and the sustaining nature of tradition which can insure a moderate rate of change and enhance an orderliness of change in the context of a rapidly changing world.[5]

Even beyond points of continuity, history serves to outline points of discontinuity with the past. For example, contemporary educational questions may be similar to those of the Middle Ages, yet those questions may be asked in a distinct way. Thus historical investigation must explore additional contextual factors beyond the educational matrix. For example, the question of how to share the Christian faith with children is a recurrent one, but as it is posed in the twentieth century with the rise of the media is quite distinct from a first-century context.

In addition to stimulating the awareness of continuities and discontinuities, history can broaden understanding beyond a limited focus upon the past and provide inspiration for current and projected educational efforts.[6] History reveals not only the ecology of education in the past, but also the pathology of education. The ecology of education is the interactive network of factors and forces that result in effective and positive educational experience. The pathology of education reveals forces of indifference, apathy, ignorance, and vested interest that result in miseducation or the lack of needed education.[7]

An understanding of both the ecology and pathology of education is needed to gain a critical assessment of the history of education. Education must be seen in terms of both its liberating and oppressive effects upon persons, groups, and society at large. The past is a mixture of both good and bad and this must be seen in the area of education. The history of the great expansion and popularization of education in the United States portrays a complex ecology of institutions that teach persons, but it also reveals the pathology of those excluded and ignored.

A third contribution of history to education is enabling persons to see the broader stream of cultural and intellectual history of which

4. Edward Shils, "Tradition and Liberty: Antimony and Interdependence," *Ethics* 68(1958):153–65.

5. Kenneth Charlton, "The Contribution of History to the Study of the Curriculum," in *Changing the Curriculum*, ed. John F. Kerr (London: University of London Press, 1968), 70.

6. Bellack, "Curriculum Thought and Practice," 291.

7. Charlton, "Contribution of History," 75.

education is just one facet.[8] In studying and practicing education, educators must explore the wider societal context and consider those economic, political, and social interests and ideologies which affect efforts to pass on wisdom and knowledge to other persons. Different views of history exist and it is important to ask which values and orientations guide a particular historical explanation and interpretation. Without asking this question and others, students of history may not be able to assess the validity of the suggested interpretation. History must be more or other than a political statement. Careful consideration must be given, for example, to the impact of science upon the life and world views of those making and writing history in the twentieth century.

History and Christian Education

Martin Luther considered history the story of divine providence and a practical guide for life. He praised historians for aiding the understanding of worldly events and for noting the wonderful acts of God.[9] The evangelical educator can also view the accounts of past efforts in Christian education as providing key insights and lessons. In response to such lessons, educators can take a stance of affirmation and/or criticism in light of both the liberating and oppressive effects of past efforts. Thus the past serves as an ever present tutor for present and future Christian education.

Christian educators do not have to reinvent the wheel. Christian educators have the potential to identify principles, purposes, and goals of education which may be eternal and unchanging through the study of history. In addition, they may adapt educational strategies and methodologies that were effective in the past to present realities. Several key questions can be posed in affirming the past: (1) What caused an awakening, renewal, or growth in godliness and how did educational efforts foster this development? (2) How did Christians effectively relate their faith to their cultures and how did they educate for this living faith? (3) How were needs of persons effectively addressed and what biblical demands were formative in this response? How were biblical demands interpreted or applied in this particular setting? and (4) What vision, conceptions, and rationale grounded effective educational work and how were these communicated to and owned by others?

George Santayana's oft-quoted insight is worth repeating: Those who ignore the mistakes of the past are bound to repeat them.[10] Christian

8. Bellack, "Curriculum Thought and Practice," 291.

9. Harold J. Grimm, "Martin Luther (1483–1546)," in *A History of Religious Educators*, ed. Elmer L. Towns (Grand Rapids: Baker, 1975), 114.

10. George Santayana, *The Life of Reason; or The Phases of Human Progress* (New York: Charles Scribner's Sons, 1905–1906) 1: chap. 12.

educators must carefully assess how social, economic, political, technological, and religious factors in the larger culture or a subculture hindered effective educational efforts and renewal. In this assessment they must be aware of the effects of classism, racism, sexism, ageism, and other forms of coercion, imposition, and oppression which have prevented the formation of whole persons, that is, persons created in God's image and reflecting that reality and potential in all areas of their lives. Much can be learned from the mistakes of the past if persons are willing to rely upon God's grace and seek the forgiveness of God and others in owning the past.

Beyond these areas of affirmation and criticism, it is possible for the Christian to appropriate history with a sense of appreciation and inspiration—despite warnings that history should not be used as straight politics or a form of evangelism which focuses solely on inspiration.[11] Inspiration is a secondary result of the pursuit of truth through historical investigation because a Christian world view affirms God as an active agent in the historical process. Christians can appreciate God's transcendent intervention in the world and God's immanent working through persons and all of creation. The Christian educator can discern how God has revealed and transmitted truths through various educational processes in the past.

Christian educators can compare and contrast past developments in Christian education from those in general and ask these questions: (1) How were Christian or biblical philosophies of education formulated, and how did they differ among different persons and groups? (2) How was the actual practice of education affected by new light and vision from Christian sources? and (3) What was the extent of cultural accommodation of the faith as compared with cultural renewal in the area of Christian education? Through such study, Christians may be inspired by realizing that others have trod a similar path, encountering and overcoming obstacles through faith in God. History reveals that persons make history and can be used of God to redirect historical developments in significant ways.

History also reveals that God is active through all persons who retain the image of God, though marred, and who are sustained divinely in their efforts. All persons discover truths of God's creation, providence, and/or redemption, but the particular challenge for the Christian is to discern what "truths" apply to the thought and practice of Christian education or what "truths" are in fact consistent with a Christian world view. This is a constantly challenging and arduous task from which no Christian is exempt in his or her sphere of responsibility and calling.

11. Bellack, "Curriculum Thought and Practice," 291.

The basic questions at stake in this task from the perspective of the history of Christian education are: To what extent were truth, love, peace, and justice practiced in the previous Christian education effort? How does this understanding and appreciation challenge and/or warn us? As was noted in the case of history in general, the responses to these questions will reveal a varied record of faithfulness and sin, of obedience and disobedience to God's will for persons and the entire creation.

Every community has a heritage or memory which can serve to guide its life. The Christian community is one such community, and the heritage or history of Christian education can help guide present and future ministries. Christian education and education in general has depended upon what Bernard Bailyn has identified as the great axles of society: family, church, community, and economy. Bailyn identified these axles in his study of education in colonial America.[12] In the context of contemporary society, education also depends upon the school, the media, and various social and community agencies and groups. As these fundamental social institutions or agencies have shifted over the generations in their relative impacts upon persons, the forms of education have also shifted.[13]

In colonial New England, the family and church were the dominant educational agencies in the lives of persons. Input from the family and church generally confirmed and complemented one another with the church being a gathering of families or households. Households represented a more inclusive group than the nuclear family, including various generations and extended family members. In contemporary society of North America the school and media are dominant influences in the education experiences of persons. Furthermore, input from the media may often contradict those values and commitments stressed by the family and church. The conflict resulting from such contradiction has necessitated the development of various strategies to resolve or avoid the conflict.

Through various epochs of history the church has developed different agencies and instruments by which it has sought to fulfill its educational task in relation to the other axles or institutions of society. Education has been the means most often utilized for initiating both adult converts and the young into the practices and beliefs of the Christian community.

12. Bernard Bailyn, *Education in the Forming of American Society* (New York: W. W. Norton, 1960), 45.
13. William Bean Kennedy, "Christian Education Through History," in *An Introduction to Christian Education*, ed. Marvin J. Taylor (Nashville: Abingdon, 1966), 21. Kennedy draws heavily upon the work of Lewis J. Sherrill in *The Rise of Christian Education* (New York: Macmillan, 1944). See the table of contents in Sherrill's work for an outline of the historical periods Kennedy suggests.

This goal is partially, though indirectly, addressed as the community participates in worship, shares its common life, and observes ethical teachings. In addition, Christian groups have almost universally developed institutions, programs, and methods for the direct pursuit of the goal of initiating others in the Christian faith and in encouraging their discipleship as Christians.[14]

Beyond their particular educational agenda, Douglas Sloan, an educational historian, points out that churches have given expression to many of the core values and life views of the larger community. They have also carried the prime responsibility for certifying, preserving, transmitting, and transforming those values and views from generation to generation. In this effort the church has employed all the traditional means of education: teachings of the Christian faith; teachers (ministers, theologians, Sunday school workers, and spiritual guides); textbooks (Scripture, creeds, and commentaries); and teaching aids (rituals, sermons, cathechisms, and spiritual disciplines). In a broader sense, too, as the outward expression of the ideas, values, convictions, and prejudices of a culture and its subcultures, Christian faith has often furnished the very material and matrix of education. Moreover, Christian movements have in various times had an impact of their own in defining reality, sanctioning and rationalizing behavior, and developing social visions and goals that can be described as educational.[15] Such a broadened view of the role of the Christian church provides the context in which to consider the Christian education heritage. We will survey this heritage from the pre-Christian sources of Old Testament and Greek education to post-Reformation developments in the United States. Only key issues will be highlighted with an emphasis upon areas of continuity.[16]

The Old Testament

Old Testament teaching included instruction and admonition. Instruction involved informing persons of God's truths and demands; admonition entailed challenging persons in their way of life. Education

14. Marvin J. Taylor, ed., *Religious Education: A Comprehensive Survey* (Nashville: Abingdon, 1960), 11.

15. Douglas Sloan, *Historiography and the History of Education: Occasion Paper No. 3* (New York: Institute of Philosophy and Politics of Education, Teachers College, Columbia University, n.d.), 16.

16. More detailed accounts are available in other sources. For example, see Kenneth O. Gangel and Warren S. Benson, *Christian Education: Its History and Philosophy* (Chicago: Moody, 1983); and John H. Westerhoff, III, and O. C. Edwards, Jr., eds., *A Faithful Church: Issues in the History of Catechesis* (Wilton, Conn.: Morehouse-Barlow, 1981).

centered in the Torah, the Law of God, first communicated orally, then written in the Scriptures which contained the very moral and spiritual revelation of God. God was the measure of all things; all of life was dedicated to God. The purpose of education in the Old Testament was for holiness and transformation. Persons were to be trained in the very ways of God and the focus was on godly character and wisdom that would issue in moral action. The Law was to be lived; obedience was the fruit of a faithful response to education.

The primary context for education was the home, and parents were responsible to instruct their children in the Law, bring them into wedlock, and to teach them a trade.[17] Beyond the centrality of the home as a house of worship, participation in communal religious life served to educate persons. Priests were experts in ritual life, bridging the gap between persons and God, and prophets spoke God's Word protesting the violation of it in personal and corporate life. Wise persons spoke to ethical questions and shared guidance for practically working out dedication to God. During and subsequent to the exile, synagogues and schools developed to teach the Hebrew language, oral tradition, and the written Scriptures.

Teaching methodology depended upon oral communication with various memory aids, including poetry, word play, and acrostics. Teaching was conducted at scheduled times and on various spontaneous occasions (Deut. 6:7), with significant time devoted to instruction (Neh. 8:3). Visual aids were used in teaching (Exod. 12:1–28; Deut. 6:4–9; Josh. 4:1–24), along with music and psalms. The guiding principle in all these teaching efforts was that persons would bring honor and credit to the name of God and their families through their lives. In relation to God, honor was expressed through an obedient life as an expression of worship and reverence. David Ng's and Virginia Thomas's account of how the Hebrew child learned to worship describes the spirit of the Old Testament educational heritage:

> How did the Hebrew child learn to worship? First through a relationship with a worshiping parent, a member of a worshiping community; through intentional education built into the rituals of home and community worship; through a multitude of sensory experiences and vivid, thought-provoking symbols and dramas; through a life of ethical actions growing out of worship; through a pattern of recurring sabbath and festivals that recreated the Hebrews' story; and eventually through a form of public,

17. William Barclay, *Educational Ideals in the Ancient World* (Grand Rapids: Baker, 1974), 16.

community gathering which made teaching an essential part of the liturgy.[18]

The Greek Heritage

In his discussion of Western education, Freeman Butts, an educational historian, makes this observation: "We think the way we do in large part because the Greeks thought the way they did. Thus, to understand our own ways of thinking we need to know how the Greeks thought."[19] Given this dependence upon Greek thought in the West, educational thought and practice reflect distinctives of the Greek intellectual heritage. Socrates maintained that knowledge itself was a virtue. For Socrates, to really know what is good was to prohibit one from doing evil. He stressed the place of reason and logic, with thinking itself viewed as objective reasoning. Human reason was the means by which to discern divine revelation and its implications for all of life. Socrates stressed the importance of moral life, but not in terms of the God of the Hebrews.

Of greater subsequent influence in the Christian community was Plato. Plato defined education as the training in excellence from youth upwards that makes a person passionately desire to be a perfect citizen and teaches him/her how to rule with justice. He viewed only the ideal as real with actualities being mere copies of the transcendent and perfect ideal. This aspect of Plato's thought was particularly attractive to Christian thinkers, who later synthesized these insights with the Christian faith. Plato's idealism fostered a concern for social and political reform as a fruit of education in the lives of those persons who grasped the ideals.

In contrast with Plato's emphasis was that of the Sophists. The Sophists advocated the use of reason and judged that metaphysical questions were beyond solution. Therefore their stress was upon human nature and human relations which resulted in the belief in the relativity of all truth. Ultimately, persons were the measure of all things, not God, who was beyond knowing. Their concern was with the world of the senses and with the effective use of reason. The perspective of the Sophists is associated with skepticism and individualism, which are dominant philosophies in the postmodern world.

Representing a mediating position between Plato and the Sophists was Aristotle. Balancing Plato's idealism and the Sophists' this-world-

18. David Ng and Virginia Thomas, *Children of the Worshiping Community* (Atlanta: John Knox, 1981), 52.
19. Freeman Butts, *A Cultural History of Western Education* (New York: McGraw-Hill, 1947), 45.

liness, Aristotle viewed matter as purposeless with form emerging as the mind or spirit transformed matter into something with life and purpose. Aristotle is associated with scientific empiricism and realism in emphasizing control of oneself and one's environment. Aristotle's golden mean stressed that nothing is to be done in excess, assuring discipline and control in the entire life process. Education was viewed as a means by which persons, through the use of reason and experience, could achieve balance and moderation in life through making right choices. Human virtue was based upon knowledge of the world and its rational principles and was evidenced by appropriate behavior in all dimensions of life.

A Greek concept of particular significance is that of *paideia. Paideia* represents a culture's consensus about what constitutes human excellence. It reflects a culture's ideals and vision that shapes the calling of a nation-state as well as its individual citizens. Socrates, Plato, the Sophists, and Aristotle all had different visions and ideals. Further differences were apparent in the distinct visions of the city-states of Athens and Sparta. In Sparta the male ideal was the well-conditioned military leader with a courageous and bold character. In Athens the male ideal was the citizen developed both in mind and body with a strong intellect. Therefore, in considering any educational heritage, one must consider the controlling *paideia* in any particular community or effort. The ancient Greeks used the term to refer to "education," "culture," or "social, political, or ethical aspiration." But significantly, as Lawrence Cremin indicates, some have considered the concept of *paideia* to be incompatible with individual freedom and growth given the stress of a corporate or communal vision that is imposed upon individuals. Nevertheless, he points out that individuality is impossible to define apart from some sort of community life.[20]

Paideia, communal vision, is a major challenge in the pluralistic society of the West. There exists a genuine quest for community on the part of many persons who do not relate that quest to a continuing and exclusive emphasis upon their private and individual lives. A renewed awareness is needed in the Christian community in affirming the public and communal dimensions of life. Apart from such awareness, individuality and private life is truncated. In addition, effective educational planning requires the articulation of a shared *paideia* within a particular faith community.

The biblical use of the term refers to nurturing, chastening, and character formation, implying that persons are genuinely committed and vitally related to one another in community. It also implies that there exists a vision for excellence within that community which directs the

20. Lawrence Cremin, *Public Education* (New York: Basic Books, 1976), 39.

process of forming character, and chastening and nurturing persons. Frank Gaebelein maintains that in Christian education those responsible have a duty to point all persons "to the highest examples of excellence—namely, the most excellent of all books, the Bible, and the most excellent of all persons, Jesus Christ."[21] This duty demands the best of efforts to pass on a Christian *paideia*, a Christian world and life view that addresses one's role in society.

In addition to *paideia*, other issues emerge from consideration of the Greek educational heritage. What is the nature of knowledge in a Christian perspective and how is knowledge related to life? How is reason related to faith? What has Jerusalem to do with Athens? To what extent can Christianity be wed to a particular philosophy or does Christianity itself imply a general philosophy and an educational philosophy? What Christian virtues should be fostered in Christian teaching? How does one balance commitments to the community with personal needs and aspirations? How does one fulfill Christian commitments in both the private and public spheres of life and educate others in these responsibilities?

Abraham Heschel, a Jewish educator, suggests a comparison of the insights from the Greek heritage with those of the Old Testament and today: "The Greeks learned in order to comprehend. The Hebrews learned in order to revere. The modern man learns in order to use."[22] Whereas comprehension and the use of learning are important, the challenge remains for Christian educators to enable persons to revere, to appreciate, to stand in awe of and worship God as a result of their teaching. This challenge applies to those who teach in homes as parents and family members, in churches, schools, and communities as teachers, pastors, and fellow Christians, and in all other settings of life.

The New Testament

Beyond the biblical foundations presented in chapter 1, additional observations can be made regarding the practice of education during the New Testament period. The disciples of Jesus followed the Jewish patterns of worship and learning. Several New Testament books evidence the use of different methods of education, most reflecting earlier Jewish customs.

Some persons learned in family settings. Timothy was influenced by

21. Frank E. Gaebelein, *The Christian, the Arts, and Truth: Regaining the Vision of Greatness*, ed. Bruce Lockerbie (Portland, Oreg.: Multnomah, 1985), 144.
22. Abraham J. Heschel, *Between God and Man: An Interpetation of Judaism from the Writings of Abraham Heschel*, ed. Fritz A. Rothschild (New York: Free Press, 1959), 37.

both his grandmother, Lois, and his mother, Eunice (2 Tim. 1:5; 3:15).
The Ethiopian eunuch was instructed by Philip before coming to faith,
and presumably received some instruction subsequent to his conversion
(Acts 8:36–40). Still others assimilated their faith into pagan and Jewish
backgrounds. Paul, for example, was thoroughly trained in the Law under
the tutelage of Gamaliel in Jerusalem.[23] He made use of this training to
become an effective advocate for the faith among both Gentiles and Jews.

Education gradually came to emphasize a distinctive way of life for
God's chosen people. Christians were identified as followers of the Way
(Acts 9:2; 24:14). Education emphasized the teachings by and about
Jesus, for in his very person he represented the way, the truth, and the
life (John 14:6). The disciples of Jesus were commissioned to teach others
to obey everything Jesus had commanded (Matt. 28:20). Education emphasized the Old Testament background for interpreting the meaning of
Jesus' lordship (Luke 24:25–27; John 5:39). Creedal summaries and hymns
(1 Cor. 15:3–8; Phil. 2:6–11; 1 Tim. 3:16; 2 Tim. 2:11–13; Titus 3:4–7)
suggest essential truths that the early Christians felt important for converts to learn. In time, certain official teachers arose after the rabbinic
pattern whose responsibilities included the preservation, transmission,
and interpretation of essential truths to the Christian community.[24]
They were called and held responsible for the stewardship of their ministry (James 3:1). Teachers were to insure the perpetuation of the Christian beliefs which were essential for the identity of the Christian
community in the midst of a hostile and pluralistic world.

The way of knowing and life in the New Testament called for active
engagement in the world in obedience to Christ's reign and in response
to the experience of Christ as Lord in the midst of life.[25] This active
engagement included the need for careful reflection upon the teachings
of the Old Testament Scriptures and the words of Christ as shared and
elaborated by his disciples and later recorded. Such reflection was to
enable a faithful response to God's calling on the part of the followers
of Jesus. Their faith was to be expressed in their way of life. The miracle
of the incarnation was to be repeated in the lives of the disciples through
the person and work of the Holy Spirit. Education was to help persons
reflect the renewed image of God through the presence of the risen
Christ. In the light of this New Testament perspective, one issue posed
for current and future educational efforts is the extent to which educational efforts foster the head, heart, and hand response of persons to the

23. Kennedy, "Christian Education Through History," 22.
24. Ibid.
25. Thomas H. Groome, *Christian Religious Education: Sharing Our Story and Vision* (San Francisco: Harper & Row, 1980), 157.

very revelation of God in Jesus Christ. Such a response is to embody in fresh ways the reality of the living Christ in the world.

Early Christianity

In the early church there was an emphasis on the faithful transmission of the Christian heritage. Up until the fourth century, this was done in a hostile society which resulted in a largely countercultural stance of contending for the faith. External and internal challenges had to be addressed in carefully reflecting on the faith. In this context the community was maintained by stressing the canon, a rule of faith, and church order. The canon identified those accepted sources which were to ground the faith and be its final authority. The rule of faith included the confession of Jesus' lordship, the Apostles' Creed, and summaries of biblical history which were to be believed by those faithfully following Jesus. Church order specified the organization and discipline necessary to define the true church and those with valid authority in directing the church's shared life.[26] These three elements served to maintain continuity without distortion as the faith addressed a Hellenistic-Roman world marked by cultural and religious pluralism.

Various educational forms emerged to deal with the challenges of interpreting the faith in the light of unfulfilled eschatological expectations. In particular, catechesis arose as an essential component of passing on the faith. John Westerhoff points out that the Greek source for this term refers to resounding or echoing, to celebrating or imitating, to repeating another's words and deeds. When the term *catechesis* was first used, it referred to instruction by oral repetition in which persons were taught by having them sing out the answers to posed questions.[27] In order to fulfill the need for catechesis, catechumen classes emerged in various localities to support home training and worship services. The form and length of this catechesis varied, but generally the training continued for three years.[28] This period served as a time of training and probation before full acceptance into the church. Among the catechumens the "hearers" were those considering Christianity, the "kneelers" remained for prayers after the hearers withdrew, and the "chosen" or actual baptismal candidates were given intensive doctrinal, liturgical,

26. William Bean Kennedy, "Background Historical Understanding for Christian Education" (Union Theological Seminary, 1980), 1.

27. John Westerhoff, III, "The Challenge: Understanding the Problem of Faithfulness," in *A Faithful Church: Issues in the History of Catechesis*, eds. John H. Westerhoff, III and O. C. Edwards, Jr. (Wilton, Conn.: Morehouse-Barlow, 1981), 2.

28. Michael Dujarier, *A History of the Catechumenate: The First Six Centuries*, trans. Edward J. Haarl (New York: Sadlier, 1979), 94.

and ascetical training in preparation for baptism and full participation in the life of the church. Following baptism, additional instruction was provided regarding the meaning of the sacraments and other mysteries of the church which had been experienced by new members.

In addition to catechumen classes, catechetical schools were formed. Christianity soon found itself needing highly educated apologists to interpret the faith in Hellenistic terms and to defend it against cultured attackers. At catechetical schools like the university in Alexandria future leaders of Christian thought and life were instructed in the various disciplines and philosophies of Hellenistic culture. Some leaders, such as Tertullian, maintained that to use the thought forms of Greek philosophy to express the gospel was dangerous and even heretical. Other leaders, such as Origen, believed that it was essential to synthesize the Christian faith with contemporary thought forms in order to address the world on its own terms.[29]

The curriculum for Christian education included the reinterpretation or interpretation of the Old Testament Scriptures. Many converts were not Jews and were exposed to the Old Testament for the first time and needed an interpretation of how Jesus' life and ministry related to God's previous dealings with people and creation prior to the incarnation. For those converts who were Jews, the Old Testament had to be reinterpreted in the light of the claims of the Messiah. In addition to the Old Testament, the gospel accounts of the life and teachings of Jesus were shared. Following the death of eyewitnesses, these accounts and their implications were codified to provide an authoritative standard. In addition to the Scriptures, the curriculum was comprised of the confession of faith and teaching of "The Way." The confession of faith was the affirmation of Jesus' lordship elaborated in the Apostles' Creed. "The Way" specified moral expectations for a follower of Christ which were clearly outlined in the *Didache*, the earliest extant form of catechetical instruction.[30] Beyond these explicit curricular components, the common life of the Christian community provided the implicit curriculum as nonformal and informal teaching and learning occurred.

As has been suggested for other historical periods, certain issues emerge from the general distinctives of the educational heritage of early Christianity. A recurring issue is continuity. An alternative to this emphasis is one that focuses upon the adaptation of the faith in light of a rapidly changing world and in some cases drastically distinct conditions. A second issue relates to the maintenance of the Christian community. In the early church the constant threat of annihilation required an em-

29. Kennedy, "Christian Education Through History," 23.
30. Kennedy, "Background Historical Understanding," 2.

phasis on order, discipline, and clear guidelines, but in a more accommodating societal and cultural context an emphasis upon ardor rather than order may be appropriate. Certainly the loss of community rather than its maintenance may be more of a contemporary concern, but the need to balance both continuity and discontinuity is posed in each historical setting of the Christian church. The tasks of education in the midst of these issues are to raise such questions and to suggest possible ways of resolving inevitable tensions.

Membership in the early church implied costly discipleship and serious commitment in stark contrast with many contemporary congregations in the West. There is a need to make church membership mean something more than occasional attendance and financial giving or even the mere appearance of one's name on a church roll. The radical demands of following Christ must be made explicit through educational efforts that move the church beyond a faithless cultural accommodation to a faithful response. A final issue is posed in terms of the inclusion of definite ethical demands as a part of the curriculum where "The Way" is specified and persons are actually expected to fulfill their ethical responsibilities, allowing for the place of forgiveness and the operation of God's grace in the midst of human frailty and sin.

The Middle Ages

After Constantine and the establishment of Christianity, the role of Christian education changed. The church no longer required intensive training for those joining its numbers. Church leaders had to find new ways to nurture large numbers of persons and lead them to a deeper understanding and appreciation of the faith.[31] With the fall of Rome and the collapse of imperial power, the church became the social institution with continuing influence. As a result of a power vacuum, ecclesiastical interest increased in the direction of all areas of human life. The emerging dominance of the church had a profound impact upon education.[32]

Worship emerged as the chief medium of Christian education. Although worship was directed chiefly toward God, the developing richness of symbolism in architecture and art taught lessons of the faith to participants. The elaborate character of worship included the mass, which was celebrated daily; the various Christian festivals associated with the liturgical calendar; and the religious drama of the morality and mystery plays.[33] Along with drama and architectural and artistic symbolism, pen-

31. Kennedy, "Christian Education Through History," 23.
32. Taylor, *Religious Education*, 14.
33. Ibid.

itential literature addressed ethical concerns.[34] All of these nonformal vehicles functioned to convey the Christian message to a largely illiterate population who for the most part had no access to formal Christian education. The very fabric of the shared life of the church with its sacraments provided cognitive input to supplement the affective input of drama and counseling, and the visual input of architecture. Thus socialization, acculturation, and enculturation provided the vehicles for educating the masses.

During this time the family declined in its relative importance in educating for the faith. Celibacy or the single life emerged as a viable option and manifested a redefinition of the Christian faith. Those intensely committed to spiritual formation could opt for life in monasteries and convents which sought to foster community and a sense of order through common discipline, manual labor, and spiritual exercises.[35] The rise of alternative communities to the family as the center for Christian education must be seen in relation to economic developments in which survival was an all-consuming concern. Primary energies were devoted to economic sustenance, and opportunities for reflection and learning were extremely limited outside of the worship experience for the common folk.

Formal education was conducted in monastic and cathedral schools as well as universities (beginning in the twelfth century). Such education was reserved primarily for a few young men entering the orders. These schools eventually broadened their curricula after 800 to include the seven liberal arts, and were the forerunners of later universities. From approximately A.D. 500 to 1000 monastic schools were centers of intellectual activity, but as large cities grew, collegiate church schools or cathedral schools emerged. Their curricula stressed the liberal arts and humanities, in addition to theology; the focus was not upon personal piety. In the twelfth century, universities grew out of the cathedral school movement; they sought to produce both a professional and scholastic mind. Their origin reflected the growth of cities, the rise of a middle class, and new intellectual interests stimulated by contacts with Moslems. The universities were not narrowly religious in focus, and most students studied law, medicine, and other secular subjects in preparation for careers outside the church. Increasingly the church, government, and theology itself were subjected to critical inquiry in the universities despite their rigid and formalized instruction.[36]

In *Children Without Childhood*, Marie Winn suggests that North

34. Kennedy, "Background Historical Understanding," 2.
35. Ibid.
36. Taylor, *Religious Education*, 14–15.

American society is moving toward a "New Middle Ages" in how it relates to and educates children.[37] She points out a shift in focus upon children being protected and differentiated from adults in the past century to a current emphasis on the preparation of children for adult life which places them in an undifferentiated position. Her provocative suggestion is that this move reinstitutes a view popular in the Middle Ages. Winn's analysis, if correct, maintains that current educational efforts have focused on children gaining awareness of responsibilities and realities of the adult world. Such an exposure assumes that children need to know about both the positive and negative dimensions of life, often in areas which they cannot handle.

The issue posed for Christian educators is whether they should maintain a guarded environment for children and youth or expose them to societal realities with adequate opportunity for dialogue and reflection. One youth worker, for example, was posed with the dilemma of being invited to view an R-rated video movie with youth with the possibility of discussing its portrayal of life with them or opting to refuse their invitation and to discourage the viewing. In this case he chose to view the video and was able to discuss the debasement of human sexuality and the alternatives suggested by the Christian faith.

Beyond the issue of children being protected or prepared, the increase in the options of a celibate or single life have resulted in persons opting out of marriage, birthing, and parenting within marriage. These developments raise the issue of the place of the family in local church efforts. In that a large portion of the adult population is single, the local church must consider educational programming that includes singles, childless couples, and others, and that is sensitive to their needs. Jesus, who was himself a single adult, may not be welcome in some churches which have an exclusive emphasis on the nuclear family. The church is a *household* of faith.

Paralleling medieval developments of increased anomaly and a plurality of visions for life, the local church in modern times must address the need for a unifying center in communal life. Without understanding the Christian call to corporate life that affects the public and wider society, a narrow concern for personal survival and a fortress mentality can emerge which isolates persons. Certainly, the church must address the genuine needs of food, clothing, and shelter, but an educational agenda must also emphasize the Christian responsibility to care for the world as God's creation and the stewardship of resources beyond the maintenance of any personal, familial, or national fortress. Beyond the

37. Marie Winn, *Children Without Childhood: Growing Up Too Fast in the World of Sex and Drugs* (New York: Penguin Books, 1981), 205–10.

walls of present-day monasteries and convents are vast areas of human enterprise which require the presence and work of Christians who can make a difference by the grace of God.

Two additional issues are suggested by the educational heritage from the Middle Ages. The increased interest in spiritual disciplines and formation which characterized monastic developments can be affirmed as they foster necessary communion with God and reflection in a rapidly paced world. Christian education efforts must seriously evaluate the extent to which persons are encouraged to grow in their personal relationship with God—provided a concern for the private sphere does not neglect the public and corporate responsibilities of Christians. An emphasis on personal spiritual piety can readily degenerate into a pietism devoid of concern for the wider community and culture. Evangelicals have been particularly delinquent in this area as they have neglected Jesus' call to work for justice and peace.

A second issue is posed by the extensive use of visual communication during the Middle Ages. A loss of the impact of the written word can be noted in a media-oriented society like the United States, paralleling the lack of availability of the written word and formal education in medieval times. To what extent should Christian educators adapt or supplement visually oriented technologies and forms to teach the Christian faith? Fewer people are reading books in the United States and the rise of various visual media demand a critical and appropriate response by Christians in order to effectively address persons without diluting the message of the gospel.

The Renaissance

The Renaissance was a reawakening, a rebirth, a renewal of learning which took place in the fourteenth, fifteenth, and sixteenth centuries. A reawakening interest in the classical sources originated in Italy, but spread to other parts of Europe. Corresponding to this classical interest was a rise in humanism, with persons and their world rather than God and heaven as the focal point of human interest. A new emphasis on individualism began to develop, reflecting a break with traditionalism and a reaction to ecclesiastical despotism that characterized medieval society. These shifts occurred in the context of chaotic societal change with great ferment in the political, social, economic, cultural, and intellectual dimensions of life.

Various areas of life affected by the Renaissance in turn influenced education. Education became important to individual cities, with rich merchants and powerful banking houses supporting and sponsoring learning. Political tensions between the papacy and various princes and rulers resulted in an emphasis on education as serving the state and society at large. A scientific revolution, beginning with Roger Bacon's inquiries, fostered a focus on the created world rather than its Creator. This new interest in science resulted in shifts in the curricula of schools. Much experimentation developed in music, architecture, literature, and the arts. In the area of religion, increased interest in differing perspectives was fostered through the printing of religious books which, though expensive, were in demand. Many Renaissance leaders and thinkers might be characterized as seeing the chief purpose of persons as glorifying human life and enjoying the world to the fullest.

A broadening aim characterized Renaissance education, with more emphasis on individual development. Individuals were viewed as increasingly separate identities from their communities, but possessing sufficient personal influence to affect those communities. The great technological advance of printing made self-education possible. Greek and Roman classics were reappropriated through Moslem and Jewish scholarship which provided vast resources for curricular expansion along with increased scholarship and study in the areas of the humanities, arts, and sciences.

Issues which emerge from the Renaissance reintroduce questions from the Greek educational heritage, in particular, the place of human reason in relation to the Christian faith. For some Renaissance thinkers, reason was enthroned above faith. There was a tendency to place the humanities, science, and arts on an equal footing with the revealed truths of Christianity.

Evangelicals, in contrast, maintain that all truth is God's truth, but not all truth is of the same order or on the same level. The question of priority is important and evangelicals assert that only the truth revealed in Christ and in Scripture comprises the ultimate and unifying perspective for learning and life. Anything less can make persons the measure of all things.[38] Faith in Christ and reliance upon Scripture are to have a higher priority over those insights gained through human reason and experience.

Augustine maintained that if one did not believe in God that person would not come to know the essential truth. Anselm of Canterbury in the eleventh century stated, "Believe that you may know." Evangelicals suggest that this principle also extends beyond religious faith to other endeavors in that believing, as commitment, leads to the knowledge of truth.[39] This stance in Christian education implies the need to empha-

38. Gaebelein, *The Christian, the Arts, and Truth*, 252.
39. Ibid., 86.

size personal belief in Christ and Scripture as the essential foundation for inquiry in the pursuit for knowledge and truth.

This reliance upon Christ and Scripture follows from the recognition of the presence of sin and the fallen nature of persons which affects the use of unaided reason, not subject to divine revelation. Given the presence of personal and corporate sin, Christian education must address the areas of moral and ethical character formation to supplement intellectual training, but not in a way that violates the worth and dignity of persons as God's creatures. How this balance is achieved presents a continual problem in the actual practice of education. For example, what is the place of doubt and questioning? The use of reason implies posing questions and having doubts, even about certain truths which Christianity has historically defended. Posing questions becomes the very occasion for discovery and inquiry using the capacities of human reason created by God.

The Reformation

Medieval patterns of education (home training, worship, pastoral teaching, and guidance) continued past the schism of the church.[40] Home training made use of a number of catechisms written for both children and adults, and parents were held responsible for the religious training of their children. Worship included the liturgy, but the sermon also took on new importance as a primary vehicle for teaching. Pastoral preaching and teaching were revised to encourage the active participation of laity as learners; pastors were to assume the educational leadership of their congregations. Guidance was provided by church leaders and parents who sought to encourage personal appropriation of the Christian faith. An additional educational form for Roman Catholics was the confessional, which provided additional personalized guidance and teaching.

The authority of the Bible was emphasized with a return to the sources of the Christian faith. Historical-grammatical exegesis of the texts in their original languages resulted in a new appreciation of biblical truths. *Sola scriptura* affirmed the sole and final authority of the Scriptures over that of the church.

There was an emphasis on justification by faith (*sola fide*). A distinction was made between faith and belief. Faith emphasized with whom one walked, whereas belief emphasized content and creed. Both faith and belief were important, but salvation was seen in terms of personal faith, a personal commitment to and trust in Jesus Christ as Lord and Savior. Hence, there was a new concern for the evangelistic dimension

40. Kennedy, "Christian Education Through History," 24.

of the Christian faith; salvation centered in personal response in addition to participation in the church's life. Another principle was the priesthood of all believers.[41] Each and every person had access to God through Christ and had significance in Christ's body, the church.

These three principles fostered a new vision for Christian education cast in terms of universal education. The aim of Christian education was to train all Christians to be priests of the living God. This was to be realized in part through translating the Bible into the vernacular. One could know God directly through reading Scripture with the eyes of faith. For education this implied that each individual was important and that reading was an essential skill for each and every person. Preaching was revitalized as well and was viewed as teaching persons to assume their personal responsibilities before God. Preaching was not evangelistic in its primary thrust, but expounded the biblical tradition in a didactive manner to foster its personal appropriation by all God's people. The home was viewed as an extension of the church for instruction of all its members.[42] Luther stressed the centrality of home instruction by writing catechisms for children and regularly encouraging parents to assume their teaching responsibilities.

Because an educated citizenry was valued and domestic training was inadequate, state-supported schools arose. These schools were supported by those in political power, often in cooperation with the church. State-supported education generally developed along two tracks or levels. On the lower level vernacular elementary schools sought to teach children how to read. On the upper level elementary and Latin grammar schools and the universities sought to teach those with promise to become future societal and church leaders. Despite these efforts, the realization of compulsory universal education awaited later historical developments.[43] Noteworthy in the efforts of the Reformers is the inclusion of girls along with boys in the schools established by John Calvin in Geneva, Switzerland, and John Knox in Scotland.

Given the potential impact of a revived Christian education, teachers had an essential role which demanded both dedication and training. Calvin, for example, stressed the need to train ministers as teachers because of their place in the community. As the major educated person in the community, the minister became the chief teacher or school supervisor, and the importance of right doctrine required that teaching be a high priority in pastoral ministry.[44]

41. Kennedy, "Background Historical Understanding," 3.
42. Ibid.
43. Kennedy, "Christian Education Through History," 25.
44. Ibid., 24.

During the Reformation, education for the sake of the community of faith—for its protection, its enhancement, or its extension—began to share primacy with education for the development of the individual. Christian education was first for one's personal response to God, but increasingly for the fulfillment of one's individual potential as God's unique creation with a contribution to make to the larger community. Thus there emerged an increased appreciation of the nature of the Christian calling or vocation to be in the world serving God and others. This responsibility belonged to each priest, each faithful believer in Jesus Christ.

By comparing and contrasting developments in the Renaissance and Reformation, it is possible to identify issues for educational thought and practice. A number of similarities between the Renaissance and Reformation can be noted. Both movements were expressions of societal renewal: in the case of the Renaissance the renewal was cultural and intellectual; in the Reformation, it was primarily theological and ecclesial. In both periods the individual was affirmed: in the Renaissance the autonomy of persons was stressed; in the Reformation a new sense of individual faith fostered personal reading of Scripture and the personal responsibilities of Christians to be God's priests in the Christian community and in the world. In terms of education, both movements expanded the curriculum beyond traditional areas of study. Finally, both movements represented a break with tradition and a questioning of existing authorities. In the Renaissance a questioning of the political power and mind-set of the state and church developed; and in the Reformation serious questions were raised about established religious norms and church traditions. These similarities indicate the potential for renewal and change that can significantly affect all dimensions of life. They also indicate the potential costs of implementing change and the need to raise questions about the limits of that change.

By way of contrast, the Renaissance and Reformation represent distinct commitments and world views. The following contrasts can be noted:

1. Whereas the Renaissance generally focused upon persons, the Reformation centered life and education upon God, evidencing a renewed consideration of persons as God's creatures with definite privileges and responsibilities.
2. Whereas the Renaissance centered primarily on the elite, the Reformation included the masses of society as well.
3. In the Reformation spiritual renewal was primary, whereas the Renaissance centered upon cultural and intellectual renewal. But spiritual renewal and cultural or intellectual renewal are not mu-

tually exclusive. In Reformation thought, human reason was viewed as fallen and subject to God's revelation in Scripture, whereas in certain Renaissance developments human reason was perceived as perfected. Given the Reformers' sensitivity to human depravity their primary source for understanding was the Bible, but biblical truths were integrated with insights gained through reason and experience.

4. In contrast with a Reformed focus on the Bible, Renaissance thinkers primarily relied on extrabiblical classical literature.

5. Reformers stressed the use of the vernacular in disseminating knowledge in contrast with the exclusive use of classical languages by Renaissance scholars who were not necessarily commited to universal education. Nevertheless, many of the Reformers were schooled in classical studies and used classical languages in their scholarship.

6. A final contrast might be stated in terms of the ultimate goal of education. In the Reformation knowledge was viewed in relation to the higher goal of commitment to and communion with God, whereas in the Renaissance traditional knowledge itself was a goal, largely irrespective of God's revelation.

In relation to each of the above contrasts, choices must be made and priorities set in relation to basic educational thought and practice. Each contrast can best be thought of as representing a possible continuum of emphases upon divine and human centeredness. A Christian world view must remain faithful to God's revelation while being sensitive to human realities.

John T. McNeill maintains that the Reformers differed from Christian humanists in that they emphasized the majesty and holiness of God, the sinfulness of persons, and the gulf between God and persons reconcilable only in Jesus Christ.[45] But in the Renaissance there were those who could be identified as moderate, radical, and Christian humanists. Erasmus best typified the Christian humanist who influenced the Reformers. The young John Calvin hoped to see humanism contained within the bounds of decent responsibility. Thus the Renaissance and Reformation pose the issue of the relationship between theism and humanism in the context of the very human enterprise of education which seeks to be faithful to God. Certainly the roots of the Reformation were in the Renaissance, but subsequent historical developments posed many questions regarding the central thrusts and emphases of educational commitments.

45. John T. McNeill, *The History and Character of Calvinism* (New York: Oxford University Press, 1967).

The United States

In dealing with the complexity of the post-Reformation, education developments in the United States will be considered in this section while recognizing that significant changes have occurred in other contexts as a result of a host of intellectual, political, economic, and social factors which include the Enlightenment, the Industrial Revolution, and increased urbanization and plurality. In addressing these complex developments, Lawrence Cremin proposes a network or configuration of institutions that educate. These social institutions include the family, church, community, school, various agencies, the media, and others. Each institution interacts with the others and with the larger society. Each institution has its own values, assumptions, and agenda which are either explicit or implicit in teaching its members or participants.[46]

Awareness of educational configurations forces the evangelical educator to consider a vast array of institutions and their interrelationships far beyond parochial concerns. For example, those primarily concerned with church education via the Sunday school cannot neglect the educational impacts of families, schools, communities, media, and the larger society in planning and implementing programs. Such influences must be considered in identifying purposes, developing strategies, implementing programs, and evaluating efforts. In addition, networks must be established with other institutions or vehicles for processing their messages, if the church is to be effective. To neglect to do so is shortsighted and consigns evangelical efforts to cultural backwaters.

The relationships among the institutions or agencies constituting an educational configuration can be described as confirming, complementing, and/or contradicting one another.[47] Institutions confirm one another by supporting the same message and encouraging compliance with certain guidelines. For example, the church can confirm the role of the family by encouraging children to honor and obey their parents and to heed the truths passed on by parents. Likewise, parents can confirm the role of the church by encouraging children to learn from, respect, and obey Sunday school teachers, pastors, and other adults in the church setting. Parents can also confirm the church's message through their

46. Lawrence A. Cremin, lecture presented at Teacher's College, Columbia University, New York, New York, 18 December 1978. See also Lawrence A. Cremin, *American Education: The Colonial Experience 1607–1783* (New York: Harper & Row, 1970); Lawrence A. Cremin, *American Education: The National Experience 1783–1876* (New York: Harper & Row, 1980); and his forthcoming volume, *American Education: The Metropolitan Experience.*
47. Ibid.

active participation and support of the church and by modeling the church's teachings.

Relationships between institutions can also be described as complementing one another in the sense of having input and impacts that supply areas lacking in the other compatible institutions. For example, schools can complement families in certain settings by supplying lunches for children from homes that cannot supply them. In a similar way, parents can complement the school by tutoring their children in subjects that teachers cannot address. Parents may be also able to complement or supplement the emphases in Sunday school curriculum through family devotional times, elaborating themes and concepts shared by teachers.

A third possible relationship is contradictory in the sense that institutions may have distinctly different messages that create dissonance and conflicts for participants. A contemporary example of this is the relationship between the agenda of certain segments of commercial television and the values supported by the Christian church or family. Commercial television generally defines the good life in terms of the abundance of goods a person possesses. This stance contradicts Christian concerns for stewardship and service in a world of declining resources. Another example of a contradictory relationship is the perception of some Christian parents that the public school's secular humanism directly opposes Christian values and truths. This perception has resulted in the increased development of Christian private and home schools which confirm and/or complement a Christian world view held by the family.

In addition to these three designations to describe the relationships among institutions in an educational configuration, configurations as a whole or in part interact with the larger society. An example of this is a Christian family that takes a strong countercultural stance and as a result decides not to own a television, attend movies, frequent public schools, or relate to local public communities. The Amish and Bruderhof communities represent guarded Christian enclaves which opt for a more cloistered and separated life in relation to the larger society.[48]

Using this concept of an educational configuration, the shifting relationships and perspectives of the constituents of Christian education efforts can be traced. Rather than attempt to recount a vast and diverse array of shifts, developments in general education in the United States as traced by Cremin will be described with implications for Christian education.

48. For a study of a fundamentalist private school that represents a guarded community, see Alan Peshkin, God's Choice: The Total World of a Fundamentalist Christian School (Chicago: University of Chicago Press, 1986).

Cremin identifies five major thrusts which characterize American education. First, there are a multiplicity of educational institutions. The impact of these institutions differs with the individual. Some people gain their education through self-education rather than through the direct efforts of a traditional educational agency or program.[49] For example, persons may be educated primarily through personal study, observation, and reflection, using resources made available through libraries or other information storage agencies. An implication for Christian educators is the need to carefully assess the particular educational configurations of persons with whom one is ministering. Persons who are primarily self-educated may need increased access to resources and opportunities to share with others what they have gained through their study and experience.

Christian educators must also assess the extent to which inputs from other social institutions and society in general confirm, complement, and/or contradict the truths and values of a Christian world view. On the basis of this assessment, decisions must be made regarding possible Christian responses to the particular historical context. The allocation of personnel, material resources, and time requires a reading of the times in the light of the past and the projected future. Christian educators must ask about the ways in which teaching in any institution, agency, or program were or are educative in terms of specified purposes. One challenge posed for current Christian education efforts is how parents, pastors, teachers, and others should respond to the increased impact of the media.

Cremin's second point in assessing developments in the United States is that at different times society has placed its emphases in different institutions. During the colonial period (1607–1783), the family and church were the educational institutions of primary importance and society was to be saved and bettered through their teaching efforts. Colonial developments did evidence distinct configurations in New England, the Middle Colonies, and the South, but the efforts of the family and church generally confirmed and complemented one another. During the national period (1783–1876), the school (in particular, the public school) along with the church was to educate persons and save society. This occurred in the context of a rapidly expanding nation and the increased separation of church and state. During the metropolitan period (1876–1986), the school and various child rearing or rehabilitative institutions were to make for an educated and good society. Each of these emphases had varied success and has been viewed differently by historians from various perspectives. Each general societal configuration was

49. Cremin, lecture, 18 December 1978.

intended to save all, but their effects varied.[50] Some people were significantly served and bettered through their educational experiences in the dominant educational configuration, whereas others were not served. Cremin's account indicates the decreased role of the church amidst the increasing secularization of life, but does not indicate that Christians cannot influence the educational efforts of society in general. This scenario suggests that the church has a key role to play in raising critical questions about the dominant educational configuration and in proposing alternatives from the perspective of a marginal status. This marginal status is implied by the decreased impact of Christian values in the wider society.

Third, in the United States a concerted effort has been made in the schools to balance the societal ideals of liberty, equality, and fraternity. Liberty can be viewed as the right to strive for educational, social, political, and economic achievement. Equality traditionally has been viewed as equal opportunity for all, but in the twentieth century has been redefined in terms of results. Fraternity can be defined as the concern for human community and the desire to build a new and good society with education at its heart. Given the ever present plurality of persons in the United States, the realization of community has necessitated an interaction and mix of persons and groups.[51] In such a mix, a constant tension exists between maintaining one's distinct identity and entering the mainstream of society. This tension has been particularly acute for those coming from cultural and racial backgrounds other than that of northern Protestant Europe. In addition, the two primal crimes of the United States, namely the genocide of American Indians and the system of chattel slavery of blacks have perpetuated a struggle with racism and discrimination. Thus the ideal of liberty must address the liberation of persons currently excluded from society along with a commitment to the responsibilities liberty entails; the ideal of equality must address the fact that some are perceived as more equal than others; and the ideal of fraternity must assess the nature of the community which has excluded some from full membership.[52]

Christian educators can relate to the ideals of liberty, equality, and fraternity in terms of the Christian gospel. Liberty can be defined as the freedom made available in Jesus Christ. Yet this freedom must not be viewed in isolation from the corresponding obligation of covenant, with

50. Ibid. Also see Lawrence A. Cremin, *Traditions of American Education* (New York: Basic Books, 1977).

51. Ibid.

52. See Robert N. Bellah for an analysis of the polarities revealed by history in *The Broken Covenant: American Civil Religion in the Time of Trial* (New York: Seabury, 1975).

responsibilities to God, other persons, and the creation. Equality can be defined as equal access to God through Jesus Christ. The gospel embodies a commitment to view each person as having infinite worth and dignity by virtue of being created in God's image. Fraternity can be defined in terms of the common humanity of all persons and the unique relationships that exist in Christian community. Christian educators can affirm these three ideals in their educational efforts, but they must always be related to the whole counsel of God as revealed in Scripture. A particular challenge is posed for Christians when these societal ideals are in conflict. For example, should Christians support the busing of school children to achieve greater racial equality in public schools?

Fourth, there has been a persistent effort to popularize education, to make it more readily available to all persons. This popularization involves access, content, and control. The advantages and disadvantages in popularization can be cited in terms of the inevitable tensions between quantity and quality. Popularization may result in the vulgarization of knowledge and truth, while lack of popularization results in an elitism which is inherently prejudicial. Cremin's fifth and final observation is that the historical record of education in the United States reveals that efforts have been both oppressive and/or liberating, depending upon the persons or groups involved.[53] Christians have been both faithful and unfaithful in sharing the faith and though the prospects of popularizing the faith are not an option, the concern is to enable every person to hear the claims of Christ in a way that enables a knowledgeable response. The call is to faithfulness over against a popular accommodation of the faith, while sharing the Christian world view in ways which others can understand. In relation to Cremin's fourth and fifth points, it must be asked if evangelical communities have vulgarized the gospel in the effort to be popular in society and have therefore oppressed those persons who need to hear the whole counsel of God. This may be the case if an emphasis on personal transformation has neglected the call for social transformation.

Recent Evangelical Educators

The contributions of evangelical educators following World War II must be viewed in relation to the earlier fundamentalist–modernist controversy. The term *fundamentalist* emerged from a series of booklets distributed from 1909 on entitled *The Fundamentals*. These booklets sought to affirm orthodox Christian doctrines in response to critical and evolutionary views of Scripture and theology which were popular-

53. Cremin, lecture, 18 December 1978.

ized through the modernist or liberal movement. One expression of the liberal movement in education was its emphasis on progressive education, supported through the efforts of the Religious Education Association founded in 1903.

During the twentieth century parallel organizations gradually emerged which supported either liberal or mainline groups or evangelical constituencies. The National Association of Evangelicals was established in 1942 in protest against some of the theological and social concerns of the Federal Council of Churches (now the National Council of Churches). Similarly the National Sunday School Association was begun in 1946 to stimulate growth in Christian education among evangelical or conservative groups.[54] From commissions of this body the current National Association of Professors of Christian Education and National Association of Directors of Christian Education emerged, parallel organizations to the Religious Education Association in providing leadership for conservative constituencies. These developments set the context in which to explore the work of Frank E. Gaebelein, Lois B. LeBar, Gene A. Getz, and Larry Richards.[55]

Frank E. Gaebelein

Frank E. Gaebelein guided the efforts of the National Association of Evangelicals in the formation of its statement on Christian education, *Christian Education in a Democracy.*[56] In 1954, Gaebelein's perspective was further elaborated in *The Pattern of God's Truth: Problems of Integration in Christian Education.*[57] As the title suggests, Gaebelein addresses how a Christian faith commitment and a Christian world and life view might be integrated with the teaching and learning of various school subjects. Gaebelein quotes Edwin H. Rian's insights on the task he undertakes: "A Christian theory of education is an exposition of the idea that Christianity is a world and life view and not simply a series of unrelated doctrines. Christianity includes all of life."[58]

Gaebelein sets out to reaffirm the perspective espoused by Augustine of Hippo. Augustine maintained that all truth is God's truth and that

54. Kendig B. Cully describes further developments in *The Search for a Christian Education—Since 1940* (Philadelphia: Westminster, 1965), 94–112.

55. The four educators highlighted here are cited in Gangel and Benson, *Christian Education,* 338–45.

56. *Christian Education in a Democracy: The Report of the N.A.E. Committee* (New York: Oxford University Press, 1951).

57. Frank E. Gaebelein, *The Pattern of God's Truth: Problems of Integration in Christian Education* (New York: Oxford University Press, 1954).

58. Edwin H. Rian, *Christianity and American Education* (San Antonio: Naylor, 1949), 236.

the Christian educator is called to the task of "spoiling the Egyptians," to the task of discerning truth as revealed in all areas of human knowledge and discovery. The discernment of truth requires a constant reference to biblical truth and to the person of Jesus Christ. Therefore, Gaebelein proposes that Christian educators adopt as their unifying principle Christ and the Bible.[59] Gaebelein acknowledges that areas of truth not fully addressed in Scripture are part of God's truth and therefore crucial for consideration. But primacy must ultimately be given to spiritual truth revealed in the Bible and incarnate in Christ.[60] This is the inherent pattern of God's truth which must be explicitly shared with students and related to every aspect of their lives.

Gaebelein's position was liberating for those who were accustomed to compartmentalizing spiritual truth in that it encouraged thinking "Christianly." He was criticized for being rationalistic in his approach.[61] But Gaebelein reminded evangelical educators that they were to do more than just *know* the truth—they were to *do* the truth in their efforts. The challenge inherent in Gaebelein's thought is that education be effectively integrated with the truth of God and thus consciously stand under the authority of Scripture. Gaebelein's four main principles are: (1) Christian education must be done by Christian teachers; (2) the Bible is the very heart of the curriculum; (3) education may be integrated with a Christian world view through excellence; and (4) Christian education, broadly considered, must be democratic in a scriptural sense.

Burgess aptly observes that "the heart of religious education, for Gaebelein, is the communication of biblical truths by teachers who are able to lead students to an understanding of these truths."[62] Gaebelein is idealistic about the advance of Christian education and in his expectation that the transmission of biblical truths will lead to personal and communal appropriation.

Lois B. LeBar

Lois LeBar's primary work is *Education That Is Christian*, written originally in 1958 but revised and updated in 1981.[63] In this work, LeBar outlines methods that consistently emphasize biblical content and the centrality of Christ. She maintains that Christian education must be centered in both the living Word of God (Christ) and the written Word

59. Gaebelein, *Pattern of God's Truth*, 20.

60. Ibid., 23.

61. Cully, *Search for a Christian Education*, 109.

62. Harold W. Burgess, *An Invitation to Religious Education* (Mishawaka, Ind.: Religious Education Press, 1975), 27.

63. Lois LeBar, *Education That Is Christian*, rev. ed. (Old Tappan, N.J.: Fleming H. Revell, 1981).

of God (the Bible).[64] She exemplifies Gaebelein's vision that Christian educators must stand under Scripture in their formulation of educational theory. LeBar consistently refers to Scripture for her insights. In doing so, she places a significant emphasis on the work of the Holy Spirit as the human teacher consciously seeks to work with the Divine Teacher in all aspects of teaching.[65]

LeBar is distinct from Gaebelein in her conscious effort to include experiential aspects of learning, drawing upon the insights of John Amos Comenius and his educational realism. Comenius emphasized the place of "nature" and the impact of education upon society. Comenius's hope was that education would transform or reform society because teaching would grapple with the practical applications of truth. Comenius was sensitive to the needs, interests, and motivations of students.

LeBar identifies three goals for Christian education, stated in terms of student outcomes: (1) to lead students to Christ; (2) to build students up in Christ; (3) to send students out for Christ.[66] In other words, the three goals of education are transformation, formation, and service.

Following in the tradition of Comenius, LeBar combines an emphasis on authoritative content with an emphasis on the actual experience of students. This is distinct from Gaebelein's subject-centered approach. She also seeks to wed an emphasis on the Sunday school with an emphasis on the home and community. In some ways she is not unlike the progressive educator John Dewey, though coming from a distinctly theistic and supernatural faith commitment. Dewey sought to synthesize child-centered and content-centered approaches in education. He also sought to combine emphases on the school and society in the hope that the school would become a microcosm of society.[67]

LeBar affirms the historical, revelational, and soteriological distinctives of Christianity, while accomplishing that which Dewey sought to accomplish in his synthesizing efforts in general education. While LeBar

64. Ibid., 212–15.

65. Ibid., 238–54.

66. Lois E. LeBar, *Children in the Bible School* (Westwood, N.J.: Fleming H. Revell, 1952), 193–94.

67. The best introduction to Dewey's educational thought is provided in Martin S. Dworkin, *Dewey on Education: Selections* (New York: Teachers College Press, 1959). From a Christian perspective, Dewey must first be criticized for his ahistorical pragmatism and presentism. Christianity is a historical faith. Second, Dewey must be criticized for his antisupernatural bias that discounts the place of revelation. Christianity is a revealed religion. Third, Dewey must be criticized for his faith in progress and education and for his assumption that education can result in the salvation of persons. Christianity maintains the reality of sin and that salvation comes through faith in Jesus Christ by the grace of God. Beyond these criticisms, much can be gained from a study of Dewey.

traces her roots to Comenius, her ideas are a sensitive Christian complement to those of Dewey in the areas of educational practice and curriculum formation. LeBar can be criticized, however, for her lack of sensitivity to some of the wider social implications of the Christian faith and for her emphasis on the formal structures of education, namely the school, to the relative exclusion of nonformal education.

Lawrence O. Richards

Lawrence O. Richards is a well-known contributor to the literature on evangelical Christian education. His most comprehensive and definitive work is *A Theology of Christian Education.*[68] In contrast with Gaebelein and LeBar, Richards is an enthusiastic advocate of nonformal education which, he maintains, better fosters change and development in the total personality of students.[69] Richards opposes a formal school approach to Christian education that depends exclusively upon a subject-centered approach to nurture persons in the Christian faith and life. As an alternative, he recommends a socialization/enculturation approach in which there is a self-conscious intention to develop a community of faith in which the Christian life is modeled and more "caught than taught." Richards's approach does not exclude a concern for revealed truth, but encourages persons to consider the implications of truth for life and the response to truth in life.[70]

Richards is a visionary who calls the church to renew its educational efforts by stressing training and discipleship. He advocates a whole-person focus that requires students to be active rather than passive in the learning process. He sets high ideals for leadership, growth, relationships, and home nurture in the effort to encourage the ministry of all believers.

Richards can be criticized, however, for his lack of sensitivity to various contextual factors. He appears to be insensitive to liturgical structures and denominational distinctives in stressing renewal. He limits the place of authority in emphasizing servant leadership and assumes the ready availability of models and disciples in the local church setting. He fails to recognize the multiple factors that can limit effective nurture in the home, including the presence of non-Christian parents. His emphasis on nurture fails to adequately stress the need for evangelism and service as equal concerns in the educational program of the local church.

68. Lawrence O. Richards, *A Theology of Christian Education* (Grand Rapids: Zondervan, 1975).

69. Ibid., 68.

70. This emphasis is expanded in Lawrence O. Richards, *Creative Bible Teaching* (Chicago: Moody, 1970).

Despite these criticisms and the potential limitations of Richards's perspective, his thought represents an alternative to a dead orthodoxy that fails to influence the lives of its adherents with the life that is Christ. His theology embodies a concerted effort to grapple with biblical foundations for Christian education outside the confines of formal education. Richards suggests an alternative paradigm for renewal in Christian education in the local church, providing essential insights for developing nonformal education and for the socialization and enculturation processes of Christian communities. Richards reminds educators that significant educational experiences are the relationships established and the modeling communicated.

Gene A. Getz

Like Richards, Gene A. Getz is a spokesperson for the renewal movement in evangelical education. He shares Richards's concern to provide an alternative vision to guide the church in its educational efforts. Basing his insights on the educational commission of Matthew's Gospel, he emphasizes the tasks of evangelism and edification in the development of disciples of Jesus Christ. Getz proposes a model that incorporates three lenses for discerning an appropriate philosophy of education.

From the first lens of Scripture, Getz identifies biblical principles essential for evangelism and edification. From the second lens of history, he suggests lessons from previous educational attempts in the evangelical church. For example, he points out that the strength of emphasizing Scripture has resulted in a loss of the importance of the active participation of individual members in the church. Getz questions whether current church activities are actually contributing to mature discipleship among all church participants. The third and final lens is that of culture.[71] Cultural considerations helpfully confront the Christian educator with the need to distinguish cultural and biblical values and to struggle with questions of contextualization.

An examination and understanding of each of the perspectives of the four educators discussed in this section (see table 4) is valuable in the attempt to appreciate the evangelical heritage of Christian education. There is a shared concern among these four theorists for the authority of Scripture and the need for faithfulness and excellence in any education that claims to be Christian. Gaebelein calls for consistency with biblical truth, LeBar for cooperation with the Holy Spirit, Richards for an impact upon life and the church community, and Getz for accountability in

71. See Gene A. Getz, *Sharpening the Focus of the Church* (Chicago: Moody, 1974) for an introduction to his work.

relation to ecclesiastical purposes.[72] Building upon this heritage is the task of evangelical educators today and in the future.

Continuity and Reaffirmation

In addressing the issue of continuity, it is helpful to be reminded of what C. S. Lewis has termed the "chronological fallacy." This fallacy dismisses ideas and values simply because they are not new and thereby makes the calendar the criterion of truth.[73] An evangelical theology implies an affirmation of basic truths on the basis of revelation and on the basis of their correspondence with reality as evidenced through the study of history. These insights provide helpful guidelines for current educational thought and practice.

While these insights provide for continuity, they also require adaptation to specific contexts. Christianity is a historical faith and history involves change over time. A Christian world and life view must be sensitive to historical developments. The development of an educational theory is an art. This art is one that includes creativity, subjectivity, and risk. Risk is inherent in our human condition. It involves the recognition that persons are embedded in the fabric of history and have responsibilities as makers of history to live out their values and commitments.

Christians have not chosen the timing for their historical journeys,

Table 4 Recent Evangelical Educators

Educator	Focus	Stance
Frank Gaebelein	Quality formal education Academic excellence under the authority of Scripture	Wise scholar/ headmaster
Lois LeBar	Spirit-filled formal education Teaching sensitive to student needs	Inspired teacher
Lawrence Richards	Nurturant nonformal education Discipling and modeling in the Body	Enthusiastic visionary
Gene Getz	Faithful local church Education (formal and nonformal) Evangelism and edification	Discerning pastor/guide

72. Additional evangelical educators could be cited for their contributions. These four represent an adequate sampling.

73. Frank E. Gaebelein provides this insight in "The Idea of Excellence and Our Obligation to It," *Gordon Review* (Winter 1962):137.

but being in a particular historical time requires learning from the past and living in the present with a concern for God's future. Viewing the past provides a rootedness from which to address the challenges of the present and future world in which the Christian vocation is to be expressed. In appreciating the light and shadows of the past, Christians can reappropriate an all too forgotten heritage, resulting in rejoicing, repentance, and renewal.

5

Sociological Foundations

In *The Social Construction of Reality: A Treatise in the Sociology of Knowledge,* Peter Berger and Thomas Luckmann maintain that reality is socially constructed. They define reality as "a quality apertaining to phenomena that we recognize as having a being independent of our own volition."[1] The task of a sociology of knowledge is to analyze those processes by which reality is socially constructed. This task is particularly important for Christian educators because education is concerned with the production and distribution of knowledge. Christian educators seek to share with their students that which is real. They seek to share knowledge that is essential for life. Berger and Luckmann define knowledge as "the certainty that phenomena are real and that they possess specific characteristics."[2] Christian educators seek to share a knowledge of God, a knowledge of God's Word, and a knowledge of reality as viewed from the perspective of the Christian community.

The Christian community is a social entity both in its historical and contemporary expressions. As a social entity, the Christian community manifests variety along with an underlying unity. Both its variety and

1. Peter L. Berger and Thomas Luckmann, *The Social Construction of Reality: A Treatise in the Sociology of Knowledge* (Garden City: Doubleday, 1966), 1.
2. Ibid.

151

unity have an impact upon the thought and practice of Christian education. Thus careful attention must be given to the sociological foundations of Christian education. In order to understand the process of Christian education, one must refer to culture and society. The very practice of Christian education assumes a cultural context. This is a given in our created world. God created persons with the capacity to create culture and to form societies. Without culture, Christianity would be an abstraction unrelated to human life.

The Social Construction of Reality

There are various ways to regard culture. G. H. Bantock, for example, sees culture as sharply divided into two kinds, high and low culture, relative to one's social class. High culture is the way of life associated with the sophisticated elite class while low culture is associated with the working class. From Bantock's perspective, education for different classes would be distinct in that each class has a distinct culture. In contrast with Bantock, a second perspective is advocated by P. H. Hirst, who ignores historical and social differences in cultures and subcultures. Hirst sees education in terms of "culture-free" knowledge, which implies sharing knowledge interculturally and transculturally. For Hirst, culture is a way of life independent of the educator's primary tasks. A third perspective regarding culture is that of Raymond Williams. Williams sees culture in terms of its historical setting and examines cultural change taking place over various periods of time. His analysis indicates that educational change has not kept pace with social and cultural change. Thus the task for educators is to make their teaching as update and relevant as possible in order to influence the lives of students.[3]

In order to discern the relative truths of these three perspectives, it is necessary to define culture in general and to consider a possible Christian perspective on culture. Clifford Geertz provides a helpful definition. He defines culture as a historically transmitted pattern of meanings embodied in symbols. It is a system of inherited conceptions expressed in symbolic forms by means of which persons communicate, perpetuate, and develop their knowledge and attitude toward life. Culture integrates

3. Dennis Lawton, *Class, Culture and the Curriculum* (London: Routledge & Kegan Paul, 1975), 9–26. For a further discussion of Williams's perspective, see Raymond Williams, *Culture* (London: Fontana, 1981), in which he seeks to develop a sociology of culture. The problem of definition is discussed on pp. 10–14 of this work. One definition sees culture as a distinct way of life with a distinctive signifying system. A second definition encompasses artistic and intellectual activities which include signifying practices. For a fuller definition of culture, see Raymond Williams, *Keywords: A Vocabulary of Culture and Society*, rev. ed. (New York: Oxford University Press, 1985), 87–93.

both the ethos and world view of a people. The ethos of a group is the tone, character, and quality of its life. It is the moral and aesthetic style and mood which characterizes the group's way of life. A world view is the picture one has of the way things are in actuality, the most comprehensive idea of order.[4]

Geertz's comprehensive definition enables the Christian educator to view the Christian faith in its particular expression as one cultural system. The Christian world and life view is a historically transmitted pattern of meanings that is embodied in symbols. It is much more than this system, given the Christian claim to supernatural realities, but for the purposes of considering the educational task it is at least this. In addition, there is an ethos that characterizes the Christian community. (Of course, there are additional cultural aspects which characterize any given group of Christians relative to their historical and sociological situation. A first-century Christian community in Asia Minor is distinct from a twentieth-century Christian community in Latin America, though there may be some remarkable similarities.)

How, then, does culture operate in the lives of Christians? As N. H. Beversluis suggests, culture for the Christian can become piety expressing itself in honesty, fairness, and righteousness. It can become participation in the world's work, making things or changing things, and doing this as an image bearer in conformity with what is understood to be God's will. Culture is working with the givens, the "materials," in the world of nature or in society. The Christian can do this work with sensitivity and accountability, with creative imagination and self-expression, giving glory to God.[5] Thus, what may distinguish the Christian's cultural activities is her or his commitment, values, and sensitivities that focus upon the revelation and will of God for human life. Herein is the potential of a Christian culture in the midst of a pluralistic society.

While Bantock recognizes the existence of social classes and different cultural expressions, a Christian world view implies the necessity of sharing the whole counsel of God with all social classes. This does not negate the need for cultural sensitivity in sharing Christian truth and the consideration of the readiness of participants, but suggests a reconciliation in Christ that unites persons of high and low culture in a common community, namely the church.

Hirst's "culture-free" knowledge necessitates careful evaluation. The Christian faith lays claim to a body of knowledge that is true by virtue

4. Clifford Geertz, *The Interpretation of Cultures* (New York: Basic Books, 1973), 126–27.

5. N. H. Beversluis, *Toward a Theology of Education: Occasional Papers from Calvin College*, vol. 1, no. 1, February 1981, 15.

of its being God's revelation. This truth is transcultural in the sense of having significance for all cultures, in all historical contexts. Yet, this truth was initially communicated with very specific cultural situations in view, and the task of the Christian in a contemporary context is to discern the implications for current life. Herein is the task of hermeneutics that calls for the interpretation, explanation, and application of the transcultural truths of Scripture for the present. The work of hermeneutics takes place within various cultural contexts and the application of transcultural truths requires a careful reading of both the cultural situation in which one ministers and the cultural situation initially addressed by biblical writers. In one sense freedom from culture is not possible given the created nature of persons as cultural beings, yet in another sense, Christ enables persons to be free from those aspects of culture that limit or oppress them and prevent them from becoming all God has intended them to be.

Williams's perspective on the historical character of culture must be affirmed from a Christian world view. Christianity is a faith rooted in history which emphasizes the significance of persons in time as God interacts with them. God in the person of Christ entered into time and space to accomplish God's redemptive purposes and the historical process gives evidence to continuing creative and providential activities. But Williams's perspective is to be questioned in emphasizing that educational change must keep pace with social and cultural change. All social and cultural change may not reflect the will of God and thus the Christian is called to be critical of change for the sake of change itself. Growth implies for the Christian not only change but continuity; not only change, but conformity to God's will in the midst of change. Thus Christians must be discerning of cultural change and be supportive of those changes which represent closer approximations of God's will.

Is there a Christian culture which Christian educators should perpetuate? There are a variety of cultures and each can embody the Christian faith in ways that glorify God. The culture in which persons are born provides them with windows on the world. But this culture can also erect walls, walls which can isolate and separate people.

Each person's culture serves as a lens through which he or she sees and understands other people. All information is filtered through that lens—beliefs about the world, people, life, God, and ultimate reality. Each person's lens can be viewed as liberating and/or oppressive to the extent to which it provides information that is true in relation to God's general and special revelation. The challenge for the Christian is to be discerning about the nature of that lens. In certain areas each culture must be affirmed and preserved given the unique understanding it provides for human life. In other areas the lens distorts things and the

Christian task is to apply the redemptive fruits of Christ's work. In some situations the lens is so faulty, as was the case in Nazi Germany, that a total transformation is necessary if human life is to continue. Making such judgments requires spiritual discernment and a serious grappling with Christian values.

What *is* the relationship between the Christian faith and human culture? What *has* Jerusalem to do with Athens? The possible responses to that question have often been described by comparing the perspectives of two early church fathers, Tertullian and Origen.

Tertullian essentially maintained that Jerusalem had nothing to do with Athens. He saw the need to affirm the place of piety in the Christian faith because Christians were called to be set apart, distinct, holy, and sanctified in relation to a culture opposed to God. Tertullian's stance, while affirming piety, has the potential of fostering pietism. Pietism is otherworldly, subjective, withdrawn, and legalistic. Pietism is neither of the world nor in the world. By comparison piety can be characterized as being not of the world while being engaged in it. N. H. Beversluis describes piety as living between doubt and faith, between guilt and renewal with hope. Piety is "the practice and celebration of the presence of God in the midst of life."[6]

Origen essentially maintained that Jerusalem had everything to do with Athens. He saw the need to affirm the place of cultural obedience in the Christian faith because Christians were called to be actively engaged in the world given that it was God's creation and the locale for Christian life and vocation. Origen's stance, while affirming engagement, has the potential of fostering cultural accommodation and secularism. Cultural accommodation is this-worldly, undiscriminating, undiscerning, and profane. By comparison, cultural obedience or engagement can be characterized as being in the world while not being of it. N. H. Beversluis describes cultural obedience as doing the world's work with discrimination and accountability. He sees this involvement as part of Christian sanctification, which takes account of sin and affirms the world while seeking to transform it.[7]

Tertullian's and Origen's perspectives represent extreme answers to the enduring question of the relationship between Christ and culture. H. Richard Niebuhr's typology, introduced in chapter 2, provides a helpful vehicle for further consideration. Each model has strengths and weaknesses for dealing with the wider society and culture; and each community response may vary with the issue under question. In addition, each model implies a distinct approach to the task of Christian

6. Ibid., 12–13.
7. Ibid., 15–17.

education. Evangelicals have usually opted for types 1, 4, and 5 of Niebuhr's models (Christ against culture, Christ and culture in paradox, and Christ the transformer of culture).[8]

Tertullian represents the model of Christ against culture. The strength of such a model is its emphasis on being set apart for God, on being not of the world, on fundamental allegiance to the holiness and righteousness of God. The weakness is its withdrawal, its ghettoism of the mind and heart from the world. Educational practice under this model tends to be guarded, disciplined, protected, purist, and isolated. Some Christian day schools and home schooling efforts attempt to stand over against the culture with its pagan philosophy and life-style. Such an education is also polemic and apologetic.

The model of Christ and culture in paradox necessitates a careful assessment of the claims of Christ and those of culture. The claims of both domains must be addressed, resulting in inevitable tensions for Christians who want to faithfully exercise their responsibility. The primary call is for loyalty to Christ, yet responsibility for culture cannot be ignored. Life is lived between a rock and a hard place. The rock is that of the Christian faith and the hard place is the world with its many demands.

The strength of this second model is its realistic portrayal of the dimension of conflict in the lives of Christians and of the radical work of God in Christ. But its weakness is that such conflict may be never resolved or resolvable. Such a stance can lead to acceptance of the status quo, antinomianism, or an incipient cultural conservatism.[9] Given the inevitability of paradox or conflict, Christians may become disinterested and distant from further engagement in the world while negotiating a reasonable peace in their personal lives. Educational practice under this model tends to be challenging, introspective, and conserving.

The model of Christ the transformer of culture highlights the need for Christians to promote renewal and revival in the wider culture as a means by which to promote God's will in human life. This model promotes the extension of Christ's redemptive work to the whole of creation. Such an approach assumes the personal appropriation of salvation in Christ and the expression of personal faith in the works of culture. The strength of this model is its conscious attempt to relate the claims of Christ's lordship to all of life and to struggle with the implications of this. The weaknesses of this model are its failure to seriously grapple

8. David J. Hesselgrave, *Communicating Christ Cross-Culturally* (Grand Rapids: Zondervan, 1979), 79–80.
9. H. Richard Niebuhr, *Christ and Culture* (New York: Harper & Row, 1956), 185–87.

with the extent of sin and its misdirected energies in seeking the conversion of culture which may rarely happen.

Educational practice under this model stresses the need for a careful
reading of the wider culture, focusing upon opportunities for renewal.
There is a constant effort to relate Christian truth claims to study in all
areas. Such an effort is inevitably optimistic while recognizing the realities of sin and human fallenness. A constant challenge in this model
is the effective use of Scripture to discern the whole of God's truth as
discovered in general revelation. Unlike the first two models, this model
holds a greater potential for compromise and cultural accommodation.

Contextualization and Decontextualization

In the discussion of theological foundations in chapter 2, contextualization was defined as the continual process by which truth is applied to and emerges from concrete historical situations.[10] Harvie Conn,
a Reformed missiologist, defines contextualization as "the process of the
conscientization of the whole people of God to the hermeneutical obligations of the gospel."[11]

Stephen Knapp identifies contextualization as the "dynamic process
through which the church continually challenges and/or incorporates—
transforms elements of the cultural and social milieu of which it is an
integral part in its daily struggle to be obedient to the Lord Jesus Christ
in its life and mission in the world."[12]

The first definition emphasizes the translation of the gospel as truth
into relevant social and cultural forms or symbols. Both Conn's and
Knapp's definitions imply not only this translation, but the additional
dimension of decontextualization. Decontextualization is the judgment
of the Word of God which transforms personal, political, economic, social, and cultural spheres of life.[13] Thus two processes are important in
relating the Christian faith to culture. The first process is contextualization, which requires dialogue between the Christian educator and the
immanent context of ministry. This process requires a hermeneutic of
the world in its social and cultural particularity. The second process is
decontextualization, which necessitates dialogue between the Christian
educator and the Scriptures. In this second process a hermeneutic of the
Word is required. Both processes complement one another and are nec-

10. See p. 55 of chapter 2.

11. Harvie M. Conn, "Contextualization: Where Do We Begin?", in *Evangelicals and Liberation*, ed. Carl E. Armerding (Nutley, N.J.: Presbyterian & Reformed, 1977), 104.

12. Stephen Knapp, "Contextualization and Its Implications for U.S. Evangelical Church and Missions," paper presented at Partnership in Mission, Abington, Pa., 1976, 15.

13. Conn, "Contextualization," 104–5.

essary for a faithful response to the gospel demand of being in but not of the world. This is the unique Christian calling and vocation.

Evangelicals have only recently begun to recognize these processes and to see their complementarity. This new interest has been largely facilitated by those involved in missions because they address the out-workings of the Christian faith in the diverse global context. Prior to this recent interest, evangelicals, while addressing the hermeneutics of the Word, have all too readily dismissed the various dimensions of the world. Ignoring contextualization, evangelicals have often reduced God's agenda to souls instead of the entire cosmos. Individual souls are of eternal significance, yet they represent but one dimension of persons and but one sphere of God's creation.

In contrast with evangelicals, liberal Christians and liberationists have tended to address the hermeneutics of the world. In so doing, they have too readily dismissed the various demands of the Word. Overlooking decontextualization, liberationists have on occasion baptized the world's agenda. The world is of great significance, but it represents God's creation, not the Creator. God the Creator has been revealed in the Word, both written and living.

In terms of contextualization, the Third Mandate Programme of the Theological Education Fund has posed some significant questions for seminaries, churches, and schools to consider in their educational efforts:

What about *missiological contextualization*? Is the seminary or school focusing upon the urgent issues of renewal and reform in the church, and upon the vital issues of human development and justice in its particular situation? (A liberationist perspective would question the notion of reform and renewal in the face of injustice and would instead propose revolution and complete transformation.)

What about *structural contextualization*? Is the church or school seeking to develop a form and structure appropriate to the specific needs of its culture in its peculiar social, economic, and political situation? (A liberationist perspective would require that the form or structure be liberating and transformational at points where the culture is oppressive.)

What about *theological contextualization*? Is the church or seminary seeking to do theology in a way appropriate and authentic to its situation? Does it seek to relate the gospel more directly to urgent issues of ministry and service in the world? Does it move out of its own milieu in its expression of the gospel?

Finally, what about *pedagogical contextualization*? Is the seminary or school seeking to develop theological training which attempts to understand the educational processes as a liberating and creative effort? Does it attempt to overcome the besetting dangers of elitism and authoritarianism in both the method and goals of its program to release the potential of a servant ministry? Is it sensitive to the widespread gap between the academic and the practical?[14]

No simple answers are possible to these questions, but these and other questions must be raised and addressed in responding faithfully to Christ in the midst of various cultures.

The Sociology of Knowlege

Lawrence Stenhouse aptly observes that the sociology of knowledge treats knowledge (or what counts as knowledge) as socially constructed or constituted. It also examines how subjects or disciplines are socially constructed as sets of shared meanings. The idea that knowledge is represented in culture implies that knowledge can be socially determined, and in particular, determined by the needs of both groups and individuals. Stenhouse goes on to point out that the determinations of groups and individuals may be departures from truth, though not necessarily intentional departures. A sociology of knowledge, then, does not deal with tests of truth, but its perspective implies a relativism of truth.

Given the strong tradition of aspiration toward absolutes, toward a notion of warranted knowledge,[15] evangelicals might readily dismiss such an inquiry or any insights that might be derived from this seemingly relativistic perspective. This would be unfortunate because, as Denis Lawton suggests, sociological inquiry must be supplemented by both philosophical and psychological research.[16] Philosophy and theology are disciplines which explore truth claims and their validity. The viewpoints of philosophy and sociology can be complementary rather than contradictory.

Berger and Luckmann, in *The Social Construction of Reality,* propose a dialectical relationship between persons as producers and the social world as their product. From their perspective the social world has three functions in relation to knowledge.

First, knowledge programs the channels through which an objective world is produced. Persons are the agents of externalization who express themselves in various activities and forms just as God is expressed in creation.

Second, knowledge objectifies this world through language and the cognitive apparatus based on language, that is, it orders the world into

14. TEF, *Ministry in Context: The Third Mandate Programme of the Theological Education Fund (1970–77)* (Bromley, Kent, England: Theological Education Fund, 1972), 31.

15. Lawrence Stenhouse, *An Introduction to Curriculum Research and Development* (New York: Holmes & Meier, 1975), 14–15.

16. Lawton, *Class, Culture and the Curriculum,* 58–59.

objects apprehended as reality. Adam named the creation and in that naming objectified its reality. God is revealed initially as the Word who spoke and brought forth all life and creation.

Third, knowledge is internalized again as objectively valid truth in the course of socialization. The world as named by God and Adam was then passed on to Adam's offspring and internalized by them as objective truth.[17]

Despite Berger and Luckmann's critical interest, their analysis can lead to an acceptance of dominant social knowledge and religious norms as functional necessities to be perpetuated. This is not a problem when continuity and the preservation of cultural forms are necessary, but if change and transformation are required, difficulties arise. This analysis can foster a sense of powerlessness for Christians; it lacks a moral perspective from which to critique the functional requisites of any given society in the light of gospel values.

Berger and Luckmann's portrayal of religion is one-sided in its emphasis on the role of religion in legitimating existing cultural forms. It fails to adequately consider the prophetic dimension of faith that questions the legitimation of social structures. Such a viewpoint reduces religious concerns to merely social and psychological factors. It emphasizes enculturation to the relative exclusion of disenculturation.

Evangelicals have been criticized for their support of the status quo in various societies, for failing to affirm the prophetic and radical dimensions of biblical faith. Although evangelicals may be attracted to Berger and Luckmann's perspective, they must also assume responsibility for the definition and perpetuation of knowledge which that analysis reveals. In other words, if the selection of knowledge tends to exclude other realities equally embodied in biblical revelation but not valued by evangelical communities, then corporate guilt must be recognized and addressed. Failure to do so represents a lack of faithfulness. One example of this oversight is the emphasis upon redemptive themes to the relative exclusion of the implications of creative themes in biblical revelation.

A second perspective on the sociology of knowledge is represented by Jerry Gill in *The Possibility of Religious Knowledge*. Gill maintains a functional view of knowledge based upon the thought of Michael Polanyi. The experience of knowing is composed of dimensional and contextual awareness, together with committed, functional response. The interaction between these two aspects calls attention to the tacit and mediated aspects of knowledge, as well as to its more direct and explicit aspects. Polanyi and Gill attempt to bridge the domains of fact and value

17. Berger and Luckmann, *Social Construction,* 57–58.

which have been viewed as separate in much of modern Western thought.[18]

Gill proposes simultaneously interpenetrating dimensions of knowledge that include (1) physical-awareness of the material world; (2) moral-awareness of other persons; (3) personal-awareness of oneself as a person; and (4) religious-awareness of transcendent reality. Gill's contextual factors include intentionality, purpose, activity, response of the knower and known, and social and perceptual conventions. Gill situates knowledge on a continuum, with explicit and tacit knowledge at opposite poles. Explicit knowledge exhibits such characteristics as precise analysis, verbal articulation, descriptive identification, observational objectivity, and an absolute distinction between the knower and the known. Tacit knowledge is characterized by intuitive awareness, bodily expressions, holistic recognition, embodied subjectivity, and a contextual distinction between the knower and the known.[19] Although Gill does not adequately explicate the contextual dimensions of his scheme, he does expand on an understanding of knowledge within a biblical perspective. Knowledge is not to be limited to explicit knowledge discerned through facts, but must include values, intuition, and personal response.

Gill does not offer a clear analysis of power relationships that operate in societal contexts. He appears to tacitly accept knowledge that is posited by disciplines, societies, or institutions. He speaks of contextual concerns, but does not radicalize them, relating these concerns to social, political, and economic structures. Whereas he considers the personal and religious dimensions, he does not broaden the individual focus to include corporate and global concerns. Beyond persons and their face-to-face encounters, structures and institutions must be reckoned with and cannot be collapsed into Gill's moral dimension. Gill's insights, while valuable, must be expanded upon in the light of the corporate and social dimensions of life addressed in the Scriptures. Evangelicals must recognize the wider global and cosmic implications of the gospel in relation to social, political, and economic structures, and must develop a theology of institutions to address the realities of an institutionalized world.

A third perspective on knowledge is that of Jürgen Habermas, a leading spokesperson of the school of critical theory at the Frankfurt Institute in West Germany. Habermas proposes three approaches to knowledge: (1) the approach of the empirical-analytical sciences, which incorporates a technical, cognitive interest and yields information; (2) the approach of the historical-hermeneutical sciences, which incorporates

18. Jerry H. Gill, *The Possibility of Religious Knowledge* (Grand Rapids: Wm. B. Eerdmans, 1971), 7, 8, 13.
19. Ibid., 119–36.

a practical interest and yields interpretations; and (3) the approach of the critically oriented sciences, which incorporates an emancipatory interest and yields analyses.

A key concern for Habermas is to maintain all three approaches in dialectical tension. The first two approaches yield nomological knowledge, while the third yields critical and transformational knowledge through self-reflection. The three possible categories of knowledge are: (1) information that expands one's technical control; (2) interpretations that make possible the orientation of action within common traditions; and (3) analyses that free consciousness from its dependence on hypostatized powers.[20]

Habermas's concern for responsibility and the corresponding ethical concern for responsible decisions in engagement with the world can be affirmed, but his stance of autonomy is inadequate from a Christian perspective. Autonomy is an independent stance that excludes adequate consideration of others. The danger of this exclusive autonomy is that it fails to recognize other autonomous persons. Theonomy, in contrast, affirms a shared humanity with others that is grounded in God. This moves beyond an individualistic, introspective, and personalistic stance. In a theonomous stance, one sees oneself realistically in relation with other persons in community. In this stance one affirms one's personhood.

This theonomous aspect of knowledge must be superimposed upon Habermas's categories. The ideal emancipated society of which Habermas speaks finds actualization in the covenant community of God and is approximated in the church as a remnant of God's choosing. The Bible proposes a prophetic stance of knowing that would enlarge Habermas's critically oriented approach to include personal and corporate responsibility to God and a knowledge that is personal. Human interest would embody commitment and engagement with appropriate and corresponding affective and volitional elements. Evangelicals can engage in the critical dialogue suggested by Habermas's work while maintaining a distinctly theonomous center for their understanding.

A fourth viewpoint is articulated by Paulo Freire. Freire maintains that persons can never be understood apart from their relationships with the world through thought-language. For Freire reality implies constant interaction between persons as thinking subjects and history and culture. Persons are both the cause and effect of history. Knowing is a form of praxis, a process in which a person begins to reflect on her/his orientation to the world by objectifying actions and reflecting upon them in order to return to new action and reflection. Freire, like Gill, seeks

20. Jürgen Habermas, *Knowledge and Human Interests* (Boston: Beacon 1971), 308–15.

to maintain both subjectivity and objectivity in a true act of knowing. True knowing also involves active engagement in the political process of transforming the world to realize liberation.[21]

Friere moves beyond Habermas in demonstrating an incarnated concern for the social activity of knowledge that includes co-intentionality. He addresses the political aspect of knowing that makes joint use of analysis, reflection, and critical consciousness to realize new potentials in society. But Freire can be criticized for his failure to deal with sin, which distorts the continuing process of conscientization or transformation.

The sociology of knowledge demands that Christian educators attend to some important considerations:

First, knowledge cannot be separated from a person's being in the world, and knowledge as proposed by societies and faith communities embodies and conditions the tasks of naming, creating, critiquing, and transforming that world by particular persons and groups.

Knowledge implies actualization and expression, but what of knowing without certainty and knowing only in part which is suggested by God's hidden nature beyond revelation? Evangelicals must acknowledge the place of mystery and incomplete knowledge in both doctrine and life which counters any stance of arrogance.

What is the relationship of knowledge to speaking, thinking, listening, and interpreting? How is knowledge embodied in each of these activities? How is knowledge assumed in those activities which largely mask personal commitments and value decisions? Evangelicals are called to be explicit about their commitments and values in light of key social issues and ethical questions.

What of a person's need to know, to realize a *nomos?* Is this quest a human given? Are persons socialized to question, and when does questioning transcend a society's accepted knowledge? What about anomie and acceptance of a state of not knowing or suspended knowing? Evangelicals are called to engage in the process of serious questioning and dialogue with nonevangelicals.

Is all knowledge part of a larger whole? In that God is the source of all knowledge, what implications are there for a person's quest for knowledge? Evangelicals can affirm their distinctive God-centered focus in response to these questions, recognizing God as the source of all truth.

Knowledge is conditioned by its context, by the questions being asked,

21. See Paulo Freire, *Pedagogy of the Oppressed*, trans. Myra Bergman Ramos (New York: Seabury, 1970); and Dennis E. Collins, *Paulo Freire: His Life, Works, and Thought* (New York: Paulist Press, 1977).

and is therefore always knowledge from a certain perspective or position. The recognition and ownership of one's perspective is important for all communities.

Knowledge is also socially distributed. It is an instrument in the struggle for survival and power and has the potential for the liberation and actualization of persons. Knowledge can be a tool for oppression or liberation depending upon its distribution and perpetuation. Knowledge as distributed by evangelical communities must be evaluated in these terms.

There are different ways of knowing. A person may draw upon an established authority or tradition (heteronomy). Through the use of human reasoning and thought, a person may ask questions, critique ideas and situations, assemble data, and use what appeals to reason and thought in the light of experience (autonomy). Personal or corporate experience may provide knowledge (autonomy). However, while Christians use reason, experience, and authority to make sense of the factual world, they acknowledge the beyondness known only by revelation. They accept both the supernatural and the reality of the concrete and practical, giving priority to the place of revelation (theonomy). Christians are to actively listen and interpret within their historical context, combining conviction with tolerance, commitment with openness.

It is possible to view knowledge as a union with the person or thing known. This does not mean that there must always be union with the object of knowledge in order for knowledge to exist. The highest knowledge possible for persons is knowledge of God. This knowledge is conditioned by faith and obedience, by a willingness to know and submit to the will of God. The known in this case is God, but God is also unknowable and unknown beyond revelation.

The Bible regards knowledge as something which arises from personal encounter. The knowledge of God is related to the revelation of God in the historic past and the promised future. Yet God is also revealed in the present earthly sphere in which God's creatures have their being and live out their history. The knowledge of God is inseparably bound up with God's revelation in time and space, in historical contexts. In the Bible knowledge implies the awareness of a specific relationship in which the individual person and corporate community stand with the person or object known. Just as the individual is considered a totality rather than a being composed of body and mind, knowledge is an activity in which the whole individual is engaged.

The exploration of insights from the sociology of knowledge brings Christians to a fuller appreciation and understanding of the various dimensions of knowledge. But the words of Paul directed to the issue of food sacrificed to idols in Corinth serve to warn Christians: "We know that we all possess knowledge. Knowledge puffs up, but love builds up. The man who thinks he knows something does not yet know as he ought to know. But the man who loves God is known by God" (1 Cor. 8:1b–3). Human knowledge is transcended by being known by God and by love. Paul's warning does not negate the quest for knowledge, but sets that quest in the wider context of faith and commitment.

The Sociology of Education

Beyond considerations of knowledge itself, sociological inquiry can also be directed to the larger effort of education itself. The works of Emile Durkheim, John Eggleston, and Rolland Paulston among others provide helpful insights for the Christian educator.

Emile Durkheim

In western Europe, sociology developed in response to the problems of rapid change. Emile Durkheim was concerned with the loss of traditional norms and values which had in the past been provided by the church and the breakdown of a once fairly stable society. Therefore, his sociology centers upon the themes of social order, social control, and consensus.[22]

Durkheim viewed education as a vehicle to restore equilibrium. The sociologist was to study generic types of education corresponding to different types of societies, seeking out the conditions on which each type of education depended and how they emerged from one another. One would thereby obtain the laws which govern the evolution of systems of education.[23]

In his analysis of education, Durkheim views education on three levels: the science of education, pedagogical theories, and the practice of education. The science of education involves research, the description of present or past phenomena, and inquiry into their causes or the determination of their effects. Such a science of education provides descriptions and analyses and encourages exploration and divergent thought. It proposes working hypotheses and draws upon various sources for its scientific content. These sources include psychology, sociology, anthropology, biology, economics, and political science.

Of these sources, psychology and sociology share a privileged position along with the study of philosophy.[24] At this level of inquiry, the Christian educator can participate in research and make use of the descrip-

22. Lawton, Class, Culture and Curriculum, 56.
23. Emile Durkheim, Education and Sociology (New York: Free Press, 1956), 95–98.
24. Ibid., 99.

tions gained as working hypotheses for pedagogical theories at the second level. In making use of these hypotheses, the guide for the Christian is her or his world view. A Christian world view centers upon the living and written Word of God and discounts any insights that are not consistent with or complementary to God's truth. Thus the constant challenge at this level is for the Christian to be discerning of any proposed insights.

The second level of Durkheim's analysis is the level of pedagogical or practical theories. The objective of this level is not to describe or explain what is or what has been in education, but to determine what should be the case. Pedagogical theories are oriented neither to the present nor to the past, but to the future. They propose and advocate prescriptions and syntheses for education. Such theories inform persons what must be done and are by nature speculative, creative, and imaginative reflections. In contrast with the divergent thought of a science of education, pedagogical theories are engaged with convergent thought.[25] Most Christian educators in the academic world have devoted their primary energies to the development of pedagogical theories on an ad hoc basis, selectively incorporating insights gained from the science of education. Fully developed pedagogical theories have not been developed by evangelicals.[26]

The third level of Durkheim's analysis is the level of practice. Practice in education describes what must be done, the procedures. Practice is concerned with the art of education and is a system of ways of doing education oriented to special ends. These ways of doing education are products of a traditional experience communicated by a community and/or the product of personal experience. Practice is creative and as an art may be illuminated by reflection. Nevertheless, reflection is not an essential element of the practice of education.[27] Evangelical Christian educators have generally emphasized the practice of education given their commitments to persons and various local church and parachurch ministries. This has often been done without adequate consideration of Durkheim's first two levels.

From the above analysis, it is possible to suggest an agenda for evangelical educators. The strength of evangelical education is its commitment to the practice of education and this commitment should not be lost. But evangelical educators must more seriously engage the challenges of formulating pedagogical or practical theories. These theories are better described as practical theologies given the concerted effort to

25. Ibid.

26. Warren S. Benson confirms this analysis in "Evangelical Philosophies of Education," in *Changing Patterns of Religious Education*, ed. Marvin J. Taylor (Nashville: Abingdon, 1984), 53.

27. Durkheim, *Education and Sociology*, 99.

relate all work to one's theology in evangelicalism. Without such practical theories or theologies, evangelical educators become context bound and unresponsive to important critical issues while being dependent on either traditional strategies or the latest educational trend. This does not need to be the case if adequate time is devoted to reflection and evaluation amidst the urgent demands of ministry.

John Eggleston

In contrast with Durkheim, John Eggleston is a proponent of a "new" sociology of education which considers how knowledge is defined, selected, organized, transmitted, and distributed in schools. He considers how knowledge is valued and the relationships of power and control among those in the knowledge business, namely among those in schools. But his inquiry is not limited to schools or classrooms, for he looks beyond them to see how they are connected to the larger structures of society, including economic and political systems. With this larger view it is necessary to consider questions of the legitimacy of current arrangements and commitments.

In his analysis Eggleston suggests five key questions to use in exploring values and commitments in a particular educational work or ministry:

1. What will be regarded as knowledge, understanding, values, attitudes, and skills (the elements of education)?
2. How should these elements be ranked in importance and status?
3. On what principles will these elements be distributed? To whom and at what times will they be made available and from whom will they be withheld?
4. What is the identity of the groups whose definitions prevail in these matters?
5. Is it legitimate for these groups to act in these ways?[28]

These questions are implicit in every educational endeavor and Eggleston is helpful in making explicit those areas often assumed or even neglected in the discussion of education. Regarding knowledge, understanding, values, attitudes, and skills, it is important to consider those areas that are neglected or forgotten—the "null curriculum." Careful consideration of excluded knowledge can identify the criteria used in determining the appropriate content. Given the wide possibilities of

28. John Eggleston, *The Sociology of the School Curriculum* (London: Routledge & Kegan Paul, 1977), 23.

knowledge, understanding, values, attitudes, and skills, some choice is necessary.

The determination of priorities is inevitable in education given that the limited resources of time and energy force both personal and corporate evaluation. This evaluation may occur in both private and public domains. In either domain careful discernment is needed to maintain an adequate exposure along with balance. Posing Eggleston's first two questions indicates the essential need for planning and periodic evaluation that wherever possible includes all participants in a particular educational work. It is often the case that these choices are not subject to public consideration and input from all constituencies in a community.

Eggleston's third question requires of educators and others who provide direction in educational work the careful articulation of principles for distributing content along with an awareness of the persons involved and their readiness to receive such content. Such principles are derived from various values and commitments. In the case of the evangelical church, biblical and theological commitments have generally served as normative categories for the derivation of guiding principles. In addition, increased attention has been paid to the insights from educational and social science research to discern the characteristics and needs of students and their readiness for learning. But beyond these areas, evangelical educators need to carefully assess their philosophical commitments and how they affect explicit or implicit principles. This assessment cannot be ignored in responding to ever present needs.

Evangelical educators must address areas which have not received adequate scrutiny. This has been the case in part because of a stance of conservatism which has extended beyond theological categories to include all areas of life. In such a stance, persons are generally reluctant to question the identity and legitimacy of those who direct and control various educational ministries. Eggleston directs evangelicals into radical and uncharted waters by raising questions about those persons who wield power and the legitimacy of the uses of that power. Eggleston's perspective suggests that those who are called to positions of responsibility and power need to be questioned and evaluated by those who are served. This is a necessity given the fallen nature of persons and the inevitable consequences of leadership that is other than moral. Examples can be cited where evangelical leadership has assumed authoritarian stances and has resisted the acknowledgment of weaknesses as well as strengths.

Rolland Paulston

A third contributor from the perspective of a sociology of knowledge is Rolland Paulston, whose work is in the area of international studies.

He develops a general conceptual framework for comparative and international educators. His major contribution is in relating different commitments in social and educational change to their underlying conceptual frameworks or ideological orientations. Table 5 summarizes Paulston's insights.[29]

Paulston indicates that educational reform theories are rooted in systematic ideological orientations concerning social reality and the social-change process. Such ideological orientations or biases constrain the abilities of educational planners and reformers to explore the full range of potentially effective strategies for educational reform. For example, a predisposition toward an equilibrium paradigm may ignore insights gained from the perspective of conflict.[30]

Paulston's insights pose a challenge to the Christian who is concerned for educational reform or renewal. Which if any of these theories are consistent with a Christian world view in light of Paulston's observation that these orientations are "not random or eclectic but rather follow from personal bias concerning theoretical and ideological orientations to social reality and social-change process"?[31] Lest evangelicals totally avoid conflict models, one must recall the revolutionary beginnings of the United States.

These various orientations have some parallels with Niebuhr's Christ and culture scheme. For those Christians who opt for the Christ and culture in paradox, Christ the transformer of culture, and Christ above culture stances, an equilibrium paradigm would seem to be consistent with their commitments. By comparison those Christians who opt for a Christ against culture stance would be more likely to opt for a conflict paradigm and in particular, the theory of cultural revitalization. It is also possible to see how Christians who opt for a Christ the transformer of culture stance might be attracted to a cultural revitalization theory if it were focused on staying and working within the existing system rather than opting out of it. The challenge would be posed for Christians to be agents of fundamental change within society at large, revitalizing it through their presence and service.

Paulston reminds evangelical Christians that they must be aware of their ideological commitments. Intellectual integrity and consistency are at stake along with the need to understand various perspectives on social and educational change. Each of the eight theories Paulston outlines contributes insights which must be carefully assessed. Paulston

29. Rolland G. Paulston, *Conflicting Theories of Social and Educational Change* (Pittsburgh: University Center for International Studies, University of Pittsburgh, 1976), vi–vii.

30. Ibid., v.

31. Ibid.

Table 5 **Theories of Social and Educational Change/"Reform"**

Social Change		Illustrative Linked Assumptions Concerning Education-Change Potentials and Processes			
Paradigms	*Theories*	*Preconditions for Educational Change*	*Rationales for Educational Change*	*Scope and Process of Educational Change*	*Major Outcomes Sought*
Equilibrium	*Evolutionary*	State of evolutionary readiness	Pressure to move to a higher evolutionary stage	Incremental and adaptive; "natural history" approach	New stage of institutional evolutional adaptation
	Neo-evolutionary	Satisfactory completion of earlier stages	Required to support "national modernization" efforts	"Institution building" using Western models and technical assistance	New "higher" state of education and social differentiation/specialization
	Structural-Functional	Altered functional and structural requisites	Social system need provoking an educational response; exogenous threats	Incremental adjustment of existing institutions, occasionally major	Continued "homeostasis" or "moving" equilibrium, "human capital," and national "development"
	Systems	Technical expertise in "systems management." "Rational decision making" and "needs assessment"	Need for greater efficiency in system's operation and goal achievement, i.e., response to a system "malfunction"	Innovative "problem solving" in existing systems, i.e., "research and development" approach	Improved "efficiency" re costs/benefits, adoption of innovations

Conflict				
Marxian	Elite's awareness of need for change, or shift of power to socialist rulers and educational reformers	Adjustment of correspondence between social relations of production and social relations of schooling	Incremental adjustment following social mutations or radical restructuring with Marxist predominance	Formation of integrated workers, i.e., the new "socialist man"
Neo-Marxian	Increased political power and political awareness of working class	Demands for social justice and social equality	Large-scale national reforms through "democratic" institutions and processes	Eliminate "educational privilege" and "elitism"; create a more equalitarian society
Cultural Revitalization	Rise of a collective effort to revive or create "a new culture." Social tolerance for "deviant" normative movements and their educational programs	Rejection of conventional schooling as forced acculturation. Education needed to support advance toward movement goals	Creation of alternative schools of educational settings. If movement captures polity, radical change in national educational ideology and structure	Inculcate new normative system. Meet movement's recruitment, training, and solidarity needs
Anarchistic Utopian	Creation of supportive settings; growth of critical consciousness; social pluralism	Free man from institutional and social constraints. Enhance creativity need for "lifelong learning"	Isolated "freeing up" of existing programs and institutions, or creation of new learning modes and settings, i.e., a "learning society"	Self-renewal and participation, local control of resources and community; elimination of exploitation and alienation

also reminds us that Christians may be called to ministry at various points of society, some working within the system seeking an equilibrium in line with gospel demands, while others are called to stand over against the system or society and through creative conflict to offer new possibilities. Spiritual discernment is crucial in order to distinguish at what points the equilibrium can be supported and at what points radical change is demanded in the effort to be faithful to God's calling in the world.

For evangelicals, Paulston's work has particular significance in addressing the widely discussed issue of schooling. Should Christian parents be educating their children in public, private Christian, or home schools? For various reasons, a number of Christian parents have judged that the public schools in their communities do not provide the best possible education for their children. In this case they conclude that a stance against the common culture of the public school is warranted and that cultural revitalization necessitates the schooling of their children in distinctly Christian private schools or in a home school where the parents are the primary educators. For these parents the purpose of education is to transmit Christian culture to the next generation.

Other Christian parents decide to send their children to public schools for various reasons. Their choice represents an explicit or implicit support of the public school system. This support may not in fact be total, but may represent some awareness of working within the existing system rather than opting for an alternative which may not in fact be viable. In addition, Christians also choose to work in various capacities within public schools and seek to represent their Christian commitments at least in deed, if not through direct words. Such choices by Christian parents and workers do not exclude the possibilities of working for change or renewal within the existing public school system, but accept this setting as the locus for life and ministry.

For many, the dilemma of these options can only be resolved by considering various dimensions, including one's perspective on social and educational life and change in the light of the Christian faith. It is the task of Christian educators and other leaders to raise the matter of schooling choices as they relate to the larger question of faith commitments and the Christian's call to be in but not of the world. Various responses are possible while recognizing the issues which Paulston's work suggests.

A Model for Sociological Inquiry

Building upon the preceding discussion, it is possible to propose a model for sociological inquiry that will enable Christian educators to consider the impacts of society and culture upon education. This model emerges from the work of Clifford Geertz (see fig. 10).[32]

The expressions and embodiments of corporate life are experienced most directly in the groups, organizations, and institutions with which persons interact each day. These include various economic, social, educational, cultural, and political organizations and institutions—from a department store chain to the local police force, from the community church to the regional Internal Revenue Service office. Persons relate to a host of groups in an increasingly institutionalized world.

On a larger scale, persons interact with the society in general and interface with economic, political, and social structures or networks. Economically, capitalist and socialist systems set different parameters for the theory and practice of education. Politically, democratic and totalitarian structures influence education in distinct ways. Differences in social class affiliation and commitment interact with educational philosophies and practices to result in distinct agendas and experiences for students.

Awareness of these various factors in terms of the expressions and embodiments of corporate life have not traditionally been subject to the critical awareness of evangelicals. Nevertheless, their impacts can be seen as liberating and/or oppressive, as redemptive and/or fallen. Most organizations, institutions, and societal structures cannot be classified as exclusively liberating or exclusively oppressive, but are a combination of both.

For example, both my wife and I were taught at the elementary level in the public school system of New York City. My experience was primarily positive given the fact that my local community in Brooklyn was predominantly Jewish and the quality of the schooling was excellent. My wife's experience was primarily negative and oppressive given the

FIGURE 10   **A Model for Sociological Inquiry**

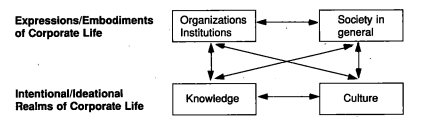

32. Geertz, *Interpretation of Cultures.* This diagram was suggested by Douglas Sloan, Teachers College, Columbus University, New York, New York, March 25, 1980 using Geertz's insights.

fact that her local community in Manhattan was predominantly Hispanic and the quality of the schooling was inferior. Other examples could also be cited where students at the public school in Brooklyn had oppressive and limiting experiences as compared to students at the public school in Manhattan who may have had liberating and expansive experiences. While recognizing this contrary and exceptional evidence, one could say that the local public schooling impact in Flatbush, Brooklyn was generally more liberating than in East Harlem, Manhattan.

During the 1960s in New York City, general consciousness had been raised regarding the effects of racism and selective economic support upon the schooling experiences in local communities. The life expectations for those attending school in East Harlem were vastly different than for those in Flatbush, and subtle messages were communicated to students in relation to academic demands and the value of their cultural heritage in relation to the larger society. Following the civil rights movement, increased awareness has occurred, but the realization of a more equitable educational experience for all the children in New York or any other major city is a continual challenge. Regretfully, the evangelical church as a whole has not been responsive to this challenge.

In returning to the model of Geertz's insights, a second level of corporate life centers upon the intentional and ideational realms of knowledge and culture. Knowledge is shared meanings, and education has primarily centered upon the discovery, accumulation, and distribution of these shared meanings. But education has also involved in a more implicit or perhaps hidden manner the transmission of culture. Culture can be defined as shared values, attitudes, and beliefs. From the broader perspective which includes the place of culture, education can be conceived as "the entire process by which a culture transmits itself across the generations."[33]

Such a broader perspective necessitates that evangelicals be less parochial and narrow in order to explore the major impacts of the wider culture upon faith communities and the extent to which aspects of the wider culture can be affirmed and/or criticized. The evangelical Christian, as every other Christian with distinct theological commitments, must discern which aspects of culture can be preserved, redeemed, or transformed. Such identification and analysis, with the subsequent development of strategies for action, must be included in Christian education if persons are to adequately represent Christ in the various cultures and subcultures in which they have been called to live, work, and minister. Indeed, the call is to make Christ's presence and transforming

33. Bernard Bailyn, *Education in the Forming of American Society* (New York: W. W. Norton, 1960), 14.

power known at all levels of corporate life. Christ is to be evident in organizational and institutional life and within larger societal structures. Christ is to be evident in the realms of shared meaning, values, attitudes, and beliefs. Such is the high calling of Christians in every society.

Why is this so? Why is this a necessary call to the Christian vocation? God is concerned for righteousness, justice, and reconciliation throughout human society in its various expressions and realms, and is concerned for the liberation of persons from every kind of oppression. This oppression includes spiritual oppression, but much more. Humankind is created in God's image and every person has intrinsic dignity and should be respected and served in the name of Christ. Christians, bearing the name of Christ, are called to be salt and light in the world as well as in the church. Our spiritual warfare involves confronting principalities and powers at all levels of society, of corporate life, which contribute to oppression, alienation, and discrimination. Evangelicals must address the interrelated complex of social problems suggested by Geertz's analysis with the mind and presence of Christ. While Christians recognize that their hope is in God and not in effective service, social action, or change, they nonetheless strive to take captive every thought and expression of corporate life to make it obedient to Christ (2 Cor. 10:5).

6

Psychological Foundations

The integration of a Christian world view with psychology is particularly problematic for a number of reasons. First, education as it is generally conceived and practiced in the twentieth century has been primarily dependent upon psychology with its varied theories, research findings, and practices. This follows from the fact that psychology as a discipline has included the study of human consciousness and behavior. Education is concerned with persons and the teaching-learning process and educators can gain much through considering the insights of psychological inquiry.

Second, there are distinct psychologies or schools of psychology including behavioral, psychoanalytic, cognitive, gestalt, humanistic, social, and transformational psychologies. Given such diverse perspectives, the issue often becomes which psychologies combined or integrated provide the best mix.

Third, the Christian is confronted with the need to think Christianly about psychology in general and/or develop a Christian psychology upon which to build educational thought and practice. Christianity embodies a perspective on human persons which has implications for their education. For example, if persons are viewed as basically good as created by God, then perhaps greater emphasis needs to be placed on freedom, discovery, and creativity in the learning process. In contrast, if persons are viewed as basically evil, as fallen in sin, then perhaps greater emphasis needs to be placed on structure, discipline, and responsibility in the learning process. An additional possibility is to view persons as being both good and evil in varying degrees, which necessitates some combination of emphases on freedom and form, on discovery and discipline, on creativity and responsibility. These examples, of course, are generalizations, but serve to point out the importance of attempting to integrate Christian understandings with psychology and views of education.

Four Approaches to Integration

To address the question of integration, it is helpful to consider the insights of Lawrence Crabb, a Christian psychologist, who has suggested four possible approaches. The first approach can be described as fragmented. It maintains two "separate but equal" tracks for viewing and relating to persons. In this approach the lives of persons are directed by psychological perspectives in all "secular" areas of life with an insistence that religious or Christian faith and development are unrelated to psychological processes and unaffected by them. This leads to religious schizophrenia and irrelevant religion. A second approach rejects psychological insights and places people in a determined religious context where their lives are totally shaped by religious insights and perspectives untainted by psychological or developmental insights. This "nothing buttery" approach maintains that nothing but the Bible or religious insights determine life and leads to a stance of heteronomy in life. A law outside of persons is imposed on them without the consideration of various insights and the personal appropriation of a world view. This approach results in a provincialism or ghettoization in life that requires constant nurture and insulation to maintain. The third approach can be described as integrated but misdirected. This is a total psychological approach to Christian education and conversion which reshapes the radical demands of faith and reduces the distinctives of evangelical theology (grace, salvation, sin and guilt, and an acceptance of salvation). This approach can be described as a "tossed salad" approach, which randomly mixes psychological and religious concepts while giving priority to psychology. A fourth and final approach is one which is integrated and directed. This approach requires openness and a candid evaluation by Christian educators about the presuppositions and goals of their psychological views. In this approach the need is to search for possible interrelationships with psychology using biblical perspectives and a Christian world view as a final authority. This approach assumes that there is discovered truth as well as revealed truth which Christians must discern with the proviso that discovered truth be consistent with revealed truth.[1]

This fourth approach was described by Augustine as "spoiling the Egyptians." It involves the search for truth in all areas of inquiry, including psychology, affirming that all truth is God's truth.[2] As the Israelites used the vessels and ornaments of gold and silver offered by the Egyptians to adorn the tabernacle in the wilderness, so Christian educators must use the wisdom gained from psychology to enrich and embellish their thought and practice to the end that God might be glorified. The potential difficulty in this "spoiling" is represented by the construction of the golden calf—an idolatry with psychologism finally holding sway over theism. Using the integrated and directed approach demands an overriding dependence upon spiritual discernment and an unwavering commitment to God's truth as revealed in Scripture and Jesus Christ. Anything less deteriorates into worship of the creature instead of the worship due to the Creator of all creation.

Questions of Developmental Psychology

Given the concern in education for the changes in persons over time as a result of educational experiences, questions of development in the field of psychology have been of particular concern to educators. Human development can be defined as "an emergent reality whereby the potential structures of the personality are given particular and varied shapes over the course of a lifetime."[3] In relation to development, Gerald R. Levin, child psychologist, has identified seven central issues with which psychologists have contended in their views of persons, and in particular, their views of children. Each issue can be viewed as representing a continuum with opposite viewpoints at each pole.

The first issue for Levin concerns developmental and nondevelopmental perspectives. The developmental point of view sees a person's psychological functioning changing so radically during the course of life that one must regard developmental changes in behavior as fundamental, as basic and profound as developmental changes in physical structure that start at conception and end when the human body is physically mature. The nondevelopmental point of view, at the other end of the

1. For a complete description of these four approaches, see Lawrence J. Crabb, *Effective Biblical Counseling: A Model for Helping Caring Christians Become Capable Counselors* (Grand Rapids: Zondervan, 1977), 31–56.

2. Augustine, *On Christian Doctrine*, bk. 2, chap. 40.

3. James E. Loder, "Developmental Foundations for Christian Education," in *Foundations for Christian Education in an Era of Change*, ed. Marvin J. Taylor (Nashville: Abingdon, 1976), 54.

continuum, assumes that a person's psychological characteristics remain essentially constant and regards the obvious changes in behavior that take place over time as superficial reflections of the continuing operation of stable, underlying processes.[4] The developmental perspective tends to stress discontinuities, whereas the nondevelopmental perspective emphasizes continuities in psychological functioning.

A second issue from Levin's analysis involves continuity and discontinuity positions. The continuity position asserts that developmental changes in behavior can be seen as a continuous series of minute changes. While the cumulative effect of these changes is dramatic, the process can be thought of as analogous to the height changes occurring between birth and maturity. Persons gain more of the same, rather than something different in development. The discontinuity position asserts that the most important changes in behavior are qualitative and discontinuous in nature. "Like the physical difference between a fertilized ovum and a newborn baby, some psychological differences involve a dramatic transformation from one stage of development to another."[5]

Levin's third issue centers upon differences between the biological position and the sociological viewpoint. For those advocating the biological position, development involves tremendous biological changes and the realization of potentials present in the genes. The helplessness of infancy, language, and sexual behavior, for example, are all products of heredity. Thus to understand normal development and its deviations, one must put the person in biological perspective. The sociological viewpoint counters this emphasis on biological factors by pointing out that development involves a great deal of learning, the acquisition of forms of behavior which are passed on from generation to generation through various cultures. The helplessness of infancy provides humans with unique opportunities for learning. Language, like other aspects of culture, must be learned through interaction with the human environment. Even seemingly biological matters such as sex take on a human character only as a result of the social context in which they are developed. Thus to understand normal development and its deviations, one views persons from a sociological perspective.[6]

A fourth issue Levin proposes considers persons as either passive, active, or a combination of both. The view of persons as passive or receptive sees them as being molded by powerful influences that are beyond their control. Driven by forces such as hunger from within and

4. Gerald R. Levin, "Child Psychology: An Orientation" (Lewisburg, Pa.: Bucknell University, 1969), 35.
   5. Ibid., 35–36.
   6. Ibid., 36.

initially helpless in solving the problems of survival, the child, for example, is almost completely dependent on the adults around him/her. As adults take care of children they shape their behavior in numerous ways, obvious and subtle, deliberately and accidently creating a figure in their own image. This shaping and imaging continues beyond childhood, with the adult largely a passive respondent to various influences. In contrast with this view is one which emphasizes persons as active. The human child is constantly active in teaching herself or himself and in seeking out more challenging problems. Even a baby will frustrate his or her parents' mealtimes by playing with food, deliberately spilling milk, and seeking out endless diversions. Most of the significant achievements of life come from a person's constant curiosity and desire to master the world than from any interest in pleasing others. Persons expend great amounts of energy in actively exploring the world.[7] John Locke saw the child as a tabula rasa, a blank slate acted upon by various influences and forces. In contrast with Locke, Jean Jacques Rosseau saw the child as a noble savage, with an innate moral sense and intuitive knowledge requiring avenues for expression and activity. Locke's perspective supports the emphasis upon passivity, whereas Rosseau's view supports viewing persons as active and dynamic.

A fifth issue for Levin centers on the relative stress placed on affective or cognitive dimensions of human persons. The affective view seeks to understand persons by examining what motivates them and what determines why they select one reaction rather than another. Priority is given to feeling and the emotional-motivational side of development. The cognitive view seeks to understand how persons know the world around them. The environment is only what people make of it, how they perceive it. Thus one must consider how persons think and what can be remembered to gain understanding of motives and emotions. Because cognitive functioning changes so radically in persons, priority must be given to this dimension.[8] The affective viewpoint has been stressed by those interested in the psychodynamics of persons, including Freud, Jung, Erikson, and other neo-Freudians. The cognitive viewpoint has been advocated primarily by Piaget, Kohlberg, and more recently James Fowler. Cognitive theorists stress the structures of persons' thoughts and consciousness as essential to understanding persons.

The sixth issue Levin highlights places in opposition macroscopic and microscopic viewpoints of persons. A macroscopic viewpoint considers as essential the broad patterns and features of human behavior which take years to develop. Confusing and secondary details are ignored

7. Ibid., 36–37.
8. Ibid., 37–38.

in order to discern major trends and what influences them. An effort is made to gain the "big picture" and how major shifts in society affect persons, and how various social structures influence individual development. A microscopic viewpoint stresses the minute details of behavior and the individual responses of persons. By examining details, the forces that affect persons can be discerned.[9] The distinctives in this issue might best be compared with the differences between wide-angle and close-up photographs, with one emphasizing the broad sweeps and trends, the other concerned with the fine details of a subject.

Levin's seventh and final issue concerns the debate between a general psychology position and a differential psychology position. The general position views persons as essentially similar, despite apparent differences among them. Similarity thus becomes the central focus and the search is for basic principles that apply to everyone. By contrast, the differential position views all persons as different, despite superficial resemblances among them. This amazing variety provides the starting point for considering persons. It is only after exploring the diversity and discerning how and when differences appear that similarities among persons should be considered.[10]

This debate can be typified in a discussion a school teacher might have with a clinical psychologist who is stressing the needs of her or his individual patient. The teacher is concerned with basic principles that will work with a large group of children and emphasizes the need for individual students to cooperate with group expectations and norms. The clinical psychologist is concerned with the best possible individualized approach that will meet the needs of a particular child within the larger classroom setting. Each practitioner will appeal to those psychological perspectives and insights which address their particular situations and needs.

Responses to these seven issues and others will greatly affect how the Christian educator will formulate an educational psychology and how one will act explicitly or implicitly in teaching or interacting with others. But it must be asked which choices within each of these issues best reflects a Christian world view and commitment. No simple choices can be made and responses may vary with the particular social, cultural, and historical context. Nevertheless, given the high dependence upon psychology in all areas of human interaction, careful thought must be given to these questions.

Some may advocate a mediating position on each of these issues, seeing truth as present in each of the opposing viewpoints or perspec-

9. Ibid., 38.
10. Ibid.

tives on persons. But the greater challenge is to rethink one's position in light of biblical revelation and theological reflection. How does a Christian view of persons interface with modern psychology in its various expressions? A consideration of cognitive, psychosocial, moral, and faith development will provide some insights for addressing this question in further detail.

Cognitive Development: Jean Piaget

The person most closely associated with cognitive development theory is Jean Piaget, a Swiss genetic epistemologist who sought to study how the structures of human thought and knowledge originated and changed with maturation, particularly from birth through adolescence. His work provided a helpful bridge between the study of biology and epistemology by viewing knowledge as bodily activity in relation to the environment. His key concepts are those of assimilation and accommodation, which refer to how persons deal with varied environmental experiences in relation to their cognitive structures. Piaget's primary concern is with reasoning and knowing, which are viewed as operations or patterns of the mind. The active body is the ground of knowledge, and interaction with one's environment is crucial for development. In relation to Levin's seven issues, Piaget opts for a perspective that is developmental, biological, cognitive, microscopic, and differential; it also emphasizes discontinuity and activity.

For Piaget, the ultimate goal of education is not to fill the child's mind with an assortment of items of knowledge, but to advance the child from one stage of reasoning within a given hierarchy to a more mature stage. The educator's main concern, then, should be *how* the child reasons and not *about what* the child reasons. Educationally this is accomplished by producing dissonance between the environment of a child and the particular stage within which he or she is.

While recognizing the place of cognitive dimensions, the Christian educator must criticize an exclusive emphasis on reasoning without a corresponding concern for motivation, feeling, behavior, and tendencies. Piaget does not ignore these dimensions, but sees them as operating consistently with intellectual functioning. In addition, Christians can criticize Piaget's underlying assumption of the fundamental goodness of humanity. Piaget assumes that if human reasoning is improved to the next higher stage, that growth, development, and maturation has occurred. Christians by contrast recognize the fallenness of humanity that affects reasoning as well as other faculties.[11]

11. Nicholas Wolterstorff, *Educating for Responsible Action* (Grand Rapids: Wm. B. Eerdmans, 1980), 27–29.

Many of the insights regarding cognitive development in Piaget's theory are true. Children do learn through activity as they organize and interpret new experiences in terms of previous knowledge. In other words, they are active and constructive in relating to the world. Children's interest and ability to learn new cognitive skills does depend on existing cognitive structures. Social interaction with peers does promote cognitive development.[12] Yet while Piaget has restored a necessary appreciation of the connectedness of persons' minds and bodies, he has opted for a psychology that focuses upon the structures or patterns of reasoning to the relative exclusion of other vital dimensions of human life.

Piaget's presuppositions as a scientific naturalist and humanist contrast with a Christian world view. Piaget would not assert that the theological and moral absolutes which Christians maintain exist and affect persons. Christians recognize an objective interpersonal reality that exists apart from culture, namely God who stands above and judges every person's and society's cognitive constructs of reality.[13] God's revelation in Jesus Christ and Scripture provides a standard for cognitive reasoning. Given this standard, true content has priority for Christian educators whereas Piaget places priority upon internal development or cognitive structures for human development. Therefore, Piaget sees growth in terms of the restructuring of one's perceptions as new cognitive structures emerge, creating one's own reality. In contrast, a Christian understanding of growth involves integrating truth as reality into one's personality by the conjoint efforts of persons and God through the agency of the Holy Spirit. This integration for Christian educators relies upon the use of Scripture to provide a framework within which persons can build their lives. In this building process, people do make use of their reason, experience, and insights from tradition and other cultural inputs. For Piaget, God's revelation in Scripture and Jesus Christ does not provide this normative function for development.[14] In fact, exposure to Scripture may be harmful as suggested by Ronald Goldman, who uncritically applied Piaget's insights to the tasks of religious education in his study of religious reasoning.[15] Therefore, while Piaget's work is help-

12. See Harry L. Hom, Jr., and Paul A. Robinson, eds., *Psychological Processes in Early Education* (New York: Academic, 1977), 17ff., for a discussion of the limitations and strengths of Piaget's theory.

13. Lawrence O. Richards, *A Theology of Children's Ministry* (Grand Rapids: Zondervan, 1983), 170.

14. The insights in this paragraph are those of Lawrence O. Richards, *A Theology of Christian Education* (Grand Rapids: Zondervan, 1975), 168–87.

15. See Ronald Goldman, *Readiness for Religion* (New York: Seabury, 1968).

ful, the Christian educator must press beyond it to address additional factors and distinctives which characterize a Christian world view.

Psychosocial Development: Erik Erikson

Erik Erikson was a psychoanalyst and professor of developmental psychology at Harvard University. Over against Freud's emphasis on abnormal and psychosexual development, Erikson's work focuses on normal development. Erikson's main interest is social roles and self-images as these change over time. He identifies eight stages of an epigenetic cycle in which persons make choices in response to a culture's established tasks and prescribed social forms.[16]

Erikson's theory combines insights from biology, ego psychology, and anthropology in analyzing how a person's sense of body, self, and role in society interface at different points in life. In other words, he maintains that the formation of the ego is a biologically based, psychologically located, socially shaped, and culturally controlled and articulated process. Development through the life span, described as epigenesis, follows a conflict/resolution process throughout life.[17] Table 6 charts Erikson's eight stages with their corresponding personal, social, and cultural contexts.[18]

In relation to Levin's scheme, Erikson's theory can be described as developmental, equally biological and social, affective, primarily microscopic, and differential; it also emphasizes discontinuity and a combination of activity and passivity or receptivity. Like Piaget, Erikson can be criticized by those who place greater emphasis on opposing or distinct stances in any of the seven issues along Levin's scheme. But beyond these criticisms, Erikson's theory must be questioned in relation to its basic assumptions.

First, Erikson assumes that the human personality develops according to steps predetermined in the growing person's readiness to be driven toward, to be aware of, and to interact with a widening social radius. Thus for Erikson, society becomes a partner in development, challenging and supporting the growing individual. Vitality comes as the developing person realizes a new sense with each successive stage.[19]

Second, Erikson assumes that society, in principle, tends to be so constituted as to meet and invite this succession of potentialities for

16. Gabriel Moran, *Religious Education Development: Images for the Future* (Minneapolis: Winston, 1983), 25.

17. Loder, "Developmental Foundations," 56–58.

18. Ibid., 59.

19. G. Temp Sparkman, *The Salvation and Nurture of the Child of God: The Story of Emma* (Valley Forge: Judson, 1983), 255.

Table 6 **Erikson's Epigenetic Cycle Model**

Stage	Psychological Crises	Radius of Significant Relations	Related Elements of the Social Order	Rudiments of Ego Strength
1	Basic trust vs. basic mistrust	Maternal person	Religion and the cosmic order	Hope
2	Autonomy vs. shame, doubt	Paternal person	Law and social order	Will
3	Initiative vs. guilt	Basic family	Theater and ideal prototypes	Purpose
4	Industry vs. inferiority	Neighborhood and school	Technological elements	Competence
5	Identity vs. role confusion	Peer groups, models of leadership	Ideological perspectives	Fidelity
6	Intimacy vs. isolation	Partners in friendship, sex, competition, cooperation	Patterns of cooperation and competition	Love
7	Generative vs. stagnation	Divided labor and shared household	Currents of education and tradition	Care
8	Ego integrity vs. despair	Humankind "My kind"	Collective wisdom	Wisdom

interaction and attempts to safeguard and to encourage the proper rate and sequence of their enfolding. Thus Erikson views the relationship between individuals and society as primarily cooperative and mutually supportive provided there is a positive resolution of each of the successive crises. Yet he does not dismiss the possibilities of negative resolutions at each stage which reappear at later stages.

Third, Erikson does not regard a given stage as an achievement. The negatives always remain as dynamic counterparts. Because persons are engaged continuously with the crises and pressures of life, no one stage is resolved once and for all.

In response to Erikson's first assumption, it can be pointed out that a Christian world view can accommodate the place of development, but perhaps not in such predetermined ways. Erikson's second assumption must be seriously questioned if one believes that individuals can influence their society. Societies vary in fostering the development of all persons; Erikson, while recognizing the place of personal choice, may diminish the role of persons as agents of transformation and reform. Erikson's third assumption indicates the open-ended character of development which is subject to changing conditions. A Christian world view affirms the continual processes of sanctification and/or deformation in human life. In this respect, Erikson is more sensitive to the exigencies of historical and cultural developments than other developmentalists, such as Piaget and Kohlberg. Whereas Erikson does not include supernatural forces as a possible source of changing conditions in human life, the Christian educator recognizes the continual operation of God in the lives of persons. The Holy Spirit is God's agent for continual renewal not only in the lives of persons, but also in the structures of society.

Erikson's conceptions of psychosocial development provide the Christian educator with working hypotheses in assessing the affective dimensions of persons' lives at various stages. The virtues of Erikson's psychosocial crises must be critiqued in relation to a lack of sensitivity to the unique distinctives of female development and Christian virtues which transcend his categories.[20] Nevertheless, Erikson's sensitivity to the larger society and cultural distinctives is noteworthy.

Moral Development: Lawrence Kohlberg

Lawrence Kohlberg is most typically associated with moral development theory. His perspective is quite similar to Piaget's in stressing the structures of cognitive reasoning in relation to moral judgment. He is not so much concerned with the content of moral development as with the structures or forms of the reasoning process that lead a person to decide on a certain solution to a moral dilemma. Moral reasoning is the primary and determinative factor in moral education for Kohlberg. He identifies three major moral levels: the preconventional, the conventional, and the postconventional or principled level (see table 7).

Movement through these three levels takes a person from the pursuit of self-interest, to adherence to external standards, to the affirmation of internal autonomous principles. This developmental sequence raises serious questions from the perspective of Christian faith. Nicholas Wolterstorff points out that Kohlberg is concerned with form to the exclusion of content or substance.[21] Moral development includes more than moral reasoning. Moral behavior can be seen to encompass moral judgment, the situation and its pressures, individual motives and emotions, and a sense of will. Moral judgment entails both moral reasoning (Kohlberg's exclusive emphasis) and moral content. Thus moral development is more complex than Kohlberg believes it to be.

In addition to Kohlberg's limited focus on form or moral reasoning, he must be criticized for his emphasis on autonomy as the highest level

20. See Moran, *Religious Education Development*, 29–40, for an elaboration of these criticisms.
21. Wolterstorff, *Educating for Responsible Action*, 79–100.

Table 7 **Kohlberg's Moral Development Model**

Preconventional Level	*Stage 1* *(ages 6–8)*	Punishment and obedience orientation (Will I get caught? Will I get punished?)
	Stage 2 *(ages 8–10)*	Instrumental, relativist orientation (What is in it for me?)
Conventional Level	*Stage 3* *(ages 10–12)*	Interpersonal, concordance orientation (What do others expect of me? How can I please adults as the nice girl/good boy?)
	Stage 4 *(ages 12–15)*	Law-and-order orientation (What does the law say? What is my duty?)
Postconventional Level	*Stage 5* *(ages 15+)*	Social contract and consensus orientation (What is the group's agreement and my personal obligation in this matter?)
	Stage 6	Universal ethical principles orientation (What is my principle that has universal significance?)

of moral development. This suggests that morality is based on universal principles derived solely from autonomous individual reasoning. Such a stance diminishes the place of a normative community and relationships within that community which are fundamental to the Christian faith.[22] Rather than a stance of autonomy, the Christian faith involves a theonomy, where persons are dependent upon God and interdependent with others within the Christian and human community. It is in this context that moral development becomes a possibility for the Christian. God introduces new possibilities into the process of moral development and addresses persons beyond the categories of Kohlberg's stages. Yet while a theistic world view emphasizes relationships in a community, it does not do so to the exclusion of individuality and autonomy within proper bounds. Such bounds include the faith premise that persons are creatures of God and must live in relation to God and all creation.

In relation to Levi's scheme, Kohlberg's viewpoint can be described as developmental, social, cognitive, microscopic, and differential, emphasizing discontinuity and activity. He is distinct from Piaget in his emphasis on the social dimension of life. But this social dimension is viewed only in terms of individuals having a reference point for their individual reasoning and not in terms of the basic human orientation of relationship and community which undergirds a Christian world view.

A number of theorists have explored Judeo-Christian alternatives to

22. Kirk E. Farnsworth, "Furthering the Kingdom in Psychology," in *The Making of a Christian Mind: A Christian World View and the Academic Enterprise,* ed. Arthur F. Holmes (Downers Grove, Ill.: Inter-Varsity, 1985), 90–93.

Kohlberg in light of his limitations.[23] Donald Joy is one evangelical educator who has made significant contributions in this area. Joy recognizes some common ground between a Christian world view and Kohlberg in the following areas: (1) justice is complex and comprehensive; (2) justice is the core of morality; (3) justice, hence morality, is a function of perception; (4) human persons are held in positive regard; and (5) human persons are morally accountable.

But moving beyond Kohlberg to evangelical distinctives, Joy suggests four hypotheses: (1) morality originates outside of humanity; (2) justice is the core of that outside morality and also is the core attribute of the character of God; (3) human morality is bestowed upon persons as the image bearers of God; and (4) since human persons are both moral and free, substantial research and theory is needed to consider moral failure, that is, sin and rebellion, in relation to the transcendent divine grace from which meaning and purpose are derived.[24]

Joy's emphasis on justice is certainly crucial in a world plagued by injustice. But an exclusive focus on justice truncates what Doug Sholl has identified as the sevenfold pattern of Christian relational content. Sholl suggests the following pattern: love and justice, truth and faithfulness, forbearance and patience, forgiveness and repentance, edification and encouragement, humility and submission, and prayer and praise.[25] Sholl's pattern indicates that moral development theory must consider the multifaceted network of human relationships which from a Christian and biblical perspective embody a plurality of virtues.

Having elaborated the positive side of moral development, it is necessary to consider amoral development. This consideration is critical given the Christian understanding that human persons are more than both moral and free; they are also fallen and responsible. But beyond the consideration of personal or individual amoral development, evangelical educators must consider the effects of amoral or immoral development on the various institutions and structures of society, including the church, family, school, and community in general.

The work of Richard H. DeLone for the Carnegie Council on Children

23. A good introductory work for exploring these alternatives is Donald Joy, ed., *Moral Development Foundations: Judeo-Christian Alternatives to Piaget/Kohlberg* (Nashville: Abingdon, 1983).

24. Donald Joy, "Kohlberg Revisited: A Supra-Naturalist Speaks His Mind," in *Moral Development Foundations: Judeo-Christian Alternatives to Piaget/Kohlberg*, ed. Donald Joy (Nashville: Abingdon, 1983), 188.

25. Doug Sholl, "Unity and Uniqueness: A Theology of Christian Relationships," in *Moral Development Foundations: Judeo-Christian Alternatives to Piaget/Kohlberg*, ed. Donald Joy (Nashville: Abingdon, 1983), 188. In addition, see Craig Dykstra, *Vision and Character: A Christian Educator's Alternative to Kohlberg* (New York: Paulist Press, 1981), 10, for a discussion of virtues other than justice.

in the late 1970s is particularly helpful in understanding the general insensitivity to corporate amoral development on the part of those concerned for the education of children and others in the United States. DeLone maintains that beliefs in child development have traditionally included the following: individual adult characteristics determine social status; those adult characteristics are substantially determined by characteristics developed in childhood; the microenvironment of the family, without reference to the society or macroenvironment in which it is embedded, is what substantially determines the way children develop. These beliefs have been maintained in a context characterized by cultural blindness to the significance of social structure and the dynamics of structure in the lives of persons. As an alternative to this belief system (which evangelicals have for the most part implicitly affirmed), DeLone suggests a theory of human development which takes account of social structures as influences in shaping individual growth, in shaping moral development. In order to do this, Christian educators must consider the significance of diverse social structures, the role of individuals as active participants in their own development, and the importance of history, both personal and social, as the medium within which development occurs.[26] Without such considerations, the Christian educator has a truncated view of development and does not move beyond a concern for moral psychology to consider a moral sociology, a moral philosophy, and a moral theology that views all of life under the lordship and sovereignty of Christ.

In considering amoral development on the corporate and societal level, evangelicals must not only assess how the local church is a positive, inclusive, intergenerational community that fosters the moral development of both individuals and the extended family of faith; they must also assess how the local church excludes certain individuals and is unresponsive to their needs resulting in alienation and the loss of community. Evangelicals must not only consider how the family can be a center for nurture and support, but also how it has been subject to various societal pressures resulting in increased neglect and abuse.

Evangelicals must not only consider how various schooling choices can foster intellectual, social, and moral development, but also how they may operate to limit persons and be agents of continued oppression in the lives of certain persons. Evangelicals must not only consider the negative impacts of the media—in particular commercial television—they may also explore and support the positive uses of various media for the extension of God's kingdom. Evangelicals must not only affirm the

26. Richard H. DeLone, *Small Futures: Children, Inequality and the Limits of Liberal Reform* (New York: Harcourt Brace Jovanovich, 1979), 113–70.

positive results of a world capitalist system which has increased the possibilities of choice by some persons living in certain societies, they must also assess the impact of this system on persons in "developing" or "undeveloped" nations and the increased poverty unaddressed by various development programs. Similar concerns must be raised in relation to socialist economies.

Moral and amoral development must be seen in these broader terms if persons are to be and become all that God has intended for those created to reflect God's image in their lives. The perspective suggested in this analysis seems to be overwhelming, but to opt for a less comprehensive focus is to deny the complexity of life as created by God and the resources present in the Christian community made available by divine grace.

Evangelical educators must also evaluate Kohlberg in terms of his approach to moral education. Kohlberg identifies three types of moral education: indoctrinative moral education, values clarification, and cognitive-developmental moral education. The indoctrinative approach includes the preaching and training of cultural rules and values. Kohlberg considers this approach an imposition. Values clarification involves eliciting a person's own judgment or opinion about moral issues or situations in which values conflict, rather than imposing the teacher's opinion on the students. The end of this effort is to enable students to become more self-aware of personal values. This approach assumes a value relativity in contrast with the identification of absolutes in the indoctrinative approach. Kohlberg prefers the cognitive-developmental approach, intended to foster movement to progressive stages of moral reasoning through the teacher's suggestion of reasoning at the next higher level to that level manifested by participants in the discussion.[27]

A Christian response to Kohlberg's cognitive-developmental approach could affirm his emphasis on discussion while recognizing his misplaced hope that discussion will so affect moral reasoning to influence moral development and behavior as well. Evangelicalism maintains the need for radical transformation in order to bring about change in moral life. Without such a transformation and the continuing operation of God's grace, moral development cannot be adequately addressed.

Nicholas Wolterstorff suggests an alternative to Kohlberg's approach in suggesting that the best way to have children internalize Christian values and a tendency to act responsibly in the light of those values is for a person (parent, teacher, friend) "who acts lovingly toward the child to combine discipline and modeling with the enunciation of a moral

27. Lawrence Kohlberg, "The Cognitive-Developmental Approach to Moral Education," *Phi Delta Kappan* (June 1975):673–75.

standard which the child perceives to fit the situations and on which he or she is willing to act."[28] Wolterstorff's suggestion must be explored as a viable alternative.

Faith Development: James Fowler

James Fowler has developed a stage theory of faith development, building upon the work of Piaget in cognitive development and Kohlberg in moral development. Fowler views faith as active, as a verb. Faith is a process of becoming rather than something a person possesses. This process involves continual growth through stages that are hierarchical (increasingly complex and qualitative), sequential (appearing one after the other in the life span), invariant (following the same order for all persons), and universal (applying to all cultural and societal settings.)

Fowler identifies seven categories which distinguish persons in various stages: form of logic, role-taking, form of moral judgment, bounds of social awareness, focus of authority, form of world coherence, and role of symbols. Fowler is concerned to distinguish the forms or structures of faith and attempts to address both cognitive and affective dimensions of faith, or the rational and the passional dimensions.

Fowler's six stages of faith development are as follows:

1. *Intuitive-projective faith.* Young children up to about age seven reflect the visible faith of their parents.
2. *Mythic-literal faith.* In later childhood the person takes on beliefs of persons other than parents. Some adults remain in stage 2.
3. *Synthetic-conventional faith.* Early teens conform to their "gang." Faith begins to synthesize life's increasing complexity. Many adults who are strongly influenced by peers are in stage 3.
4. *Individuative-reflective faith.* In late teens and early adulthood, the focus is on adult responsibility for one's own commitments and beliefs—doubting, questioning, and rejecting traditional assumptions. This is the period in which individual values are developed.
5. *Conjunctive faith.* A mature faith-stage, seldom found before age thirty (and often never reached), incorporates the integrity of positions other than one's own, and responds to an identification beyond race, class, or ideological boundaries. Stage 5 adults integrate traditional positions, their own doubts, and the views of others into a meaningful whole.
6. *Universalizing faith.* Persons in this stage are rare, with few "spir-

28. Wolterstorff, *Educating for Responsible Action,* 109.

itual giants" achieving it. Faith is a universal in which the individual identifies beyond self with God as a felt reality.[29]

In relation to Levin's categories, Fowler's work can be described as developmental, social, primarily cognitive (though inclusive of affective dimensions), microscopic, and differential; it also emphasizes discontinuity and activity rather than passivity. Criticisms can be raised from opposing stances on each of these issues, but the dominant Christian critique of the research and basic assumptions of faith development theory as advocated by Fowler is the exclusion of God as a key factor in the faith process.

Fowler basically seeks to generalize his concept of faith so it has significance for all persons—whether or not they espouse a theistic world and life view. Fowler's "faith" stands in contrast to the Reformation concept of faith as solely the gift of God's grace, given uniquely in Jesus Christ. Fowler himself recognizes that critics protest his use of the term *faith* which is an indigenously Christian category.[30]

Furthermore, Fowler's methods of individual interviews, though providing some helpful insights for ways in which persons describe their faith commitments, restrict the relational and communal complexity of faith which must include consideration of the mysterious workings and relationships of God with persons. Fowler essentially opts for the use of the science of developmental psychology to discern the dimensions of faith. This poses a particular problem if one distinguishes faith and science.

The discussion in the previous chapter on the place of science in relation to epistemology serves as background to Huston Smith's pertinent observations. Smith points out that science values control, prediction, objectivity, numbers, and signs. In contrast to science, faith values surrender, surprise, subjectivity and objectivity, words, and symbols. In other words, science primarily deals with the instrumental values of utility, usefulness, service, and control; whereas faith deals with intrinsic values.[31] If one accepts these distinctions, then the limitations of Fowler's efforts must be recognized in addressing the realm of Christian faith.

Although developmental psychology can provide some intellectual concepts or working hypotheses for dealing with the faith of persons,

29. This description was developed by Kenneth Stokes from James W. Fowler, *Stages of Faith: The Psychology of Human Development and the Quest for Meaning* (San Francisco: Harper & Row, 1981), 117–213.

30. Fowler, *Stages of Faith*, 91.

31. Huston Smith, "Excluded Knowledge: A Critique of the Modern Mind Set," *Teachers College Record* (February 1979):419–45.

additional dimensions of faith must be considered beyond Fowler's seven categories. These additional dimensions must recognize the person and work of God and the response of human persons to God which includes surrender, surprise, reverence, awe, and subjectivity. These dimensions are not readily available to scientific inquiry and require of the Christian educator a recognition of the mystery and majesty of faith. Fowler has opted for an understanding of faith that is isolated from the content and beliefs of the Christian faith and that centers upon mental structures instead of the relationships of persons with a living and active God in the context of a Christian community.[32]

A radical alternative to Fowler's work is that suggested by Ruth Beechick, who has adopted the work of Robert Havighurst in outlining the spiritual development of Christians. Havighurst identifies different roles which persons assume in life, such as child, friend, organization member, worker, spouse, parent, church member, and user of leisure time. In relation to each of these roles Beechick defines key developmental tasks which persons are to fulfill at various ages.[33] Beechick's work can be summarized in the following outline of spiritual developmental tasks.[34]

Spiritual Developmental Tasks

I. Preschool Years
   A. Experiencing love, security, discipline, joy, and worship
   B. Beginning to develop awareness and concepts of God, Jesus, and other basic Christian realities
   C. Developing attitudes toward God, Jesus, church, self, and the Bible
   D. Beginning to develop concepts of right and wrong
II. Elementary School Years
   A. Receiving and acknowledging Jesus Christ as Savior and Lord
   B. Growing awareness of Christian love and responsibility in relationships with others
   C. Continuing to build concepts of basic Christian realities
   D. Learning basic Bible teachings adequate for personal faith and everyday Christian living

32. See Moran, *Religious Education Development*, 107–26, for an expanded critique of Fowler's perspective.

33. See Robert J. Havighurst, *Developmental Tasks and Education* (New York: David McKay, 1961), 72–98. Havighurst defines developmental task as a task which arises at or about a certain period in the life of the individual, successful achievement of which leads to happiness and to success with later tasks, while failure leads to individual unhappiness, social disapproval, and difficulty with later tasks.

34. Ruth Beechick, *Teaching Juniors: Both Heart and Head* (Denver: Accent Books, 1981), 24–25.

       1. Prayer in daily life
       2. The Bible in daily life
       3. Christian friendships
       4. Group worship
       5. Responsibility for serving God
       6. Basic knowledge of God, Jesus, Holy Spirit, creation, angelic beings, heaven, hell, sin, salvation, Bible history, and literature
   E. Developing healthy attitudes toward self

III. Adolescence
   A. Learning to show Christian love in everyday life
   B. Continuing to develop healthy attitudes toward self
   C. Developing Bible knowledge and intellectual skills adequate for meeting intellectual assaults on faith
   D. Achieving strength of Christian character adequate for meeting anti-Christian social pressures
   E. Accepting responsibility for Christian service in accordance with growing abilities
   F. Learning to make life decisions on the basis of eternal Christian values
   G. Increasing self-discipline to "seek those things which are above"

IV. Maturity
   A. Accepting responsibility for one's own continued growth and learning
   B. Accepting biblical responsibilities toward God and toward others
   C. Living a unified, purposeful life centered upon God

Beechick's work represents an effort to provide practical guidelines for the direction of spiritual development in a general ground plan for a Christian education program. This ground plan must be adapted to individual needs and the specific beliefs of given Christian communities, but it does recognize the role of content and the dimension of relationships. Some may interpret this focus as imposition because it appears to program the work of God in persons' lives (e.g., an individual may not come to a personal faith in Jesus Christ until after elementary school). In addition, Beechick's emphasis is on behavior and cognitive concepts to the relative exclusion of essential values, intentions, virtues, affections, and attitudes which characterize the Christian faith.

While both Fowler's and Beechick's work can be criticized, their insights can be helpful in evaluating the effectiveness of existing programs in addressing the unique needs of persons in their faith or spiritual development. Their insights can provide descriptive categories for gaining understanding, rather than exacting prescriptive guidelines for present and future programs. Randall Furushima suggests three implications from this work: (1) programs must be intentionally developed and maintained; (2) curriculum and teaching resources must be critiqued in the light of dominant characteristics which persons in various stages generally manifest; and (3) Christian educators must be trained in the knowledge and anticipation of the multiple dimensions of life through which faith can be expressed. Stages and developmental tasks cannot serve as restrictive labels and categories in which persons are placed, for they must be subject to the greater freedom and creativity of the Holy Spirit who works in the lives of persons.[35] The freedom and creativity of the Holy Spirit are not readily discerned through the methodologies of developmental psychology, but must be valued from a Christian perspective.

Developmental Presumptions

By way of review of the developmental foundations analyzed above, it is possible to identify five presumptions which undergird developmental perspectives. Donald E. Miller has identified these presumptions in his analysis of the developmental approach to Christian education. First, development presumes a ground plan, some sort of preexistent structure through which persons move. For Kohlberg the ground plan is the six stages of moral development, while for Erikson it is the eight stages of epigenesis or psychosocial development. Second, development presumes an invariable sequence. Any stage presumes the previous stage and leads to the next stage. Furthermore, no stage can be skipped, and difficulties in one stage may cause difficulties in a later stage. A person cannot jump from stage 1 to stage 4 in Kohlberg's scheme; and if a child does not develop sufficient basic trust in others at Erikson's stage 1, later development is hindered. Third, development presumes the integration of increasingly complex elements. This integration or synthesis remains stable until challenged by elements that will not fit, at which time the individual is driven through a period of crises toward a new integration. From Erikson's perspective, the growing capacities of the child and the increasing independence from the parents lead to a crisis of the basic trust established and a testing of the parental relationship through a new independence. The toddler is posed with a crisis: Should I obey or should I venture out? A fourth presumption of development is that individual persons interact with their environment. Active interaction with

35. Randall Y. Furushima, "The Developmental Faith of Youth," *New Conversations* 5(Winter 1980–1981):41–42. Also see Randall Y. Furushima, "Faith Development in a Cross Cultural Perspective," *Religious Education* 80(Summer 1985):414–20, for an additional evaluation of Fowler's work.

the physical environment provides a sense of reality; active interaction with the social, cultural, and religious environment provides a sense of selfhood, identity, and responsibility. The fifth and final presumption is that development has a goal or end. Development does not just terminate, but rather moves toward a final level of integration that is usually referred to as maturity.[36] For Erikson stage 8 holds the potential of integrity, whereas for Kohlberg, stage 6 represents morally principled maturity as evidenced in the lives of such persons as Gandhi and Martin Luther King, Jr.

In relation to these five presumptions, it is possible to suggest responses from a Christian world view. Christians have not generally specified a detailed ground plan like developmentalists because of their reverence for the complexity of persons created in God's image and their recognition of both the place of history and culture which intrude upon any given structure. Nevertheless, Christians have also affirmed the reality of structure and form in God's creation and the place of development in created life.

In relation to an invariable sequence, a Christian view of persons might be more prone to affirm the place of radical transformation and conversion along with development in understanding changes over time. An emphasis on development provides key insights for Christian commitments to the processes of nurture and sanctification, but such an emphasis appears to be contradictory with Christian commitments to personal and social transformation. Miller suggests such a judgment: "Faith development is contradicted if conversion is so defined that it includes only a one-time dramatic reorientation."[37]

Evangelical or conversionist theology assumes a one-time conversion or justification, but does not exclude the operation of God's prevenient (before coming to saving faith) grace which operates in persons' lives to draw them to Christ. It also does not exclude God's grace as operating subsequent to justification. For some evangelicals, sanctification is an ongoing process along with edification, which is a process of growing in Christ in relation to others. Glorification is the ultimate end or goal of these processes, but nevertheless, these processes assume development. Thus a person can be described as "saved" in being justified, as "being saved" in the process of sanctification and edification, and as "to be saved" in terms of ultimate glorification at the appearing of Jesus Christ. Miller's judgment is correct if conversion as justification is only in view,

36. Donald E. Miller, "The Developmental Approach to Christian Education," in *Contemporary Approaches to Christian Education,* eds. Jack L. Seymour and Donald E. Miller (Nashville: Abingdon, 1982), 76–77.
37. Ibid., 100.

but a fully orbed conversionist theology allows for development in sanctification and edification. Christian persons are being saved on a moment-to-moment basis as God's grace continues to operate in their lives at different stages of development.

In response to the third and fourth presumptions of development, a Christian educator can both affirm the integration of increasingly complex elements and the interaction of persons with their environment. One proviso is the recognition of God as active and intrusive. In other words, interaction with the environment must include the supernatural environment, where God's presence and/or work may intrude upon development to bring out a result that is not directly attributable to what has gone before. This recognizes the place of transformation and conversion through the sovereign operation of the Holy Spirit. The work of the Holy Spirit may build upon and/or negate existing elements of development in ways that bring a creative and dynamic integration which otherwise was not possible.

The fifth presumption of development can also be critiqued in the light of Christian commitments. Christian educators emphasize the ultimate goal or end of glorifying and enjoying God. In relation to Jesus Christ, the goal of Christians is that they will be like him at his appearing and that all creation will be renewed. This complex integration of all of life transcends the categories of developmental schemes yet also includes them to the extent to which they embody God's will. Is it God's will that all persons be at stage 6 of Kohlberg's and Fowler's schemes? This question is indeed problematic when the vision of life shared by Christian sources is compared with these attempts to provide a description of maturity, wholeness, and integrity. The Christian vision focuses upon the person and work of Jesus Christ, who is the author and perfector or finisher of faith. Descriptions of the goal or end of development grow pale in the light of his face.

One final question to be raised in relation to the developmental perspectives surveyed in this chapter is one which was raised earlier in relation to Kohlberg's work. A focus upon individual or personal development must not exclude consideration of corporate and social structures and relationships which impinge upon development. These too are realities of the created world and must be scrutinized in relation to the demands of the gospel and the development of persons. To neglect the corporate dimension is to truncate a Christian world view.

An Interactive Biblical Model

In the effort to provide some form and structure in what may appear to be a web of psychological chaos, the following model is proposed which seeks to integrate developmental concepts with a biblical anthropology (see fig. 11).[38] This model is but one model and must be supplemented by other models in the attempt to provide some understanding regarding persons. The terms which designate different points on this network are those current in the field of human development. Human development theorists place different emphasis on these terms suggested, nevertheless the attempt here is not to advocate one or another emphasis. Rather, this model serves to identify the various dimensions of persons suggested by biblical sources which must be considered in ministering to and teaching persons.

God's sovereignty and grace serve as both the umbrella and foundation of this model. God's providential care and grace is a faith understanding that follows from the doctrine of creation. Questions have been raised regarding God's sovereignty in the midst of human exigencies and suffering, but a Christian world view affirms this perspective on human life.

Heredity is the genetic and structural nature and makeup of persons which they receive from parents and ancestors. There are biological, cognitive, and emotional aspects of heredity. At the beginning of life the social fabric is evident; a biblical perspective also suggests the presence of a spiritual heritage or inheritance which operates in the human family. This spiritual heritage centers upon the faith affirmations that persons are created in God's image, male and female; that persons are fallen in sin; and that persons can be recreated or transformed by Christ. By

FIGURE 11   Integration of Developmental Concepts
with Biblical Anthropology

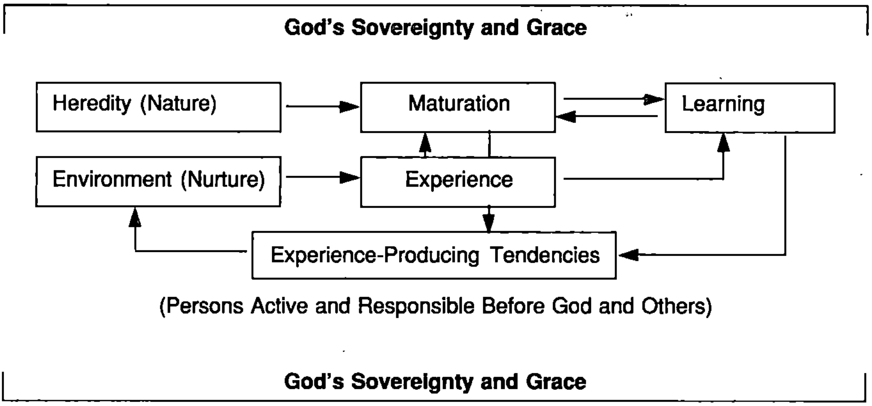

38. I am indebted to Gerald R. Levin for this model, taken from his lectures at Bucknell University, Lewisburg, Pa., September–December 1969.

virtue of their created nature, persons have intrinsic dignity and are worthy of respect, love, and service in all areas of their lives. By virtue of their fallen nature, persons are in need of instruction, correction, and discipline which recognizes the necessary operation of God's grace. Sin is manifest in both personal and social interactions and amoral as well as moral development is a concern. By virtue of Christ's life, death, and resurrection, persons can potentially experience renewal and transformation in their lives at various points and in various dimensions that include both personal and corporate realities.

Maturation refers to biological growth processes that unfold the hereditary nature of persons. Maturation is distinguished from learning. If a behavior matures through regular stages irrespective of intervening practice, the behavior is said to develop through maturation and not through learning. One example of maturation is the reflexes which newborns manifest at birth irrespective of practice and intervening experience. Having made this distinction, it must be pointed out that many activities develop through a complex interplay of maturation and learning. The Old Testament uses various words to describe children at different ages, suggestive of a maturation process:

yeled—a newborn baby (Exod. 1:17)

yônēq—a nursing child (1 Sam. 15:3)

'ôlēl—a young child beginning to ask for food (Lam. 4:4)

gĕmûl—a weaned child (Isa. 28:9)

ṭap—little children clinging to their mothers (Jer. 40:7)

naar—a growing child who "shakes free" (Isa. 11:6)

bāḥûr—a young adolescent, twelve to fourteen years of age (a "ripened one," Isa. 31:8)

In 1 Corinthians 13:11, Paul states "When I was a child, I talked like a child, I thought like a child, I reasoned like a child. . . ." Children's ways of knowing are distinct from those of adults and change as a result of maturation. The observation of infants and children at various ages confirms the biblical descriptions.

As a psychological term, learning has been defined as the process by which behavior or the potentiality for behavior is modified as a result of experience. Learning can also be defined as the process of change in knowledge, beliefs, values, attitudes, feelings, skills, or behaviors as a result of experience with the natural or supernatural environment. In relation to their created nature, persons are called to learn to love, live in, and obey God within the grasp of their understanding and ability.

God's grace enables persons to learn in ways that fulfill divine expectations for and gifts to humanity. The greatest challenge is for Christians to be involved in lifelong learning in communities that provide such access to them at points of readiness. Learning most often involves a handling of a cultural heritage in one form or another.

Environment denotes the total context in which a person grows or develops. Physical, psychological, familial, communal, economic, political, social, cultural, educational, aesthetic, and religious dimensions of the environment affect persons. Those theorists and practitioners in the field of human services who emphasize the impact of the environment upon persons are said to maintain a "nurture" stance as compared with those who emphasize the impacts of heredity upon persons (a "nature" stance). Locke stressed the role of the environment upon persons viewed as blank slates, whereas Rousseau emphasized the unfolding of each person's nature given at birth. Key biblical passages emphasize the need for adults to consider the environment for the nurture of children. Both Deuteronomy 6:4–10 and Psalm 78:1–8 emphasize parental responsibilities for passing on to the next generation God's commandments and accounts of God's historical activities. Ephesians 6:4 admonishes parents not to exasperate their children, but to bring them up in the training and instruction of the Lord.

The environment in its variety of expressions influences people via experiences. Personal experiences are the only direct experiences persons have. In particular, the world of children is an experiential world and persons who raise or teach children must be aware of this. The Book of Proverbs is a guidebook of practical wisdom for supervising the experiences of others. A frequently quoted verse addressing the experiences of children is Proverbs 22:6: "Train a child in the way he should go, and when he is old he will not turn from it." "Way" can refer to the child's natural endowments and disposition or the intention of the child's mentors.[39] The first interpretation is to be preferred, as it emphasizes the need to be sensitive to each child, respecting her or his unique, God-given individuality. This perspective stresses the need to allow for creative self-fulfillment and a careful reading of each person's character. In raising children, the stress is upon choosing what God wants them to be and do and not forcing them to conform to the parents' way.[40] These insights regarding children also apply to the experiences of youth and adults.

39. J. Coert Rylaarsdam, "The Proverbs," in *Peakes's Commentary on the Bible,* eds. Matthew Black and H. H. Rowley (London: Nelson & Sons, 1962), 454.

40. Marvin J. Wilson, "The Hebrew Model of Education," lecture presented at Gordon-Conwell Theological Seminary, South Hamilton, Mass., 17 September 1977.

Although people are influenced by their inborn nature and the nurture they receive, they are active as well as receptive. In Isaiah 29:22–23, children's very presence is said to be a reminder of God's faithfulness. Scripture affirms the place of children in ministering to God and others (1 Sam. 1–3). The psalmist declares that from the lips of children and infants God has ordained praise (Ps. 8:2). From the very beginnings of life, persons are active and responsible before God at the level of their understanding and competence. They have experience-producing tendencies.

God created persons with minds and wills and a disposition to gain competence and abilities in a vast variety of endeavors. Often despite limitations, people express their curiosity, creativity, and uniqueness. Where diversity is affirmed in human responses, educators in the home, church, school, and community witness the capabilities of persons to initiate activity and gain experience which affects the environment and potentials for learning. As indicated in the model, a person's experience-producing tendencies are influenced by previous learning and maturation, and the impact of nature and nurture cannot be precisely predicted given the reality of a person's own active engagement with such influences. Therefore, no guarantees of what outcomes will occur can be assured in any educational setting. This means, for instance, that identical twins may have similar home and educational influences and yet gain different perspectives and learn different things.

A complex web of elements must be accounted for in considering a biblical view of persons. Various theorists have stressed one element or another, but careful consideration must be made of each of the suggested elements in the model. In recent scholarship and research, serious questions have been raised regarding dominant developmental understandings which have excluded and devalued the unique characteristics of women in their development. In particular, the work of Carol Gilligan in *In a Different Voice: Psychological Theory and Women's Development* has served to pose fundamental challenges for traditional ways of understanding persons.[41] Gilligan points out the need to consider attachments along with separations in development, and the need to affirm affiliation and interconnection as well as achievement. She focuses on responsibility and care in addition to justice and personal rights in considering moral development. These conceptions, along with others, serve to promote the formulation of a wholistic understanding of persons more in harmony with a Christian world view. As God's creatures, per-

41. Carol Gilligan, *In a Different Voice: Psychological Theory and Women's Development* (Cambridge: Harvard University Press, 1982).

sons are multifaceted in their makeup and relationships, and this must be reflected in both theoretical and practical conceptualizations.

The interactive model proposed above does not claim to be the final word in considering the psychological foundations of education, but it does suggest a framework for considering the unique complexities of persons created by God. Beyond the insights of such an analysis is the affirmation that persons are whole and that each individual is unique, and worthy of our consideration, concern, and care. To do otherwise is to distort the image of the Creator in each one of us.

7

Curricular Foundations

The Christian educator must make decisions that directly affect the actual practice of education. These decisions are particularly necessary in the planning, implementation, and evaluation of curriculum. Christian educators must explore curricular foundations with a focus on concrete realities and a concern to develop practical guidelines.

An issue of immediate concern in considering curriculum is that of definition. Various definitions and conceptions of curriculum have been suggested reflecting distinct value orientations and commitments in the field. Among suggested definitions are the following:

1. Curriculum is the content made available to students. (Dwayne Huebner)[1]
2. Curriculum is the planned and guided learning experiences of students. (John Dewey)[2]
3. Curriculum is the actual experiences of a student or participant. (Alice Miel)[3]

1. Dwayne F. Huebner, "From Theory to Practice: Curriculum," *Religious Education* 77(July–August 1982):363.
2. John Dewey, *Experience and Education* (New York: Macmillan, 1944), 16, 86.
3. Alice Miel, *Changing the Curriculum: A Social Process* (New York: Appleton-Century-Crofts, 1946), 9.

4. Generally, curriculum includes both the materials and the experiences for learning. Specifically, curriculum is the written courses for study used for Christian education. (Iris Cully)[4]
5. Curriculum is the organization of learning activities guided by a teacher with the intent of changing behavior. (Lois LeBar)[5]

Some theorists refer to curriculum as that which is planned or intended by educators, whereas instruction is that which is actually experienced by students. In this case, that which is experienced may be quite similar or quite distinct from that which is planned or intended. In contrast with this distinction, the definition of curriculum must include aspects of instruction. Curriculum is that content made available to students and their actual learning experiences guided by a teacher. This definition implies that the teacher must assume responsibility in terms of content and experience in the planning, implementation, and evaluation of teaching.

In justifying this perspective, the comments of LeBar are helpful. She observes that Christian content without experience is empty and that experience without content is blind.[6] The challenge in curriculum construction is to merge both Christian content and experience so that the minds and lives of students are influenced and transformed by God's truth. An exclusive emphasis on content in orthodoxy (right belief) can ignore the essential dimension of Christian experience, without which Christian education is empty. Likewise, an exclusive emphasis on experience in orthopraxis (right practice) can ignore the essential dimension of Christian content, without which Christian education is blind. An effective curriculum weds Christian content and experience and thereby is life transforming.

No simple formula to accomplish an adequate blending of content and experience exists, but certain guidelines can be shared. The teacher is called to be knowledgeable and sensitive to dimensions of the content and to the various experiences of the students. Through this knowledge and sensitivity, a teacher can tailor the presentation of material to her or his students. This blending implies complementary concerns for truth and love in a Christian world view.

Truth is the essential content of Christian teaching—truth as revealed in Scripture through the ministry of the Holy Spirit, and truth as dis-

4. Iris Cully, *Planning and Selecting Curriculum for Christian Education* (Valley Forge: Judson, 1983), 11–12.

5. Lois E. LeBar, *Education That Is Christian*, rev. ed. (Old Tappan, N.J.: Fleming H. Revell, 1981), 211.

6. Lois E. LeBar, "Curriculum," in *An Introduction to Evangelical Christian Education*, ed. J. Edward Hakes (Chicago: Moody, 1964), 89.

cerned in the creation. All truth is God's truth. Love is the medium through which truth is effectively communicated. Christians are commanded to love and witness about their faith through this love (John 13:34, 35). The Scriptures blend these two virtues in the exercise of Christian ministry. In Ephesians 4:15, Paul describes the need to speak the truth in love. In 2 John 1–2, John describes his relationship with the chosen lady and her children, most likely referring to a church and its members. He states that he loves these persons in the truth because of the truth that lives within them. Therefore, in order to blend both content and experience, the Christian teacher must faithfully live out a concern for both truth and love in the content of his or her teaching and the experience of students.

A concern for truth not tempered by an equal concern for love can lead to harshness. A concern for love not tempered by an equal concern for truth can lead to license. Truth without love becomes hard, whereas love without truth becomes soft. Too often evangelical Christians have so proclaimed the truth to a world in need of love, that the gospel message has gone unheeded because it is inappropriately hard. Likewise, liberal Christians have so often emphasized love to a world in need of hearing God's truth that the gospel message has been viewed as insignificant because it is inappropriately soft. This limited analysis of evangelicals and liberals points out the desperate need for a balanced curriculum in dealing with just these two essential Christian virtues.

Basic Questions

Decisions regarding curricula are crucial because it is through the curriculum that educational values and commitments actually become embedded in practice. Curriculum is the vehicle or medium through which educational vision takes roots. In relation to decisions regarding curriculum, several basic questions are either explicitly or implicitly answered by those involved in the process.

What specifically should be taught? In answering this question, areas of knowledge, understanding, values, attitudes, and skills can be identified by the Christian educator. Biblical and theological basics are essential to set down at this point along with areas of the Christian life that are to be addressed. Even at the youngest ages, theological concepts can be experienced by children.

Why should these areas be taught? In answering this question, the educator outlines general purposes and specific goals as discerned through Bible study, prayer, conscious dependence upon the Holy Spirit, and careful assessment of student needs. Needs must always be compared with God's demands and our responsibilities before God. There are genuine needs, but a culture may define needs which must be questioned in relation to biblical values.

Where is the teaching being done? One's situation affects what can be reasonably accomplished with the given resources and limitations. Unique cultural, social, and economic factors must be considered by the educator. The context of teaching may set clear limits that affect curricular decisions.

How is the teaching to be done? One must consider the most appropriate methods for teaching. A variety of methods consistent with the truths being taught can be used in teaching. In addition, a media-oriented Western society necessitates the use of more visual materials to maintain the interest of students. This "how" question also involves decisions regarding the organization of the content to be taught and the interrelationship of various components of the curriculum that may facilitate the integration and transfer of learning to other situations.

When should various areas be taught? Christian educators discern the readiness of students and teachers to deal with the various areas of the Christian faith selected for teaching. Chronological age and spiritual maturity are factors to consider. A sense of timing is important in relation to previous and anticipated learnings and in relation to unanticipated events.

Who is being taught and who is teaching? Understanding the lives and the needs of students provides an important basis for the choice and development of any curriculum. In addition, Christian educators must understand their own unique gifts, strengths, and weaknesses. All those involved in educational ministries are in need of the personal support and encouragement that characterizes Christian fellowship. Relationships become a vehicle for communicating God's living truth.[7]

Answering these essential educational questions will enable the Christian educator to make specific decisions about the curriculum from an informed perspective. Various other criteria must be explored in dealing with specific ministries. In using teaching materials that are distributed by denominational and independent publishing houses, educators should be in basic agreement with how curriculum writers and editors have answered these six questions and supplement the published curriculum in areas of disagreement. In developing one's own curriculum, agreement may be assured, but the writing of curriculum can be consuming in terms of material and time resources.

If one chooses to use published curriculum, several key areas must be explored. First, does the theology of the publisher and curriculum

7. Thomas Groome poses these basic questions in *Christian Religious Education: Sharing Our Story and Vision* (San Francisco: Harper & Row, 1980), xiv.

writers agree with the theology of the particular church or ministry? Are theological concepts appropriate for various age levels and comprehensive in exposure?

Second, does the curriculum affirm the Scriptures as authoritative? Is the whole counsel of God addressed in the sequence of the curriculum across the age groups?

Third, are the activities for learners varied and relevant to their life situations? Are students actively involved in the learning and challenged to deal with appropriate questions of the Christian faith?

Fourth, do the lesson plans allow for adapting materials to deal with time constraints, available resources, class size, and differing student ability? Can inexperienced teachers effectively use the materials?

Fifth, does the material deal with the needs, interests, and concerns of students? Are students provided with appropriate ways in which to apply Christian truth and encouraged to respond to the lordship of Christ in all areas of their lives?

Finally, are the layout, colors, and quality of the materials attractive and attention-getting? Are racial and sexual representations appropriate? Can the curriculum be used more than once?

The comparative importance of positive responses to each of these questions must be determined by those evaluating a variety of published curricula. Evaluators need to be aware of the strengths and weaknesses of published materials and the unique needs of their particular education setting. It may be helpful to develop scales for comparing curricula in the areas mentioned. Additional questions beyond those suggested may need to be asked. Once a curriculum is chosen, the greater task is equipping teachers to effectively use and adapt that choice to their individual classes. Teacher training sessions can be planned to assist teachers in this area.

If the choice is made to develop one's own curriculum, the Christian educator must consider questions of continuity, sequence, and integration. Continuity is a measure of the extent to which biblical, theological, or life-related themes are adequately repeated for any one age group throughout the course of study. Sequence is a measure of how current teaching and learning builds upon previous learning and contributes to future learning. Integration assesses the extent to which efforts in one aspect of the educational program, such as church school, relate to other aspects, such as Sunday worship and youth group activities. These are questions that are generally addressed by publishers, but are frequently overlooked in personalized curricula.

Any decision concerning curriculum must be eclipsed by a greater concern for the life and ministry of the teacher herself or himself. The teacher needs to consciously rely upon the guidance of the Holy Spirit and demonstrate a genuine love for his or her students. God's curriculum transcends published or developed materials, and teachers must be flexible in the use and adaptation of the curriculum. The teacher herself or himself is a key element of the curriculum in teaching ministries. Paul's instructions to Timothy illustrate this perspective in 1 Timothy 4:11, 12, 16: "Command and teach these things. Don't let anyone look down on you because you are young, but set an example for the believers in speech, in life, in love, in faith and in purity. . . . Watch your life and doctrine closely. Persevere in them, because if you do, you will save both yourself and your hearers." Timothy is encouraged to consider not only his teaching or doctrine, but also his life, as it teaches by way of example.

Proposed Metaphors for Curriculum

Herbert M. Kliebard has provided an insightful analysis of the metaphorical roots of curriculum design. He identifies three metaphors that have influenced the thought and practice of curriculum making in both general and Christian education: production, growth, and travel.[8] Figure 12 places these metaphors along a continuum. One pole emphasizes teacher direction and the other pole, student direction.

It is helpful to explore these metaphors as they relate to curricular decisions. Each of these metaphors will be discussed in terms of its general description, view of the teacher and teaching, advocates, and potential strengths and weaknesses.

The Metaphor of Production

In this metaphor, the curriculum is the means of production in education, while students are the raw material which will be transformed into a finished and useful product under the control of highly skilled technicians, namely, the teachers. The outcome of production is carefully plotted in advance according to rigid design specifications with a concern to eliminate waste and maximize efficiency. Other descriptors of this approach are "teacher-directed education," or "pedagogy," refer-

FIGURE 12   Curriculum Metaphors

Metaphor	Production	Travel	Growth
Emphasis	Teacher-directed	Mutually directed	Student-directed
View of Teaching	Science	Science–Art	Art

8. Herbert M. Kliebard, "The Metaphorical Roots of Curriculum Design," in *Curriculum Theorizing: The Reconceptualists,* ed. William Pinar (Berkeley: McCutchan, 1975), 84–85.

ring to the art and science of teaching children. Student learning goals in this metaphor are structured competitively by teachers with a concern to shape students in relation to predetermined objectives.

The teacher is viewed as a sculptor or social engineer, actively shaping and chipping away at the raw material of the students. Wherever possible, teaching is viewed as a science which specifies, measures, and combines various factors to maximize its impact in the lives of students.

The strongest advocate of this conception in general education is B. F. Skinner, who has stressed the need to shape the behavior of persons through careful and systematic conditioning or behavior modification. In addition, there have been various advocates in the area of instructional design, such as Robert Mager, Robert Gagne, and William E. Hug, who have emphasized efficient management of various educational elements. In the area of curriculum formation, Ralph Tyler developed a rationale that is the dominant framework for curricular planning and writing. The four basic steps of this rationale are identifying education objectives, selecting appropriate learning experiences, organizing learning experiences, and evaluating the learning.[9]

An extensive analysis of Tyler's metaphor is warranted given its dominance in the curriculum field of Christian education. First, its strengths:

1. This framework has generally been successful and popular given its basic rationality. A logical and sequential order is provided.
2. Tyler's framework does not stress minute details in the writing of objectives as compared with Mager and others working in the area of instructional design and technology.
3. It is a powerful model for the technical aspects of curriculum, those aspects that can be measured, quantified, and readily evaluated.
4. Tyler emphasizes a neutrality or value-free position in dealing with competing conceptions for objectives.
5. Tyler defines education as the "process of changing the behavior patterns of people." In so doing, he uses behavior in a broad sense to include thinking, feeling, and action.
6. Tyler views the learner as active in the sense of responding to appropriate input. Learning experiences are to balance discipline and freedom. Thus Tyler's emphasis is distinct from Skinner's

9. Ralph W. Tyler, *Basic Principles of Curriculum and Instruction* (Chicago: University of Chicago Press, 1949). Also see Robert F. Mager, *Preparing Instructional Objectives* (Palo Alto: Fearson, 1962); Robert M. Gagne, *The Conditions of Learning* (New York: Holt, Rinehart & Winston, 1970); and William E. Hug, *Instructional Design and the Media Program* (Chicago: American Library Association, 1975).

commitment to discount the place of human freedom and dignity in education.
7. Tyler's rationale diverts a focus upon testing in curricular planning, placing it instead on objectives of the educational program.[10]

Next, the weaknesses of the metaphor:

1. Philip Jackson, in *Life in the Classrooms*, suggests that Tyler's understanding is oversimplified in relation to what actually goes on in classroom teaching. The ordinary teacher is too busy to focus on preplanned objectives exclusively. Teaching, and therefore curriculum planning, must view the opportunistic nature of classroom interactions. Because the teacher must work with a high degree of uncertainty and ambiguity, albeit creative ambiguity, Tyler's rationale is inadequate.[11]
2. Curriculum planning and implementation is more an art or craft than a science. The imposition of a scientific and systematic approach is therefore not appropriate for the best results.
3. Tyler's rationale can exclude other considerations, such as differing styles of teaching and learning that would limit the effectiveness of identifying common objectives for any group. A teacher must be aware of responsiveness, variety, and flexibility in teaching which this framework does not adequately encourage.
4. The statement or formulation of objectives, which is the crucial step in Tyler's rationale, may not adequately encourage the consideration of one's values and philosophy. Nor may it allow for adequate collaboration with others, including students when appropriate.
5. It is questionable whether stating objectives, when they represent external goals allegedly reached through the manipulation of learning experiences, is a fruitful way to conceive of the process of curricular planning. A broader and more comprehensive approach is called for.
6. Tyler's concept of a learning experience—the interaction between the learner and external conditions in the environment—fails to address interpersonal relationships which are fundamental to teaching and learning.
7. Evaluation may ignore latent outcomes in concentrating on man-

10. Herbert M. Kliebard, "The Tyler Rationale," *School Review* 78(February 1970): 259–72.
11. Philip W. Jackson, *Life in the Classrooms* (New York: Holt, Rinehart & Winston, 1968), 165–66.

ifest and anticipated ones. Latent outcomes, those unanticipated insights or results of teaching often described as incidental learning, may be just as important as stated objectives.[12]

The Metaphor of Growth

In this metaphor, the curriculum is the routine care provided in a greenhouse situation where students grow and develop to their full potential under the wise and patient attention of the teacher. The plants that grow in the greenhouse are of every variety, but the gardener cares for each plant in unique ways so that each comes to flower. Each person is taught in accordance with personal needs; individualized instruction is the norm.

The teacher is viewed as a gardener caring for the individual needs of each growing plant or life. The teacher needs a great deal of sensitivity and insight in order to maximize appropriate growth at various points in development. Every effort is made to accurately discern the unique characteristics of students and the best-tailored plan to foster growth. Teaching from this perspective is perceived as an art, similar to the patient art of nursery care or gardening.

Given the impact of psychology in education, Carl Rogers has been most associated with this perspective.[13] In the field of education, those emphasizing progressive education in the tradition of John Dewey have placed a similar emphasis upon growth and nurture.

The strengths of this metaphor include a focus upon individual needs, a concern for persons beyond their responses, and a freedom to emphasize differences and distinctives. A weakness of this metaphor is its assumption that students are to a certain extent self-directed and capable of pursuing tasks on the basis of increased intrinsic motivation. This metaphor can potentially de-emphasize the place of structure and discipline as necessary prerequisites for growth and creativity. Growth in itself may be an inadequate goal if it is misguided and random.

The Metaphor of Pilgrimage

This metaphor represents a balance between teacher- and student-directed approaches. Students are relatively interdependent with teachers, as compared with being primarily dependent in the teacher-directed metaphor of production and being primarily independent in the student-directed metaphor of growth. Student learning goals are structured in a

12. Kliebard, "Tyler Rationale," 259–72.
13. For an introduction to Rogers's work, see Carl R. Rogers, *Freedom to Learn* (Columbus, Ohio: Charles E. Merrill, 1969); and Carl R. Rogers, *On Becoming a Person: A Therapist's View of Psychotherapy* (Boston: Houghton Mifflin, 1961).

cooperative or collaborative way which assumes a degree of responsibility on the part of students. Teaching is related to a pilgrimage or route over which students will travel under the leadership of an experienced guide or companion. Each traveler or student will be affected differently by the journey since its effect is at least as much a function of the expectations, intelligence, interests, and intentions of the travelers as it is of the contours of the route and the skills of the guide. No effort is made to anticipate the effect on the traveler. But great effort is made to plot the route so that the journey will be as rich, as fascinating, and as memorable as possible.

The teacher is the experienced guide and companion who cares for and stimulates those with whom she or he is traveling. Teaching is viewed as a cooperative endeavor that employs both artistic and scientific elements in such a way that creativity from the realm of art and validity from the realm of science are both preserved.[14]

Those theorists who have emphasized the place of pilgrimage as communicated through story support this metaphor. Both James Fowler and Richard Peace have emphasized the place of pilgrimage as related to development or growth.[15]

This metaphor is appealing given the story nature or narrative quality of human experience. Teachers have served as guides and companions with students in exploring various areas of studies. Possible weaknesses of this metaphor include the time necessary in order to develop personal relationships between teachers and students. It also assumes a measure of creativity and flexibility on the part of the teacher in responding to unique characteristics of the route and the students.

Which metaphor is best and should therefore guide curriculum conceptions and decisions? No simple answer can be given. Sensitivity is required in relation to purposes, content, and student/teacher needs and styles. In teaching a highly technical skill, the metaphor of production would be warranted. In teaching a creative sensitivity that entails individual learning, the metaphor of growth would be best. In teaching a survey course of a richly diverse subject, the metaphor of pilgrimage would be the choice. A larger question at stake in the choice of a metaphor or metaphors in curriculum planning is the question of values.

The Place of Values in Curricular Planning

A curriculum embodies values in relation to those understandings, attitudes, skills, and behaviors shared with students. Values are generally

14. James Michael Lee describes teaching in these terms in *The Flow of Religious Instruction* (Dayton, Ohio: Pflaum/Standard, 1973), 215–21.

15. See James W. Fowler, *Stages of Faith: The Psychology of Human Development and the Quest for Meaning* (San Francisco: Harper & Row, 1981); and Richard Peace, *Pilgrimage: A Workbook on Christian Growth* (Los Angeles: Acton House, 1970).

defined as conceptions to which worth, interest, and goodness have been attributed. Once Christians identify values in education that are consistent with a Christian world and life view, they are under certain obligations to consider those values in curricular planning and teaching. These obligations are fourfold.[16]

First, Christians must own and live out the values they profess. This is a call to integrity in curricular decision making and planning. If Christians affirm the value of individuals as created in the image of God, they must adapt or adjust teaching styles to enable various persons to learn and apply God's truth in ways that are both consistent with God's demands and with their own learning styles. If this is not the case, curricular planning and teaching is subject to the inappropriate imposition of content and method upon students.

If Christians affirm the view of a heavenly parent who disciplines children for their benefit, they must uphold appropriate discipline and order in curricular planning and teaching that benefits students and glorifies God. This obligation is an especially difficult task in a generally undisciplined and unrestrained societal context that ironically also struggles with abuse of various kinds in epidemic proportions. If Christians affirm the creative potential of each person who has been created creative, they must allow for creative expression in curricular planning. A slavish adherence to behavioral objectives in curricular planning may in fact stifle the freedom and open-ended responses necessary for creative expression in the classroom.

A second obligation in curricular planning can be noted. In order to live out Christian values, Christians must translate their values into the purposes and goals of the curriculum. It is often the case that purposes and goals are stated without questioning their relation to the underlying values of a Christian world view. The result is a truncated educational experience that can claim to be Christian in name, but not in substance. For example, all truth is God's truth. This implies the necessity of enabling students to think "Christianly" about any area of study. It also implies the need to integrate truth in various areas to God's truth as revealed in the Bible wherever possible. Furthermore, love and truth must be balanced. In the curriculum, this implies the need to teach the truth and encourage students to love the truth. It also implies the necessity of encouraging love between teacher and students and among students. Whereas these purposes may be viewed as simple and assumed in curricular planning, they are in actuality profound and pervasive in their impact.

A third obligation involves the need to pursue values in the institutional orders of everyday life. These institutional orders include the

16. See the discussion of values in chapter 3, pp. 90–96.

home, the church, the school, the community, the society, and other groups. Values can become so privatized that there is a loss of rootedness in life. Life is inherently social and corporate. Institutions, groups, and communities embody various values which unfortunately are often unexamined. These unexamined values can run counter to those stated values and purposes in the curriculum.

A fourth obligation is related to the constant need for renewal in curricular formation, the need to reaffirm basic values and goals. The real danger of "morphological fundamentalism" exists in curriculum. This term refers to the fact that certain forms or structures may take on the character of being sacred and therefore exempt from question or examination. They become fundamental and essential. With curriculum, this danger implies the need for constant evaluation and adaptation. Change and transformation are realities to consider and plan for in developing any curriculum. Those who use a curriculum must be encouraged to adapt the material to their particular group and setting. Without a certain degree of flexibility and adaptability, a curriculum can become outdated and inappropriate.

The Hidden Curriculum

Elizabeth Vallance points out that the "hidden curriculum" identifies those nonacademic and systematic side effects of education that are sensed, but which cannot be adequately accounted for by reference to the explicit curriculum. She suggests three dimensions along which aspects of the hidden curriculum can be considered:

1. Hidden curriculum can refer to any of the contexts of education, including the student-teacher interaction, the classroom structure, or the whole organizational pattern of the education establishment as a microcosm of the social value system.
2. Hidden curriculum can bear on a number of processes operating in or through schools, churches, or homes, including values acquisition, socialization, and maintenance of a social structure.
3. Hidden curriculum can embrace differing degrees of intentionality, and of depth of "hiddenness," ranging from incidental and quite unintended by-products of curricular arrangements to outcomes more deeply embedded in the historical social function of education in different communities.[17]

17. Elizabeth Vallance, "Hiding the Hidden Curriculum: An Interpretation of the Language of Justification in Nineteenth-Century Educational Reform," *Curriculum Theory Network* 4(1973–1974): 5–21.

How do Vallance's insights relate to Christian education? Examples from one educational context may help. An evangelical college or theological seminary may maintain the following hidden curriculum:

1. Each person in the community should have had a personal experience with Jesus as Lord and Savior.
2. Scholarship, service, discipline, or piety is the highest ideal in Christian ministry.
3. Liberals are to be viewed as enemies of the evangelical faith.
4. Graduates of specific evangelical colleges or institutions are to be revered.
5. A faithful evangelical is a member of the Republican party; a thinking evangelical is a member of the Democratic party.
6. Evangelicals are not communists, social activists, or successful capitalists. Evangelicals are suspect if they are inappropriately aligned politically or economically.
7. Evangelicals are the backbone of middle-class society in the United States.
8. Evangelical faith is the faithful embodiment of historic orthodox Christianity in the modern world.
9. If Jesus were alive today, he would be an evangelical.

These aspects of the hidden curriculum are held in varying degrees and with varied effect upon students.

Lawrence Richards, in his analysis of seminary training, maintains that the hidden curriculum of most programs also includes the conceptual structuring of content. As a result, students are often trained to study and master Scripture in an intellectual rather than a personal or relational way. The hidden curriculum also includes a largely impersonal learning setting which transfers to an impersonal style of ministry following seminary. The emphasis is on Bible information over against modeling the Christian life. Finally, in Richards's analysis, seminary training emphasizes that learning is primarily individual and competitive to the relative exclusion of corporate and cooperative patterns.[18] Richards's insights are generally accurate, but developments since 1975 indicate some movement from this pattern of seminary training.

It is Richards's contention that the hidden curriculum is the most powerful educational force with which Christian education deals. This is the case not only at the seminary level, but at all levels of education. This contention naturally follows from his emphasis on socialization

18. Lawrence O. Richards, *A Theology of Christian Education* (Grand Rapids: Zondervan, 1975), 251–52.

and nurture through modeling. Richards, in fact, defines the hidden curriculum as those elements of every setting in which believers interact which support or inhibit the transformation process.[19] This transformation process for Richards is the essence of Christian education which commmunicates the Christian faith as life.

In relation to Richards's contention, both explicit and hidden curricula require equal attention. Both are powerful forces and need to complement one another. An emphasis on the hidden curriculum should not diminish a concern for the explicit, academic dimensions of the curriculum. Likewise, an emphasis upon the explicit curriculum should not diminish a concern for the hidden curriculum. The Christian educator is called upon to assume responsibilities in both areas and to complement academic and nonacademic emphases wherever possible. Both content and experience must be addressed. Both formal and nonformal educational components are matters for curricular planning. Both explicit and hidden curricula are concerns for the Christian educator in planning for and implementing an effective educational program.

In addition to both the explicit and hidden curricula which operate in any educational setting, be it the church, home, or school, it is possible to identify the "null curriculum." Elliot Eisner defines the null curriculum as that which is not taught in a particular teaching setting by choice or oversight. It is his thesis that what is not taught may be as important as what is taught because ignorance affects the options one is able to consider.[20]

A Larger Vision

A survey of most printed curricula reveals that a vast majority specify what students are to know, feel, or do as a result of a particular class or course. This results from emphasizing behavioral objectives in teaching and learning. Clarity and specificity in relation to purposes, goals, and objectives are to be affirmed, but a larger vision is suggested by exploring biblical models. In curricular matters, how does the dominant model, emphasizing the identification, realization, and evaluation of behavioral objectives, compare with a model implied in the context of a New Testament ministry? In relation to this question, the Book of Titus provides some helpful insights:

19. Ibid., 321.
20. Elliot W. Eisner, *The Educational Imagination: On the Design and Evaluation of School Programs*, 2d ed. (New York: Macmillan, 1985), 97. Also see Ronald T. Habermas, "Even What You Don't Say Counts," *Christian Education Journal* 5(Autumn 1984):24–27.

You must teach what is in accord with sound doctrine. Teach the older men to be temperate, worthy of respect, self-controlled, and sound in faith, in love and in endurance.

Likewise, teach the older women to be reverent in the way they live, not to be slanderers or addicted to much wine, but to teach what is good. Then they can train the younger women to love their husbands and children, to be self-controlled and pure, to be busy at home, to be kind, and to be subject to their husbands, so that no one will malign the word of God.

Similarly, encourage the young men to be self-controlled. In everything set them an example by doing what is good. In your teaching show integrity, seriousness and soundness of speech that cannot be condemned, so that those who oppose you may be ashamed because they have nothing bad to say about us.

Teach slaves to be subject to their masters in everything, to try to please them, not to talk back to them, and not to steal from them, but to show that they can be fully trusted, so that in every way they will make the teaching about God our Savior attractive.

For the grace of God that brings salvation has appeared to all men. It teaches us to say "No" to ungodliness and worldly passions, and to live self-controlled, upright and godly lives in this present age, while we wait for the blessed hope—the glorious appearing of our great God and Savior, Jesus Christ, who gave himself for us to redeem us from all wickedness and to purify for himself a people that are his very own, eager to do what is good.

These, then, are the things you should teach. Encourage and rebuke with all authority. Do not let anyone despise you. (Titus 2:1–15)

Titus was a gentile convert to Christianity who became a fellow worker and assistant to Paul. Paul's letter to Titus finds him in Crete, where he has the responsibility of supervising the work of the church. Part of this supervision involved teaching various groups with distinct needs and responsibilities. Paul addresses the content and methods of teaching these various groups (older men, older women, younger women, younger men, and slaves). Titus is advised both what to teach and how to teach. Paul outlines age-graded specifics along with general guidelines for the curriculum. Paul's insights are suggestive for current efforts.

In general terms, Titus is encouraged to teach various groups *to be* something or other. No doubt knowing, feeling, and doing are implied in the call to be, but a concern for being implies a larger purpose, a larger vision. Titus is to be concerned with character formation. Good works and conduct flow from sound doctrine and from a person's being in a right relationship with God and others. Christian educators must be concerned for Christian values and virtues which persons are called upon to embody in their very lives.

Titus is to teach the older men *to be* temperate, worthy of respect, self-controlled, and sound in faith, in life, and in endurance. Titus is to teach the older women *to be* reverent in the way they live, not to be slanderers or addicted to much wine, but to be teachers of what is good. Younger women are *to be* taught by older women to love their husbands and children, to be self-controlled and pure, to be busy at home, to be kind, and to be subject to their husbands. The young men are *to be* taught to be self-controlled. Titus, himself a young man, is to be an example by doing what is good and to show integrity, seriousness, and soundness of speech. By implication other young men are to be encouraged to be like Titus. Slaves are taught *to be* subject to their masters in everything, to try to please them, not to talk back to them and not to steal from them, but to show they can be fully trusted. This curriculum, even in terms of each age and social group, is quite extensive. How is Titus to accomplish this task? How can teachers teach others *to be?*

Several answers can be suggested. In commenting on Titus 2, Wilbur Wallis maintains that God's grace not only saves persons but also teaches and trains them in sober and godly living.[21] This is one possible answer. Every Christian teacher can confess the need for God's grace to accomplish any results in the lives of students. God's grace is realized not only through the abilities and sensitivities of teachers and students alike in the classroom, but also through the medium of prayer as all participants rely on God's wisdom and work. Thus prayer and the expectation of the work of the Holy Spirit are essential elements.

A second possible answer is also suggested in the text of Titus itself. Titus is encouraged to set an example by doing what is good and by showing integrity, seriousness, and soundness. Titus was to teach others "to be" by "being" himself. Likewise, teachers can encourage students to be of a certain character by embodying that very character themselves. This ministry does not eliminate the possibility of students surpassing their teachers and manifesting abilities and aspects of character beyond their examples. But teachers must be aware that they are examples or models.

A third answer involves the Christian virtues of love and truth. Titus is instructed by Paul to teach what is in accord with sound doctrine (2:1) and to rebuke with all authority (2:15). Titus is to affirm the standard of God's truth. This standard requires that persons say "no" to ungodliness and worldly passions and live self-controlled, upright, and godly lives. A concern for truth implies a serious grappling with God's standards for holiness and purity in both personal and corporate life.

21. Wilbur B. Wallis, "The Epistle to Titus," in *The Wycliffe Bible Commentary*, eds. Charles F. Pfeiffer and Everett F. Harrison (Chicago: Moody, 1962), 1395.

In addition to this concern for truth, Titus is instructed to encourage various persons in their need to be taught. For him to effectively accomplish this, he needs to love them, a theme not specifically addressed here but clearly taught in other portions of Scripture. Some Christians in the past have used this text to support slavery, whereas others have raised serious questions about the presence of Christian love with the existence of slavery. This indicates the need for critical awareness of what one is in fact teaching using the biblical sources and how one is appropriating a text or context.

In conclusion, Titus is to teach others by relying on the grace of God, by being himself an example, and by teaching in truth and in love. These are simple yet profound answers to questions of how to encourage others to be in Christ. To live out these answers requires the diligent efforts of a teacher in a working relationship with God.

This chapter completes the survey of the various foundations which Christian educators should consider in their thought and practice. No final answers have been provided, but the hope is that grappling with such matters will make a difference in the advance of God's work in our time. The important task of formulating principles and guidelines for practice remains for the Christian who seeks to be faithful in the various dimensions of Christian education.

Select Bibliography

Biblical Foundations

Barclay, William. *Educational Ideals in the Ancient World.* Grand Rapids: Baker, 1974.

Boys, Mary C. *Biblical Interpretation in Religious Education.* Birmingham, Ala.: Religious Education Press, 1980.

Bruce, A. B. *The Training of the Twelve.* Grand Rapids: Kregel, 1971.

Brueggemann, Walter. *The Creative Word: Canon as a Model for Biblical Education.* Philadelphia: Fortress, 1982.

Grassi, Joseph A. *Teaching the Way: Jesus, the Early Church, and Today.* Washington, D.C.: University Press of America, 1982.

Heschel, Abraham J. *Between God and Man: An Interpretation of Judaism from the Writings of Abraham Heschel.* Edited by Fritz A. Rothschild. New York: Free Press, 1959.

Horne, Herman H. *The Teaching Techniques of Jesus.* Grand Rapids: Kregel, 1920.

LeBar, Lois. *Education That Is Christian.* Old Tappan, N.J.: Fleming H. Revell, 1981.

Marino, Joseph S. *Biblical Themes in Religious Education.* Birmingham, Ala.: Religious Education Press, 1983.

Stein, Robert H. *The Method and Message of Jesus' Teaching.* Philadelphia: Westminster, 1978.

Theological Foundations

Beversluis, N. H. "Toward a Theology of Education." *Occasional Papers from Calvin College.* 1 (February 1981): 1–32.

Bushnell, Horace. *Christian Nurture.* Grand Rapids: Baker, 1979.

DeJong, Norman. *Education in the Truth.* Nutley, N.J.: Presbyterian & Reformed, 1969.

Fackre, Gabriel. *The Christian Story: A Narrative Interpretation of Basic Christian Doctrine.* Rev. ed. Grand Rapids: Eerdmans, 1984.

————. *The Christian Story: Authority: Scripture in the Church for the World. Vol. 2, A Pastoral Systematics.* Grand Rapids: Eerdmans, 1987.

Foster, Charles R. *Teaching in the Community of Faith.* Nashville: Abingdon, 1982.

Freire, Paulo. *Education for Critical Consciousness.* New York: Seabury, 1973.

————. *Pedagogy of the Oppressed.* Translated by Myra Bergman Ramos. New York: Continuum, 1970.

Gaebelein, Frank E. *The Christian, the Arts, and the Truth: Regaining the Vision of Greatness.* Edited by D. Bruce Lockerbie. Portland, Oreg.: Multnomah Press, 1985.

————. *The Pattern of God's Truth: Problems of Integration in Christian Education.* New York: Oxford University Press, 1954.

Getz, Gene A. *Sharpening the Focus of the Church.* Chicago: Moody Press, 1974.

Giltner, Fern M., ed. *Women's Issues in Religious Education.* Birmingham, Ala.: Religious Education Press, 1985.

Goodwin, Bennie E. *Reflections on Education: A Christian Scholar Looks at King, Freire, and Jesus as Social and Religious Educators.* East Orange, N.J.: Goodpatrick, 1978.

Groome, Thomas H. *Christian Religious Education: Sharing Our Story and Vision.* San Francisco: Harper & Row, 1980.

Little, Sara. *To Set One's Heart: Belief and Teaching in the Church.* Atlanta: John Knox, 1983.

Marthaler, Berard. *The Creed.* Mystic, Conn.: Twenty-Third, 1987.

Moore, Mary Elizabeth. *Education for Continuity and Change.* Nashville: Abingdon, 1983.

O'Hare, Padraic, ed. *Foundations of Religious Education.* New York: Paulist Press, 1978.

————. *Tradition and Transformation in Religious Education.* Birmingham, Ala.: Religious Education Press, 1979.

Richards, Lawrence O. *A Theology of Christian Education.* Grand Rapids: Zondervan, 1975.

Schipani, Daniel S. *Conscientization and Creativity, Paulo Freire and Christian Education.* Lanham, Md.: University Press of America, 1984.

Seymour, Jack L., Robert T. O'Gorman, and Charles R. Foster. *The Church in the Education of the Public, Refocusing the Task of Religious Education.* Nashville: Abingdon, 1984.

Thompson, Norma H., ed. *Religious Education and Theology.* Birmingham, Ala.: Religious Education Press, 1982.

Van Til, Cornelius. *Essays on Christian Education.* Nutley, N.J.: Presbyterian & Reformed, 1977.

Westerhoff, John H., III. *Will Our Children Have Faith?* New York: Seabury, 1976.

Wilhoit, Jim. *Christian Education and the Search for Meaning.* Grand Rapids: Baker, 1986.

Wolterstorff, Nicholas. *Educating for Responsible Action.* Grand Rapids: Eerdmans, 1980.

Philosophical Foundations

Burgess, Harold William. *An Invitation to Religious Education.* Mishawaka, Ind.: Religious Education Press, 1975.

Durka, Gloria, and Joanmarie Smith, eds. *Emerging Issues in Religious Education.* New York: Paulist Press, 1976.

Graendorf, Werner C., ed. *Introduction to Biblical Christian Education.* Chicago: Moody Press, 1981.

Harper, Norman E. *Making Disciples, the Challenge of Christian Education at the End of the Twentieth Century.* Memphis: Christian Studies Center, 1981.

Heckmann, Shirley J. *On the Wings of a Butterfly, A Guide to Total Christian Education.* Elgin, Ill.: Brethren Press, 1981.

Knight, George R. *Philosophy and Education: An Introduction in Christian Perspective.* Berrien Springs, Mich.: Andrews University, 1980.

Little, Sara. *To Set One's Heart: Belief and Teaching in the Church.* Atlanta: John Knox, 1983.

McKeachie, Wilbert J. *Teaching Tips: A Guidebook for the Beginning College Teacher.* 7th ed. Lexington, Mass.: D. C. Heath, 1978.

Moran, Gabriel. *Interplay: A Theory of Religion and Education.* Winona, Minn.: St. Mary's Press, 1981.

Palmer, Parker. *To Know As We Are Known: A Spirituality of Education.* San Francisco: Harper & Row, 1983.

Perry, David W., ed. *Making Sense of Things: Toward a Philosophy of Home-grown Christian Education.* New York: Seabury, 1981.

Sanner, A. Elwood, A. F. Harper, et al. *Exploring Christian Education.* Grand Rapids: Baker, 1978.

Seymour, Jack L., and Donald E. Miller, eds. *Contemporary Approaches to Christian Education.* Nashville: Abingdon, 1982.

Wren, Brian. *Education for Justice: Pedagogical Principles.* Maryknoll, N.Y.: Orbis Books, 1977.

Zuck, Roy B. *Spiritual Power in Your Teaching.* Rev. ed. Chicago: Moody Press, 1972.

Historical Foundations

Bailyn, Bernard. *Education in the Forming of American Society.* New York: University of North Carolina and W. W. Norton, 1960.

Bellah, Robert N. *The Broken Covenant: American Civil Religion in Time of Trial.* New York: Seabury, 1975.

Cremin, Lawrence A. *Public Education.* New York: Basic Books, 1976.

———. *Traditions of American Education.* New York: Basic Books, 1977.

Cully, Kendig B. *Basic Writings in Christian Education.* Philadelphia: Westminster, 1960.

———. *The Search for a Christian Education—Since 1940.* Philadelphia: Westminster, 1965.

Dworkin, Martin S. *Dewey on Education: Selections.* New York: Teachers College, 1959.

Gangel, Kenneth O., and Warren S. Benson. *Christian Education: Its History and Philosophy.* Chicago: Moody Press, 1983.

Greven, Philip. *The Protestant Temperament: Patterns of Child-Rearing, Religious Experience, and Self in Early America.* New York: Alfred A. Knopf, 1977.

Kennedy, William B. *The Shaping of Protestant Education.* New York: Association Press, 1966.

Knoff, Gerald E. *The World Sunday School Movement: The Story of a Broadening Mission.* New York: Seabury, 1979.

Lynn, Robert W., and Elliott Wright. *The Big Little School: Two Hundred Years of Sunday School.* Rev. ed. Birmingham, Ala.: Religious Education Press, 1980.

Peshkin, Alan. *God's Choice: The Total World of a Fundamentalist Christian School.* Chicago: University of Chicago Press, 1986.

Seymour, Jack L. *From Sunday School to Church School: Continuities in Protestant Church Education.* Washington, D.C.: University Press of America, 1982.

Sherrill, Lewis J. *The Rise of Christian Education.* New York: Macmillan, 1944.

Towns, Elmer L., ed. *A History of Religious Educators.* Grand Rapids: Baker, 1975.

Westerhoff, John H., III, and O. C. Edwards, Jr. *A Faithful Church: Issues in the History of Catechesis.* Wilton, Conn.: Morehouse-Barlow, 1981.

Sociological Foundations

Berger, Peter L., and Thomas Luckmann. *The Social Construction of Reality: A Treatise in the Sociology of Knowledge.* Garden City: Doubleday, 1966.

Durkheim, Emile. *Education and Sociology.* New York: Free Press, 1956.

Eggleston, John. *The Sociology of the School Curriculum.* London: Routledge & Kegan Paul, 1977.

Geertz, Clifford. *The Interpretation of Cultures.* New York: Basic Books, 1973.

Gill, Jerry H. *The Possibility of Religious Knowledge.* Grand Rapids: Eerdmans, 1971.

Habermas, Jurgen. *Knowledge and Human Interests.* Boston: Beacon, 1971.

Hesselgrave, David J. *Communicating Christ Cross-Culturally.* Grand Rapids: Zondervan, 1979.

Lawton, Dennis. *Class, Culture and the Curriculum.* London: Routledge & Kegan Paul, 1975.

Lines, Timothy A. *Systemic Religious Education.* Birmingham, Ala.: Religious Education Press, 1987.

Paulston, Rolland G. *Conflicting Theories of Social and Educational Change.* Pittsburgh: University Center for International Studies, University of Pittsburgh, 1976.

Stenhouse, Lawrence. *An Introduction to Curriculum Research and Development.* New York: Holmes & Meier, 1975.

Psychological Foundations

Beechick, Ruth. *Teaching Juniors: Both Heart and Head.* Denver: Accent Books, 1981.

Crabb, Lawrence J. *Effective Biblical Counseling: A Model for Helping Caring Christians Become Capable Counselors.* Grand Rapids: Zondervan, 1977.

Cully, Iris V. *Christian Child Development.* San Francisco: Harper & Row, 1979.

Dykstra, Craig. *Vision and Character: A Christian Educator's Alternative to Kohlberg.* New York: Paulist Press, 1981.

Dykstra, Craig, and Sharon Parks. *Faith Development and Fowler.* Birmingham, Ala.: Religious Education Press, 1986.

Erikson, Erik H. *Childhood and Society.* 2d ed. New York: W. W. Norton, 1963.

Fowler, James W. *Becoming Adult, Becoming Christian: Adult Development and Christian Faith.* San Francisco: Harper & Row, 1984.

————. *Stages of Faith: The Psychology of Human Development and the Quest for Meaning.* San Francisco: Harper & Row, 1981.

Gilligan, Carol. *In A Different Voice: Psychological Theory and Women's Development.* Cambridge: Harvard University Press, 1982.

Goldman, Ronald. *Readiness for Religion.* New York: Seabury, 1968.

Havighurst, Robert J. *Developmental Tasks and Education.* New York: David McKay, 1961.

Joy, Donald M., ed. *Moral Development Foundations: Judeo-Christian Alternatives to Piaget/Kohlberg.* Nashville: Abingdon, 1983.

Kohlberg, Lawrence. *Essays in Moral Development.* Vol. 1, *The Philosophy of Moral Development.* San Francisco: Harper & Row, 1981.

Loder, James E. *The Transforming Moment: Understanding Convictional Experiences.* San Francisco: Harper & Row, 1981.

Moran, Gabriel. *Religious Education Development.* Minneapolis: Winston Press, 1983.

Peatling, John H. *Religious Education in a Psychological Key.* Birmingham, Ala.: Religious Education Press, 1981.

Richards, Lawrence O. *A Theology of Children's Ministry.* Grand Rapids: Zondervan, 1983.

Rizzuto, Ana-Maria. *The Birth of the Living God.* Chicago: University of Chicago Press, 1979.

Sparkman, G. Temp. *The Salvation and Nurture of the Child of God: The Story of Emma.* Valley Forge: Judson, 1983.

Wilcox, Mary M. *Developmental Journey.* Nashville: Abingdon, 1979.

Curricular Foundations

Colson, Howard P., and Raymond M. Rigdon. *Understanding Your Church's Curriculum.* Nashville: Broadman, 1981.

Cully, Iris V. *Planning and Selecting Curriculum for Christian Education.* Valley Forge: Judson, 1983.

Dewey, John. *Experience and Education.* New York: Macmillan, 1944.

Eisner, Elliot W. *The Educational Imagination: On the Design and Evaluation of School Programs.* 2d ed. New York: Macmillan, 1985.

Guide to Curriculum Choice. Elgin, Ill.: Brethren Press, 1981.

Jackson, Philip W. *Life in Classrooms* New York: Holt, Rinehart & Winston, 1968.

Miel, Alice. *Changing the Curriculum: A Social Process.* New York: Appleton-Century-Crofts, 1946.

Lee, James M. *The Flow of Religious Instruction.* Dayton, Ohio: Pflaum/Standard, 1973.

Tyler, Ralph W. *Basic Principles of Curriculum and Instruction.* Chicago: University of Chicago Press, 1949.

Index

Acculturation, 44, 131
Aesthetics, 83, 90–91
Anthropology, 83, 84
Apostles' Creed, 60–63, 128, 129
Aristotle, 124–25
Assensus, 41, 53
Augustine, 134, 144, 179
Authority, biblical, 49–51
Autonomy, 162, 164, 187, 188
Axiology, 83, 86, 90–96

Bailyn, Bernard, 78, 121, 174
Bantock, G. H., 152, 153
Basileia, 43–45
Beechick, Ruth, 194–95
Behaviorism, 107–8, 112
Berger, Peter L., 151, 159, 160
Beversluis, N. H., 153, 155
Bible, 62, 98, 135, 136, 138, 145: as
   critical instrument, 11
Body/soul dualism, 62
Burgess, Harold W., 96, 103, 106, 145

Calvin, John, 136, 138
Canon, 128

Capitalism, 191
Caswell, Hollis L., 111–12
Catechesis, 51, 128
Celebration, 24, 44
Church, 27, 36, 50, 62: as extended
   family, 27
Church order, 128
Colossians, 36
Communion of saints, 62
Conscientization, 69
Contextualization, 55, 67, 157–58
Continuity, 209
Conversion, 50, 51–53
Cosmology, 83, 85
Covenant: of creation, 63; of
   redemption, 64
Cremin, Lawrence A., 79–80, 81, 86, 125,
   139–43
Cultural accommodation, 155
Culture, 152, 174: and Christ, 58–59
Curriculum: definition of, 205–6;
   hidden, 216; metaphors, 210–14; null,
   167, 218

Decontextualization, 157

DeJong, Norman, 81, 82–83, 86
DeLone, Richard H., 189–90
Development: biological, 180; cognitive, 183–84; continuity and discontinuity, 180; faith, 192–94; moral, 187–88; psychological, 185–87, sociological, 12, 180
Dewey, John, 108, 112, 146–47, 205, 213
Diakonia, 42, 45
Didache, 129
Discipline, 30
Discipling, 30, 33, 130, 148
Discrimination, 142
Disenculturation, 44, 79, 101
Durkheim, Emile, 165–66

Edification, 36, 42, 197
Education, 53, 125, 165, 174: biblical, 19–20; Christian, 24, 49, 57, 80–81; definition of, 77–80, 211; in early Christianity, 128–30; evangelical, 60; in the Middle Ages, 130–33; moral, 191; in the New Testament, 126–27; preparadigmatic, 13–14; in the Post-Reformation, 139–43; in the Reformation, 135–38; Reformed view of, 63–68; in the Renaissance, 133–35
Educational mandate, 18–19
Eggleston, John, 167–68
Enculturation, 79, 81
Environment, 104–5, 201
Ephesians, 35–36
Epistemology, 83, 85: biblical, 87
Equality, 142–43
Erikson, Erik, 181, 185–87, 196, 197
Eschatology, 31
Essentialism, 107, 112
Ethics, 30, 83, 90
Ethos, 153
Evaluation, 105–6
Evangelicalism, 49–50, 54, 55, 57, 59, 64, 93, 133, 134, 144, 158, 160, 163, 166–67, 168, 190
Evangelism, 52–53, 71: educational, 53–54
Exhortation, 27
Existentialism, 110–11, 112
Experience, 50
Exposition, 27
Ezra, 27–28

Faith, 41, 192, 193: and science, 88–89, 193
Fall, 63–64, 135
Family, 27, 131–32
Fellowship, 41–42
Fiducia, 41, 53
First Corinthians, 34–35
Formation, 146
Fowler, James, 181, 192–94, 195, 214
Fraternity, 142–43
Freire, Paulo, 68–72, 109, 162–63
Fundamentalism, 143

Gaebelein, Frank, 54, 126, 144–45, 146, 149
Geertz, Clifford, 152–53, 173, 174, 175
Getz, Gene E., 148–49
Gill, Jerry, 160–61
God, 54–55, 70, 84, 113, 120, 124, 126, 137, 160, 164, 184, 193, 194: as Creator, 60, 199; as teacher in biblical education, 19; as source of wisdom, 28, 76
Groome, Thomas H., 57

Habermas, Jürgen, 161–62, 163
Hebrews, 39
Heredity, 199
Hermeneutics, 154
Heschel, Abraham, 45, 99, 126
Heteronomy, 164
Hirst, P. H., 152, 153
Historical method, 116–17
History, 116: and Christian education, 119–22; and education, 117–18
Holmes, Arthur, 76
Holy Spirit, 34–35, 39, 61, 70, 146
Hope, 44
Huebner, Dwayne, 93–95, 205
Humanism, 133, 138, 140
Humanization, 68

Individualism, 124, 133
Instruction, 41 n. 21, 206
Integration, 209

Jesus Christ, 24, 32, 34, 43, 52, 61, 64, 67, 70, 102, 127, 135, 145, 175: as Master Teacher, 32–34, 38
John, 207
Justice, 189

Kerygma, 40, 41, 45
Kingdom consciousness, 43–44
Kingdom of God, 30–31, 63
Knight, George R., 85–86, 88, 90, 92, 96
Knowledge, 87, 151, 159–60, 164, 174: explicit, 161; tacit, 161
Kohlberg, Lawrence, 181, 187–88, 191, 192, 196, 197, 198
Koinonia, 41, 45
Kuhn, Thomas, 13

Law of God, 22–23, 123
Lawton, Denis, 11, 159
Learning, 200–201
LeBar, Lois, 98, 145–46, 149, 206
Leitourgia, 44, 46
Levin, Gerald R., 179–82, 193
Levite instruction, 27
Lewis, C. S., 80, 149
Liberation, 23–24
Liberation theology, 65–68
Liberty, 142
Love, 19, 42, 43, 207
Luckmann, Thomas, 151, 159, 160
Luke, 32–34
Luther, Martin, 119, 136

Marxism, 72
Mason, Charlotte, 75
Mason, Harold, 52, 53
Matthew, 29–31, 148
Maturation, 200
Maturity, 36, 39
McKeachie, Wilbert J., 100–101, 102
Metaphysics, 83–84
Miller, Donald E., 196–97
Mission, 30, 31
Moses, 18, 22, 67

Nehemiah, 27–28
Niebuhr, H. Richard, 58, 155–56, 169
Nomos, 117, 163
Notitia, 41, 53
Nurture, 42 n. 51

Ontology, 83, 84–85
Origen, 129, 155
Orthodoxy, 50

Paideia, 125–26
Palmer, Parker, 87, 90

Parents, 20, 21, 140
Paul, 34–38, 51, 76, 84, 164–65, 200, 207, 219
Paulston, Rolland, 168–69, 170
Perennialism, 106–7, 112
Personality, macroscopic and microscopic viewpoints, 181
Philippians, 37
Philosophy, 76: Christian, 76
Piaget, Jean, 181, 183–84, 187, 188, 192
Pietism, 155
Piety, personal, 50, 58–59
Plato, 124–25
Practice, 166
Preaching, 136. *See* Proclamation.
Priesthood of all believers, 36, 136
Proclamation, 27
Progressivism, 108–9, 112, 144
Psychology: developmental and nondevelopmental, 178–80; general and differential, 182; and education, four approaches to integration of, 178–79

Racism, 142
Reality, 151
Reason, 50, 134
Reconstructionism, 109–10, 112
Redemption, 50
Reformation, 64
Relationships, interpersonal, 37–38, 62
Religion, 160
Revelation, 29: biblical, 50
Richards, Lawrence O., 20–21, 147–48, 149, 217–18
Romantic naturalism, 110, 112
Rule of faith, 128

Salvation, 70, 136
Sanctification, 36, 42, 155, 197
Science, 88–90
Scientism, 88–90
Scripture, 19, 46, 49–51, 76, 135, 137, 157, 184: as ultimate arbiter of truth, 113
Self-education, 81, 134, 141
Sequence, 209
Service, 140, 146
Shalom, 44
Sin, 60, 62, 84, 135, 163, 189
Skepticism, 124
Smith, Huston, 88, 193

Socialism, 191
Socialization, 78–79, 81, 101, 131
Socrates, 124–25
Sola fide, 135
Sola scriptura, 135
Sophists, 124–25
Stewardship, 44, 140
Students, 102–4

Teachers, 29, 100–102, 136, 206, 209–10
Television, 140, 190
Tertullian, 129, 155, 156
Theology, 83: and Christian education,
   56–57; evangelical, 49–60, 83;
   liberation, 65–67, 158; propositional,
   49; Reformed, 63–66
Theonomy, 162, 164, 188
Tillich, Paul, 93–94
Titus, 219–21
Tradition, 50
Training, 41 n. 21

Transformation, 69, 146
Truth, 38, 88, 206–7
Tyler, Ralph, 211–12

Unity, 36

Vallance, Elizabeth, 216–17
Values, 91–96, 215: in curricular
   planning, 214–17; spiritual, 94

White, Lynn, Jr., 91–92
Williams, Raymond, 152, 154
Winn, Marie, 131–32
Wisdom, 28–29, 34–35, 36–37
Wolterstorff, Nicholas, 187, 191
Women, 202
Word of God, 22–23: as essential content
   of Christian teaching, 23
World view, 75–76, 153
Worship, 44, 45, 130
Wyckoff, D. Campbell, 104–5